Portugal

Fifty Years of Dictatorship

Portugal

Fifty Years of Dictatorship

Antonio de Figueiredo

Holmes & Meier Publishers, Inc.
New York

Published in the United States of America 1976 by
Holmes & Meier Publishers, Inc.,
101 Fifth Ave., New York, N.Y. 10003

First published by Penguin Books Ltd.,
Harmondsworth, Middlesex, England.

LIBRARY OF CONGRESS CATALOGING IN PUBLICATION DATA

Figueiredo, Antonio de, 1929-
   Portugal: fifty years of dictatorship.

   Bibliography: p.
   1. Portugal—History—1910-1974. I. Title.
DP680.F53   946.9′042   75-33644
ISBN 0-8419-0237-2

PRINTED IN THE UNITED STATES OF AMERICA

Foreword

Fortunate is the reader who has been led to Antonio José Wunderly Simões de Figueiredo's new book by a desire to understand what the revolution in Portugal is all about. For here is the story of how dictator Salazar plunged Portugal into a night that lasted fifty years: how Salazar seized power, how he held on to it and with what tragic consequences, and how finally the stage was set for the ancient people of Portugal to become, in one great burst of revolutionary enthusiasm, the youthful vanguard of Europe. Seldom has a revolution followed a more confusing and paradoxical course, one made all the more baffling because over the years, academic foreign area experts seem virtually to have forgotten that Portugal existed. And to the extent that anything newsworthy appeared to be happening in that obscure Westerly fringe of the Iberian Peninsula, it was not because of events in Portugal, but rather because of events in Africa where the Portuguese had somehow managed to stay on long after every other major colonial power had been driven out. And even as the bloody liberation struggles in Guinea, Mozambique and Angola ground on year after year, they went unnoticed until the very end; indeed, their significance for the future of Africa has yet to be placed in proper perspective.

Portugal, Fifty Years of Dictatorship, uniquely serves to enlighten us not only about Portugal but about Portuguese Africa. This represents an achievement for which there are some rather stiff requirements: you have to know Africa as well as you know Portugal; you have to know the revolutionary movements from the inside; you must be able to interpret all this to an English speaking readership. Antonio de Figueiredo meets these requirements perhaps to a degree unmatched by anyone else. He was born and reared in rural Portugal; emigrated to Mozambique as a young man, and has spent his

v

maturity in England, to which he fled after serving in the anti-Salazar underground.

The good fortune to which I referred at the outset has another dimension, no less valuable than those just mentioned. To read this book is not only to learn about the political economy of Portugal and Portuguese Africa, and about dictatorship, empire, liberation and revolution, but it is also to come into contact with an extraordinarily warm, intelligent and gifted human being. When Antonio de Figueiredo speaks to us of the plight of the ordinary people of Portugal and Africa during Salazar's rule, it is with an authenticity which belongs only to those who have endured and overcome great suffering on their own. Viewed merely as testimony to the indomitable will of an illiterate Portuguese peasant boy to demystify his world through the exercise of an intellect intended by church and state to remain forever dormant, this book would be a notable achievement. But Antonio de Figueiredo, writing in a self-taught language about subjects whose mastery he acquired virtually without benefit of formal schooling, has produced something of a literary gem. The pages which follow glow with subtle warmth and civilized commentary even when the events depicted plunge to the bottom of the pit. Some passages about Salazar are even funny, and I know that the author would not consider it in poor taste if you laughed out loud. True, there is over-all a vast sadness to the story of modern Portugal; but if we cannot also on occasion laugh, we only make it sadder.

There is much more to tell about Antonio de Figueiredo, but I am hoping that he will tell it for himself in the not too distant future.

MARVIN HARRIS
Columbia University

Contents

1

Acknowledgements

Since I came into exile in London in 1959, I have been indebted to a number of people for help and hospitality. The first person to help me in a concrete way was Basil Davidson. I had known him previously only through his books, which had exercised a great influence on me, and I contacted him soon after my escape from Portugal. In more recent times he paved the way for the publication of this book. Thanks must also go to the Juniper Fund Ltd, of Birmingham, for their financial assistance.

I am grateful to Richard Clements and Tribune for providing me with a platform for more than twelve years, and to the editors and staff of *Anti-Apartheid News* for publishing many of my articles over the last few years. I have also been a regular contributor to the BBC External Services, and I am thankful to James Duffell, now retired, James Nadler and my colleagues Antonio Cartaxo, Luis de Sousa, Paulo David, Saul Custodio, Carlos Alves and others for their help with news and research in the past.

I have worked with many British journalists over the years on a number of newspapers and magazines, and I would like to express my gratitude to some of the men who have influenced me, following a purely chronological order: Roy Perrot, Mark-Arnold Forster, Colin Legum, Neal Ascherson, Patrick Keatley, Roy Lewis, Richard Bourne, Michael Walsh, Peter Deeley, Nicholas Carroll, Nicholas Ashford, Campbell Page, Ian Wright, Harold Jackson, Peter Niesewand, James McManus, Jonathan Steele, Peter Pringle, Dennis Herbstein, Stephen Fay. To all of them I owe a further advance in my knowledge of English and of life in general.

For my wife Katherine,
and all those who have helped me
in Britain

Portugal

Fifty Years of Dictatorship

Introduction

On 28 May 1926 there occurred a military *coup* which led to the dictatorship of Antonio de Oliveira Salazar and, later, Marcello Caetano. Their régime was in turn overthrown by another *coup* on 25 April 1974. But it is only for the sake of convenience that the birth and death of a régime are known by given dates. The timing of the factors that brought them about cannot be so closely defined. This book therefore covers a period spanning well over fifty years. Moreover, the rule of Salazar was bound up with an attempt to rebuild the Portuguese overseas empire, and the régime collapsed after ten years of colonial wars. Thus the history of this period is also intertwined with the histories of the peoples of Guinea-Bissau, Angola, Mozambique and São Tome, which have now emerged as independent African nations.

I have drawn a portrait of Salazar the man as I develop the themes underlying Portuguese culture and politics. I am aware that a dictator does not operate in a vacuum and that he is only the embodiment of a power generated by interlocking economic, social, religious and class interests. But if ever there was a man who controlled the destinies of millions of people for generations virtually single-handed, it was Salazar. I have thus made him appear and reappear on the scene through the crucial events which shaped Portugal's development – the high tide of Fascism and Nazism in the 1930s, the Spanish Civil War, the Second World War, Portugal's own colonial wars, as well as through long periods of routine domestic repression. This is intended to give a psychological perspective to the gruelling years of Salazar's rule and his absurdly rapid disappearance into oblivion.

I see the comparatively short period of Caetano's rule as an indecisive episode in a rapidly deteriorating situation. I describe the *coup* of 25 April 1974 and the subsequent swift process of decolonization as the dramatic collapse of the system Salazar had held together for forty years. Finally I touch on the uncertain developments which have taken place under the new revolutionary régime, showing how they reflect the delayed effects of decades of repressive rule. The development of the 'guided democracy' envisaged by the Armed Forces Movement as the best transitional solution for Portugal is likely to be influenced by such after-effects for some time to come.

Moreover, this book is the product of a lifetime of experiences under the régime, and it is therefore relevant that I explain the relation between my personal background and the events I describe. As it happens I was born after Salazar came to power; my father's family are mostly illiterate peasants from a hamlet at Campo de Besteiros, in the valley of Caramulo, near where Salazar was born and brought up. Hence my knowledge of the region, where I have interviewed many people who knew Salazar from his schooldays. Like Salazar, my father rose to the ranks of the educated through a Catholic seminary, and, again like Salazar, did not take the final vows. Instead he married my mother, who was from a middle-class family from a fishing and tourist town, Figueira da Foz. Both of them died when I was only a child. I would have gone to the seminary myself but I did not show the required inclination. And so I went to work at the age of 10. This mixed background gave me first-hand knowledge of the class system and the gap there is between the mass of rural people and the minority urban population, in living standards and styles, in mobility and outlook.

Childhood experiences at Campo de Besteiros were to have a lasting influence on me. Reading and writing letters for illiterate peasants made me understand that poverty takes many cruel forms other than occasional hunger. It taught me how the peasants make do with visual signs, colours and figures in place of the written word, and how this afflicts them as if it were a kind of blindness. I well remember how wives and mothers peered over my shoulder as I took dictation for their letters as if trying to make sure I was taking things down right. I sensed how my intrusion must have inhibited them and saw how inarticulate they were – sometimes they would touch the writing-paper or stare at it as if in this way it could better carry their

10

messages of love or anxiety. Although conditions may vary between regions, the mass of peasants either work in large family estates for ridiculously low wages, or try to earn a bare hand-to-mouth living from diminutive holdings. Some of them are desperately poor. A farm labourer and part-time gravedigger, a widower with five children, was once dictating to me an anxious plea to his absentee landlord not to throw him out of his small house and piece of land for having fallen into arrears with the rent. He promised things would soon get better, and at one stage he added: 'Your Excellency, please understand that the air around here is good and as nobody is dying I cannot make a living.' When I timidly looked towards him to suggest a better turn of phrase he was wringing his hands and had tears in his eyes. And I already knew that misery is no laughing matter.

Portuguese peasants live in a pre-technological age, using archaic farming methods which have hardly changed in centuries. They live in a near-animal condition. Theirs is a male-dominated and child-exploiting society, in which the old have to cling to their grown-up sons and daughters because there are neither adequate pensions nor social care. They are seldom helped, but systematically misused. Even their religion, which is supposed to be Catholicism, is a form of sub-Christianity, for in their simple minds instead of love there is a superstitious fear of a God of Terror. The local priest, like a tribal witchdoctor, teaches them a doctrine which holds that challenges to the local and national patron saints can be punished with crop failure or the affliction of their animals and children. They are allowed to pay their sacrament fees either in money or in kind according to an arbitrary tariff which always keeps the priest on the same social level as the local doctor (if there is one) or the richer farmers and shopkeepers.

I also remember the shock of discovering at an early age that illiteracy or semi-literacy were not a product of casual neglect but part of the established social order. One day during the Second World War, as I ended an afternoon reading session in a gathering of peasants eager to listen to the speeches of President Roosevelt promising freedom, I was suddenly seized by a rural Republican Guard who had been watching me for some time.

He threatened to beat me up if I persisted in disturbing the minds of local people with that 'Communist poison', as he put it. I swore to myself that I would one day be able to explain the motivations and the power behind that rural guard.

This set me on a self-education course that was to last throughout my life. At seventeen I was sent as an emigrant to Mozambique, where I lived for twelve years, up to 1959. By the age of nineteen, I had joined the Portuguese underground as a member of the youth wing of the Movimento de Unidade Democratica (Democratic Unity Movement). Indeed, most of the Portuguese Ministers who emerged after the 25 April *coup*, as well as many leaders of the African liberation movements, were members of this group. I was detained by the police for the first time in 1949, when the PIDE was in the process of suppressing the DUM. Almost upon arrival in Mozambique I had discovered that the blacks were in the same plight as the peasants at home. However, they were not regarded as 'poor': they were called 'natives'. Their condition was not the result of 'fate' or 'God's trial' – they were naturally inferior, and it would take them a long time before they could even attain the status of 'poverty'.

The Portuguese régime benefited in a negative way from comparison with South Africa and Rhodesia, where racial supremacy was institutionalized. Laws in Angola and Mozambique were conceived in Lisbon by men like Salazar who had never visited the overseas 'provinces' where blacks were to be 'assimilated' into Portuguese nationhood. Their schemes were based upon paternalistic concepts of racial 'tolerance' which nevertheless implied a deeply ingrained, though perhaps unconscious, belief in their own cultural and racial superiority. But after many years of first-hand observation of conditions in Southern Africa, and study visits to Brazil and other countries, I realized that racialism varies according to socio-economic circumstances and environmental pressures, but requires neither an institutionalized ideology nor a legislative framework. The Lisbon empire-builders made the laws, but the local settlers made the rules, and the degree of social and economic exploitation of blacks appeared even more extreme in Portuguese

12

Africa than in the richer white-dominated neighbouring countries.

In those days all forbidden political subjects had been driven down to the level of oral culture, and there was no way in which I could make systematic research of the economic and political situation as a whole. I describe this crippling inability to communicate with the outside world in greater detail in the book. However, one day a young American anthropologist, Marvin Harris from Columbia University, came to Mozambique on a one-year field study visit. He provided me with an opportunity to broaden my horizons, and we have remained close friends ever since. But while he was to become one of America's foremost anthropologists and the author of many scholarly books, I was to undergo a long series of experiences at the hands of the PIDE, the Portuguese security police. When they finally caught up with me at the age of twenty-nine I was arrested, interrogated about my way of thinking and the smallest details of my private life, tortured, left in solitary confinement, and finally deported to Portugal, where, not surprisingly, I took refuge in a psychiatric hospital with a temporary reactive neurosis. I then planned my own escape into exile in London where I knew I could find many books and study facilities.

For fifteen years, while based in London, I was associated with the Portuguese democratic and African liberation movements and knew a number of great and brave Africans – Amilcar Cabral, Agostinho Neto, Eduardo Mondlane, Marcelino dos Santos, Jonas Savimbi and others. I was a close friend of the late General Humberto Delgado, former presidential candidate, and of several Portuguese underground leaders, such as Mario Soares, who became Foreign Minister after the *coup*, H. Palma Inacio, well known for his daring bank raids carried out for the purpose of raising funds. From these men I learned that courage is a far rarer quality than intelligence and that those who make of political ideas and theories merely an intellectual exercise are as irrelevant to democratic struggles as if they had devoted themselves to more abstract interests. At least five of my Portuguese and African fellow liberation fighters were murdered not long after I last saw them, and this knowledge is amongst the many psychological scars that linger in me. Finally, after the 25 April *coup*, I shared in the joys of liberation in Portugal and in the expectations of independence in Mozambique and Angola which I saw growing into nationhood. I try to describe these events in the last chapter dealing with the collapse of the Salazar–Caetano régime and the empire.

Since then I have revisited Portugal, Angola and Mozambique as well as other Portuguese-speaking and neighbouring countries to study new developments; I was also an adviser to the 29th General Assembly of the UN in New York at the end of 1974, which was a useful experience in international politics. But although I suddenly found myself with a considerable number of friends in positions of leadership in the governments and political parties of Portugal, Mozambique, Angola, São Tome and Guinea-Bissau, I have refrained from involvement in partisan politics. I prefer to combine the study of political theories, which are about people's needs and aspirations, with direct sociological observation of what people are, how their loyalties divide and how they behave. I also believe that in situations of chronic or critical economic scarcity the impact of short-term class or group interests is far more powerful than that of long-term theories. Thus, while understanding the meaning of imported revolutionary slogans to the effect that 'a united people will never be defeated', I accept as an objective fact that, although Portugal is conventionally regarded as an old country, it is still a nation in the making. Unlike advanced and integrated countries, both East and West, Portugal still has achieved no uniform social and technological development. While jumbo jets land at Lisbon, Oporto and Faro airports, down below people still use the Roman ox-cart and water-well.

After almost fifty years of Salazar's régime, Portugal is a country riddled with internal divisions. The foremost is that which keeps the majority of the rural population in the neglected role of providers of cheap food and wine so as to give viability to the prevailing economic system. In this context, all urban classes, including law-makers and industrial workers, have at least an immediate vested interest in maintaining the peasants' subordinate condition. Such are the dichotomies of mind induced by a long habit of class division that a social code of behaviour still discriminates against the rural population as if they were an alien subject race.

The second great division is that which arises from the patriarchal subjection of the female half of the population, reducing women to mere shadows of men. A notable book by three women writers – *New Portuguese Letters* – published in the United States and Britain in 1975, describes the insidious inequality of rights between male and female in matters of sex, work and education, at all levels of society and at all stages in life. The 25 April *coup*, which was by definition military, and which arose from all-male war experiences, conspiracies and decisions was still very much a 'man's revolution'. So much so that when during the first days after the *coup*, an army spokesman was asked by a female foreign journalist at a press conference, 'And what about women?', he was nonplussed enough to pause for some seconds and even to look under the table, such was his complete obliviousness to the issue.

There is also a rigid social hierarchy based on educational qualifications, more often than not obtained through circumstances of inherited privilege. According to this hierarchy academic honours, diplomas and degrees have replaced the nobility of old. Thus university professors are the equivalent of dukes and marquesses; doctors, lawyers and engineers are the equivalent of counts; ordinary Ph.D.s, as well B.A.s and B.Sc.s, rank as viscounts and barons. Many of them, while addressing peasants with first-name paternalistic familiarity, still expect to be addressed in return as *'senhor doutor'*, or 'your excellency'.

I have, of course, gone back to Portugal many times since the days of liberation. New generations of my relatives are still living in Red Indian-like 'reservations' of a past European social age which attract the curiosity of tourists from industrial nations. The peasants' real plight has gone largely unnoticed. Even industrial workers leave them out of the scope of their solidarity. The general stigma of belonging to a colonizing country has been extended to them, whereas in reality they

15

themselves have been the victims, rather than the beneficiaries, of colonial exploitation. If they ever had a notion of a remote empire overseas it was because successive generations of their ancestors provided the shipbuilding craftsmen, sailors, soldiers and settlers that were recruited for the continuous wars of conquest, occupation and repression. In modern times those faraway lands of Guinea-Bissau, Angola and Mozambique only conjure up cruel memories of pain and mourning for lost and mutilated sons, brothers and friends.

Since they have as from 1975 been given the right to vote, the peasants have become a decisively important section of the electorate. But urban party organizers have made the mistake of coming out to the countryside to teach before trying to learn, and the result has been that the peasants have often thrown them out of their villages. In their own ancestral environment a number of factors still combine to keep the peasants impervious to political theories. Their vocabulary is often composed of only a few hundred words, and it certainly does not include comparatively 'modern' (post-feudal) terminology, for describing democratic concepts or institutions. Even when they can read, they cannot afford newspapers, TV sets or radios. Psychologically they are more insecure than outsiders assume. Their small houses and holdings are all they have – property as well as profession and livelihood. The power of the Church contributes to making them suspicious of any ideology that might lead to agrarian reform or changes in the family customs on which their socio-economic system is based. Their instinctive conservatism arises from the fact that, whereas capitalist property might be concerned with profits, their type of property is related to survival.

They are conditioned to accept the prevailing hierarchy and authority, and the late General Delgado's memorable impact on them during the 1958 presidential elections had a lot to do with the fact that he was a member of the military establishment, though his personal charisma must have helped. At any rate many peasants referred to him as a '*manda-chuva*', 'rain-maker', a title they reserve for those whom they think are powerful, in an allusion to the age-old experience of drought. Even under the impact of modern ideas they still confide that 'if collectivization has to come to improve these poor lands, it cannot be entrusted to just anyone, least of all townspeople and students'. Lately I rejoiced when I saw the young officers of the Armed Forces Movement holding political teach-ins for peasants to explain to them the meaning of liberation. It seems that many of the officers are determined to act as a fourth 'liberation movement' and apply in Portugal the lessons learned from the PAIGC, Frelimo and MPLA freedom-fighters in Africa.

One year after the 25 April *coup* and during the first elections within the new régime, a novel scheme has begun to take shape. This would seek a middle road betweeen European democratic models and the African revolution. On one hand there would be a representative government, parties and institutions dedicated to the problems of administration and the maintenance of democratic values, seeking to integrate Portugal into the mainstream of European life. On the other there would be a shadow military Revolutionary Council and National Assembly and other parallel institutions dedicated to the socialization of Portugal. At any rate it could be a breakthrough that so many young people in Portugal have begun to realize that, in the same way that blacks were a colonized race in the former overseas empire, the mass of peasants was a colonized class at home.

Chapter 1
Salazar – the seminarist and nationalist

> *'I know that in Europe the science of
> history is steadily and fast advancing and
> that if we Portuguese do not have the
> courage to tell ourselves the truth, others
> will tell it to us with blunt frankness'* –
> ALEXANDRE HERCULANO (1810–77)[1]

Nationalism and religious faith were two of the main features in the life of Antonio de Oliveira Salazar, and they both served him well. The Catholic Church provided for his education and social promotion; nationalism was his way to political power.

He was born on 28 April 1889 at Vimieiro, a small place adjacent to the village of Santa Comba Dão. The fact that he was born exactly eight days after Adolf Hitler was to be regarded later as a curious link between two statesmen who shared so many ideological concepts and who had such admiration for each other.

At the time of his birth, Santa Comba could hardly have had more than a few hundred inhabitants and there was no building higher than the local Catholic church. Situated in a picturesque wine-producing region, almost half-way between the district capital of Viseu and the ancient university town of Coimbra, Santa Comba still has comparatively little contact with the outside world. Life is hard for the average poor peasants who live in the surrounding rural area. Many of them can reach old age without even having the thrill of 'seeing the sea', though the coast may be less than one hundred miles away.

But Salazar's parents were far from being day-labourers, as they themselves, following social prejudice against manual workers, would be the first to claim. His father was Antonio Oliveira and his mother Maria do Resgate Salazar. According to Portuguese custom, their young son should have been named

1. From *Historia de Portugal*, Preface (Bertrand, Lisbon, 1920).

Salazar Oliveira, instead of the other way round. Since no one has found a satisfactory explanation for this rare departure from tradition, one is inclined to presume that the choice was due to the fact that Salazar is a far less common-sounding name than Oliveira.

In 1889, at the time of Salazar's birth, his father was already in his fifties and his mother was forty-three. This means that Salazar's parents had been brought up before the middle of the nineteenth century, decades before the opening of the local railway station and when the pace of life in the region was set by the Roman ox-cart and the horse-drawn carriage.

Antonio Oliveira looked after the interests of absentee landlords. He had a reputation for being as strict with the '*jornaleiros*' (day labourers) and the '*rendeiros*' (tenant farmers) as he was subservient to the establishment above him. And, significantly, he was locally known, amongst rural workers and neighbours, as 'O Manholas' – 'The Crafty One'.

The couple's conservative outlook owed as much to their austere and religious upbringing as to the pressures in a social environment where men have to race for the few opportunities of income and promotion. Moreover, they had been brought up within living memory of the Napoleonic wars and were still living under the impact of the political agitation caused by the so-called 'Liberal Wars'. Although these were primarily civil wars of succession between two royal brothers, they embodied the intense ideological struggles of the time. The wars had brought constitutional monarchy to Portugal and this was seen by many reactionary people as a disruption of the established order.

At the time of Salazar's birth, Santa Comba was still a long distance away from the age of electricity which was just beginning in the world outside. Even today, the region, for all its rural beauty, is somewhat secluded from tourists, and has a parochial perspective on the world. Horizons are narrowed by the limited financial resources of most of the people, including the local middle class.

Seen from Santa Comba, the district capital Viseu, a town of only 20,000 inhabitants, is a big trade and judicial centre. The university town of Coimbra is a bustling 'city of doctors' and, further away, and already qualifying by Portuguese standards as a 'long journey', is Lisbon, 'the capital of the empire', which excites the imagination of most rural people as a European centre of power, finance and cosmopolitanism. That Salazar, first as a student of the Seminary of Viseu, later as a student and professor at Coimbra University, and finally as Prime Minister in Lisbon, was to reach beyond the social and geographical horizons of his birthplace is largely due to the shrewdness of his father.

The middle-aged couple, who already had four daughters, obviously had big plans for their only son's future. But the social and economic situation of the time was not encouraging. Well over 80 per cent of the Portuguese population worked on the land and was illiterate. The biggest opportunity of all was to emigrate abroad – but that would entail exile in distant Brazil or, worse still, in the African colonies. For those of the peasant class who remained behind there was little hope of social promotion.

Apart from a few opportunities of working their way up as rich men's stewards, peasant people could only obtain a free education or hope to ascend to a better class in two ways: if they were girls they dreamed of a good marriage; if they were boys they could at least try for one of the free places made available every year in the Catholic seminaries throughout the country.

The latter possibility emerges from a set of socio-economic circumstances which are easy to understand. The Church needs as many priests as it can find. Pay and conditions, however, despite the added incentive of heavenly rewards, are apparently not enough to attract middle-class paying students in adequate numbers, for they can anyway join the Church without passing through the lower seminaries. Therefore, a very considerable number of free or privately subsidized places are open every year to those peasant boys who have shown the right religious 'vocation' and civic behaviour and can produce the appropriate recommendations. The pressure of social conditions is such that it is not unusual to find boys coming forward who have the necessary degree of religious inspiration.

From the point of view of the Church there is, however, a snag in the system. A considerable percentage of seemingly devout boys undergo a change of heart as ordination approaches and when they have attained useful qualifications. The seminaries try to minimize their losses by working within a curriculum which does not easily find an equivalent in the secular school system; but the Church has to resign itself to this percentage loss, and consoles itself with the hope that when it has lost a priest it has gained a faithful lay friend.

Salazar's middle-aged and experienced parents saw the opportunity offered by the system. If their son, who appeared to be as frail as a middle-class boy, was to avoid the worrying prospect of having to work on the land for others, a seminary solution would have to be found. It would be up to young Salazar to make the most of it and eventually to find a career which would raise him above his family's social condition.

When one follows the initial steps of Salazar's education one finds a pattern of events only too common in Portugal. Antonio Oliveira, seeing that his young and precious only son was not getting the best results in the overcrowded primary school at Santa Comba, decided to send him first to a private class held in the village by an enterprising local schoolteacher, and later to a small Catholic school in Viseu not very far from the seminary and the bishop's mansion. While studying at the primary school and already being helped financially by a rich family that employed his father, the young Salazar developed a precocious and very thorough-going vocation for an ecclesiastical career. And at the age of eleven Salazar duly entered the Seminary of Viseu.

According to one of his official biographers Salazar 'grew up in the shade and studied in solitude'. In his own reminiscences he was to admit later that he lived 'absorbed with his ideas and work and was, in short, a boy with a serious mind'.[1] This is unsurprising if one takes into account that during the time he stayed in Viseu, his life alternated between the cloistered and

1. Luiz Teixeira, *Perfil de Salazar* (Secretariado de Propaganda Nacional, Lisbon, 1939), pp. 13, 17.

disciplined atmosphere of the seminary, occasional visits to his benefactors, and frequent holidays at home, where his mother was then in her middle fifties and his father in his sixties. This unusual gap of two generations between parents and son obviously left its mark upon Salazar, who always remained suspicious of youth and modernity.

If Salazar's Catholic convictions sprang from paternal influence, cultural tradition and indoctrination, his nationalistic beliefs were clearly rooted in the conventional values upheld by the dominating classes. Such values are the basis of all Portuguese education, from primary school to postgraduate studies at the country's three universities.

In fact, while living in the shade of solitude of the seminary, the young Salazar was following the trend of events in Portugal and could not have been indifferent to the decadence of his country. The struggles for the establishment of a secular republic and the desperate reformist efforts of the then dictator João Franco were only symptoms of a wider national crisis.

How contemporary events influenced his life is seen by the crucial decision Salazar took when, in 1908, he announced to his superiors at the seminary that he did not intend to proceed to the priesthood. Already nineteen years old, and having taken minor orders, his decision was so unexpected and inconsistent with his previous intentions that many of his biographers cannot explain why he should have chosen to follow the example of so many other defectors from the priesthood. Some believe that his decision was at least partly connected with the historic event of 1 February 1908, the day when both the reigning monarch, Carlos I, and the heir to the throne were murdered by two republican revolutionaries in one of Lisbon's main squares. According to the Catholic writer, Hugh Kay, who wrote an extensive biography of Salazar, his decision was partly motivated by this turn of events – 'with a secularist republic clearly on the way ... what future there could be for priests was anybody's guess'.[1]

1. Hugh Kay, *Salazar and Modern Portugal* (Eyre & Spottiswoode, 1970), p. 11.

Salazar himself was to acknowledge his passage through the seminary in more sentimental terms:

A poor man, the son of poor people, I owe to that house a great deal of my education which, otherwise, I would not have been able to obtain; and although I might have lost the faith in which they brought me up, I shall never forget those good priests who maintained me, almost without payment, during so many years (1900 to 1908) and to whom I owe, besides much else, my upbringing and intellectual discipline.[1]

Since, later in life, Salazar himself encouraged suggestions that he had always been a reluctant politician and statesman, others believe that his decision to abandon his ecclesiastical career was merely prompted by his wish to follow an academic career. But according to a letter written by Salazar to João Franco, the last dictator under the monarchy, which was recently published after Salazar's death, a different picture emerges.

The background to the letter is simple enough. In 1929, when former dictator João Franco was seventy-four years old and had long returned from exile to live in retirement in Portugal, he had written to Salazar to congratulate him for his firm action in the government. In his answer Salazar referred to events in 1907, while he was still at the seminary and most people assumed that his ideas had still gone no further than believing that Portugal was the 'daughter of Mary', the mother of Christ and Portugal's patron saint, or the 'daughter of the Church'.

According to Salazar, by 1907, the year parliamentary rule was suspended by the King, Portugal had been aroused by João Franco 'with an outcry of reaction against the disrupting administration of the country'. His rule had been followed by the 'healthier and most disinterested part of the nation with more than tenderness – with faith'. 'Someone, then an obscure man, still in his green years, had been touched by the same faith,' and now, from a situation of more authority, this man was thankful for the 'providential design' that had provided

1. A. de O. Salazar, *A Minha Resposta* (França Amado, Coimbra, 1919), p. 34.

the occasion to acknowledge this fact to the ageing former dictator.[1]

The statement and the choice of words clearly provide some evidence that the young Salazar, for all his ability to hide his innermost feelings, had had an early concern for national affairs and authoritarian rule. This fact is very much in keeping with his singular determination of character and his subsequent political career.

The years at Coimbra

Political life for Salazar really began in 1910, as soon as he moved to Coimbra. This was two years after he had left the seminary and after he had acquired the qualifications necessary to enter the Faculty of Law. As he was settling into Coimbra, the hurriedly crowned successor to the throne, Manuel II, found himself unable to resist the mounting revolutionary pressures and left for exile in London. The Republic was proclaimed on 5 October.

It is difficult to understand today the psychological impact this event had both at home and abroad. In 1910, with a few exceptions, all Europe, from the distant tsarist Russia to neighbouring Spain, remained under the rule of reactionary monarchies and reformist governments. The rest of the world (with the exception of the US) was still made up of political dependencies, and if they had a diplomatic voice, it could not be heard. To the dominant powers of the time and to neighbouring Spain, where the unpopular reign of the young Alfonso XIII was in its sixth year, the double assassination of King Carlos and the young heir to the throne was both an emotional shock and an omen of revolutionary danger. The resources and influence of international diplomacy, royalist family connections and the Catholic Church combined to isolate the revolutionary, anti-clerical little republic. According to contemporary reports one of the aims of the 'Republic of Terrorists' was to see that the

1. *Vida mundial* (Lisbon), 31 July 1970. This issue was devoted to Salazar in commemoration of his death.

'last king would be strangled with the entrails of the last priest'.[1]

'The Great Powers in Europe were averse to any recognition of the Republic' – that is how Sir Arthur Hardinge, the British Minister in Lisbon summed up the diplomatic situation. And, indeed, at various royal courts in Europe the diplomats of the new republic were made to feel that Portugal had become an outcast in the 'concert of nations'. The great Christian powers – that is Britain, Germany, France and Italy – looked upon Portugal very much in the same way that reactionary circles in the Americas were to look upon Cuba after Castro came to power.

Inside Portugal, whether you shared the enthusiasm for a sudden social and political awakening, after centuries of obscurantism, or lived in panic of the consequences of materialist and egalitarian subversion upon your faith and income, the first years of the republic were indeed a great emotional upheaval. But as the majority of the then six million Portuguese had hardly any income, faith alone did not justify any widespread resistance to the first republican governments. On the contrary, although largely confined to the middle classes and urban centres, the republican revolution enjoyed popularity even amongst the uneducated rural class.

At first the revolution was primarily cultural, rather than social. The core of republican intellectuals had formed themselves into a Republican Party in 1876 and through persistent struggles all republican factions agreed that if the King and the aristocracy were overthrown, the Church was the next revolutionary target. On 8 October 1910, three days after the proclamation of the republic, a decree was promulgated to curb the activities of the Jesuits and the remaining religious orders. On the 18th the religious oath was abolished; on the 22nd, Catholic teaching in the schools was prohibited; and on the 23rd the Faculty of Theology in the University of Coimbra closed down. The rule of the Church was challenged in other ways as well – on 26 October twenty-six holy days became working days; on 3

1. V. de Bragança-Cunha, *Revolutionary Portugal (1910–1936)* (James Clarke, London, 1937), pp. 147, 161.

November divorce was established in Portugal, and soon afterwards the marriage ceremony became a civil function. This was seen by many Catholics as 'equivalent to free love', 'turning marriage into legalized prostitution'. Moreover, the final blow, under the form of a Law of Separation of Church and State, whereby Catholicism would cease to be the established religion of the land, was being planned. Under this law all ecclesiastical property, from cathedrals to seminaries, would be claimed by the State.

When the young Salazar, no doubt making the sign of the cross and shaking his head, entered the University of Coimbra, even that citadel of traditionalism had been contaminated by revolutionary fervour. Students, whom the local police had been unable to trace, had slashed the portraits of the former Portuguese kings in the sacred Hall of Doctors at the university, riddling them with bullets; other students, without fear of disciplinary or divine punishments, had torn the robes of their theology professors. For the moment it appeared that all a good Catholic could do was to cling to the rosary, go no further than confessing reactionary temptations to the parish priest, and wait.

If he was anything, Salazar was a man who knew how to wait. So when he arrived in Coimbra he became the secretary of a Catholic study and social group, the CADC (Centro Academico de Democracia Cristã – Academic Centre of Christian Democracy) which had been founded in 1901 and temporarily closed by the new republican régime.

For the next few years the CADC would be the most important nucleus of Catholic intellectuais in the country. It was to be a common link in a generation of men who later held the highest positions in the government, Church and universities. The ideological conspirators were intellectuals who turned towards Rome and Paris, and they were just as alienated from the mass of ignorant Portuguese peasants as their republican counterparts were. Owing to the ignorance of the mass of Portuguese people the CADC could never have aspired to build anything like a party or a grass-roots movement such as Hitler and Mussolini had before they came to power. Unlike the

27

German dreamers of a New Order, many of the CADC members gazed fixedly towards the past and hoped to restore an absolutist monarchy; instead of party uniform, they wore the traditional black cloaks that make the University of Coimbra look so much like a medieval centre of learning; and of course, instead of beer, they usually drank wine.

Under the editorship of another promising young man, Manuel Gonçalves Cerejeira, who later was to become the Cardinal Patriarch of Lisbon for the duration of Salazar's rule, the CADC published their own weekly magazine somewhat misleadingly called the *Imparcial* (*Impartial*). Reading their collected issues, one can learn much about the Portuguese pioneers of fascism, who had already formed a cohesive group by 1919, when Hitler founded the National Socialist German Workers' Party and Mussolini his Fascia di combattimento.

Years before Hitler published *Mein Kampf* in 1923, the Portuguese Catholic–monarchist thinkers, more in keeping with the historical and cultural connections between Latin nations, were studying such political guides as Pope Leo XIII's nineteenth-century encyclical *Rerum Novarum* and the works of French right-wing writers such as Charles Maurras and Léon Bloy. In essence these doctrines offered the organic and hierarchical concepts and the corporate character of medieval society as the alternative to what they considered to be the excessive egalitarianism and individualism of the French Revolution, the mechanistic notions of the Industrial Revolution and the atheism and internationalism of Marxism. They had been further adapted to Portuguese conditions by the traditionalist writer Antonio Sardinha and others who promoted the ultra-nationalist doctrines known as 'Lusitanian integralism'. Again, in contrast with the cases of German, French and Italian fascist thinkers who were allegedly concerned with the industrial future of their societies and the welfare of workers, Portuguese 'integralism' was emphatically spiritualist, a sentimental abstraction more devoted to resurrecting a romanticized past than to creating a new future. Their nationalism, later to be extended to the overseas empire, was based upon élitist concepts and the perpetuation of the social structures of Portugal. Their fierce

anti-internationalism was prompted by the instinct for pre-
serving a subjected community of peasants and colonial peoples
from the infiltration of 'foreign ideals' and the interference of
international institutions.[1]

Salazar himself, either under his own name or under a pseudonym, was making contributions to several magazines besides
Imparcial, such as the *Revista de Estudos,* also connected with
the CADC, and newspapers published in the bigger cities of
Oporto and Lisbon. But his stolid style was more adequate for
economic and financial studies such as 'The Gold Agio, its
Nature and Causes (1891–1915)', 'The Problem of Wheat Production, Some Aspects of the Commodity Crisis', and even a
study on labour relations under the curious title of 'The Peace
of Christ among the Working Class'. Wise enough not to engage
in the abstruse philosophical flights of the 'integralists', his political concepts at the time were at least clearly expressed, as the
following passage from a Catholic address shows:

> It is needful for the Portuguese of today to create in the glorious
> Portugal of tomorrow a strong Portugal, an educated Portugal, a
> moral Portugal, a hard-working and progressive Portugal. Is it neces-
> sary for this purpose that we should love our country deeply? Oh! it
> is always necessary to love one's own country. Just as we love our
> mother deeply, so let us love our country, the great mother of us
> all.[2]

According to a commemorative issue of the CADC's *Revista de Estudos,* published in 1944, the young members used to
hold their meetings in one of the largest halls on the premises of
the group and which they had named 'Hall of the Assault on
Portugal'. One of their slogans – 'Wherever it may be necessary
to serve to save Portuguese society' – evokes a sense of mission
and urgency. A revealing hint about the way Salazar was reacting to the situation Catholics were facing at the time is given in
a book of memoirs by Salazar's lifelong friend Cardinal Cerejeira. 'Salazar was then writing, under the pseudonym of Alves

1. Raul Proença, *Acerca do integralismo lusitano* (Seara Nova, Lisbon,
1964), p. 98.

2. Luiz Teixeira, op. cit., p. 19.

da Silva, some of his best articles ... And in the evenings we would go to the Church of St. John to attend the "Month of Mary" ceremonies – with *mocas* [clubs] under our cloaks.'[1]

Curiously enough Cardinal Cerejeira admits in the same book that he himself used to carry a gun. But then Cerejeira always was more dynamic than Salazar. He once confided that while passing through Paris with Salazar, to attend a Catholic Congress of Working Youth in Liège, while he himself had taken the opportunity to have a look round Paris, the serious, black-and-grey-minded Salazar had hardly been out of the headquarters of various Paris Catholic Associations. And this, it must be recalled, was to be the only major trip abroad Salazar ever made in his life.

The list of student members of the CADC, also published by *Revista de Estudos*, gives an idea of the influence the nucleus was to have on later political developments in Portugal. Apart from Salazar and Cardinal Cerejeira, the group included several bishops and other high-ranking ecclesiastical figures, Mario de Figueiredo who later became 'leader' of the National Assembly, ten men who were to become ministers at one time or another, and no less than twelve who had become university professors and members of the National Assembly, who were all well known for their extreme right-wing views.

Despite his involvement in active politics, which at the time already extended to the newly formed 'Catholic Centre' in Lisbon, Salazar still had time to pursue his academic career. Needless to say he always passed his exams with the highest marks; when he graduated in law in 1914, he obtained 19 marks out of a possible 20. In 1917 he became assistant lecturer in economics and in 1918, already celebrated as one of the country's best financial and economic experts, he obtained his doctorate.

The details of his private life are somewhat vague. Whilst he has often been described as an emotionally cold man it is known that he was extremely attached to his ailing mother – so much so that it is alleged that he considered renouncing his career

1. Manuel Gonçalves Cerejeira, *Vinte anos de Coimbra* (Lisbon, 1943), p. 221.

rather than be separated from her in the last years of her life.

His love life is also somewhat ambiguous and many people have accused him of being misogynist. According to some of his biographers Salazar was jilted by the daughter of the rich family who employed his father and who had patronized his studies; according to others it was the girl's mother who, out of social prejudice and financial concern, had him rejected as a suitor. It is also said that upon being rejected Salazar was seen to cry by his friends for the only time in his life. But the Brazilian writer and former Ambassador to Lisbon, Alvaro Lins, reported in his book *Mission to Portugal* a revealing chat he had had with Salazar's friend Cardinal Cerejeira, the source of many insights into Salazar's character.

One day while still a law student Salazar thought of getting married. It was to be with a young millionairess from Lisbon who was staying for a time in Coimbra.

Salazar decided then to consult his old friend Cerejeira. The future Cardinal told him that he did not know the girl well enough to be sure of her qualities but pointed out that since she was rich, Salazar might not be in a position to maintain her in the standard of life she was used to. Besides, he knew Salazar was proud enough not to want to accept living off his wife's family money.

Salazar replied that, in what concerned her qualities, that was no problem – 'Even if she had none, I would lend her some of mine.' And he added thoughtfully: 'The main thing, however, is to make a decision, one way or another, and think no more about it.'

After this he went to his quasi-bride-to-be who was returning that same day to Lisbon and simply said to her: 'If within a month you get no letter from me, that is because I have decided not to get married.'

And nobody ever talked about the matter again. Neither him, nor the girl, nor anybody else.[1]

Although Salazar was to die unmarried, certain aspects of his life suggest that he was not exactly a lonely bachelor. In fact the type of domestic life he was to adopt is both revealing of his selfish character and his integration into a social pattern which is traditional to the ostensibly celibate Catholic priesthood. Be-

1. Alvaro Lins, *Missão em Portugal* (Civilização Brasileira, Rio de Janeiro, 1960).

tween 1915 and 1928, Salazar, as is normal among Coimbra students and academics who return home for their long annual holidays, shared a flat and living expenses with his two close friends and political collaborators, Manuel Conçalves Cerejeira and Mario de Figueiredo. The three also shared the services of a young maid, inevitably called Maria – Maria de Jesus Caetano. She later followed Salazar to Lisbon and remained his housekeeper to the end. It is known that her relationship with Salazar was very close. When arriving with a visiting French journalist to one of his homes, Salazar once commented: 'We are now coming into the kingdom of Maria . . . She has an authoritarian nature and does not like to have many people around. With Maria on guard, it is not just anyone who gets here. She protects me better than the police!'[1]

Maria was a permanent feature in the background of Salazar's home life, and, just as a parish priest's housekeeper might be known locally, she was known throughout Portugal as 'Dona Maria'. She always addressed Salazar as *Senhor Doutor* or *Senhor Presidente* and was never seen to eat at his table. She brought up Salazar's two adopted girls, Micas and Maria Antonia, who were apparently her own nieces.

This domestic situation closely resembles that of many priests who live in concubinage and often have children, but who, on account of their celibacy vows and attitudes to sex, deem it necessary to keep up social appearances. The Church, for practical reasons, turns a blind eye to a situation which has gained tacit recognition over the centuries. Inevitably, in the case of Salazar, his relationship with Dona Maria gave rise to some gossip and many people think that, since he was not bound by celibacy vows, he was deterred by his own provincial sense of propriety and class prejudice. Indeed, an ironic situation arises whereby any righteous denial of an intimate connection in a relationship that lasts for about fifty years between a man and a woman of considerable personal charm, would make them appear, to the outsider, even more abnormal than otherwise would be the case. All in all, the whole situation suggests that

1. Christine Garnier, *Ferias com Salazar* (Antonio Maria Pereira, Lisbon, 1952), p. 66.

Maria, for all her devotion and her promotion to 'Dona Maria', was just one of the countless victims of the egocentric patriarchy of Portuguese society. And it also seems to confirm that Salazar, who preserved his 'cultural purity' by hardly ever travelling abroad, was even in this respect very much a traditional type of Portuguese.

Salazar's nationalism

One cannot understand Salazar and the emotional force behind Portuguese nationalism without taking into account certain features of Portugal's geography and social and cultural development. Salazar's introvert character and egocentrism were well adjusted to the very nature of Portuguese national feeling.

Portugal is a small and poor country, with a long and exciting history which lends itself to romanticism. It is a coastal belt surrounded on the west and south by the sea and on the north and east by like-minded Spain, which isolates the Portuguese from the main stream of European life. Since being Portuguese is a denial of being Spanish, Portugal's links are directed either towards overseas countries, Britain, Brazil and the empire, or beyond Spain, towards France and the Vatican. Even for the educated middle class, Portugal has been as much an economic and political colony of Britain as an intellectual colony of France and a religious colony of Rome – but Spain is simultaneously there and non-existent. But for the majority of Portuguese the horizons of the 'Portuguese language world' were Brazil and the empire. The ascendancy and the connections that arose from overseas expansion at the expense of even more backward societies only helped to reinforce illusory notions of self-sufficiency and superiority. Most Portuguese lived very much in a world of their own and for many of those who filled the cadres of the administration, the army, the Church and educational establishments, it was possible to travel and live thousands of miles away in the empire without really going outside 'Portugal'.

The condition of the country as an obscure, enclosed society, developing its own institutions at its own calculated pace, is not new. Having been by-passed by the major revolutions of modern times – the Industrial, the French, the Communist, the Technological – Portugal has undergone a painfully slow process of evolution.

The authoritarian character of the government, the intimate connection between State and Church, the decisive role of the military, are almost permanent features of Portugal's past. The Holy Inquisition, which imposed repression on Portugal for over two and a half centuries in the name of God, was succeeded by police bodies and censorship boards acting on behalf of the Nation.

But in order to perpetuate structures and class privileges from generation to generation, it was not enough to seclude Portugal through censorship and repression from the influence of the great internationalist ideologies or revolutionary movements in the world outside. It was necessary actively to reject them and offer in their place a nationalistic system of ideas, based upon religious principles and a glorified mis-reading of history.

Salazar was not only conditioned by his upbringing to accept the inherited nationalist ideology; he added to it. His vision of Portugal's past, as a small, gallant nation fighting for survival, as a people chosen to carry out a civilizing mission in the four corners of the earth, as the possessor of an empire, contains emotional elements similar to those of other nationalist ideologies for which the young and the naïve are prepared to die.

Many of the notions and tenets of Portuguese nationalism are traced back to centuries-old books, such as the long epic poem *The Lusiads* by Camões, first published in 1572. Although this poem was also subject to censorship by successive inquisitorial boards it has now been elected as a kind of nationalist Bible from which extracts can be taken out of context to illustrate any lesson.

Salazar himself defined Portuguese nationalism in the following emotive terms:

Crushed in the western strip of the Peninsula, between powerful neighbours and the ocean, our existence is necessarily one long drama: but by the favour of Providence we can count eight cen-

34

turies of toil and suffering, struggle and liberty, and if the danger remains, the miracle remains also ... Here and afar we have right on our side, the right of occupation, conquest, discovery and colonization, of the substance and blood of the Portuguese watering the earth in all parts of the world, cultivating the soil, opening up wastelands, trading, pacifying, teaching. It is the will of the people; it is the call of national conscience ... It was in the twelfth and thirteenth centuries that Portugal assumed its present frontiers in the Iberian Peninsula, in the fifteenth and sixteenth centuries that it acquired vast dominions in Africa, Asia, Oceania, and America, defending Roman and Christian civilization against Islam and spreading civilization through new worlds. And this victory, of transcendental importance to humanity, was won by us at a time when the other nations of Europe were immersed in the strife of dynasties, schisms and heresies which steeped them in blood ... We are the sons and heirs of an ancient civilization whose mission it has been to educate and train peoples to a higher idea of life, to form real men through the subjection of matter to spirit, of instinct to reason ... [1]

For Salazar and the young generation of like-minded Catholic nationalists, who had such exalted views of Portugal's distant golden past and 'civilizing mission', life under the republican régime must have been a torment.

However, if, for the sake of simplification, one were to divide Portuguese middle-class politics at the time into two main groups, one comprising the triumphant progressive republicans and the other the disgruntled traditionalist monarchists, one would find between them a general consensus of opinion over the need to awaken Portugal from the appalling decadence into which it had fallen. Neither of the contending factions seemed to be resigned to accepting the reality of Portugal's historical condition and limitations. And paradoxically, while imperialism might have provided other nations with the means to promote industrialization and high standards of living, the empire for Portugal was perhaps the greatest single factor contributing to decadence and stagnation.

Many other small nations in Europe, which were equally 'crushed' between the sea and powerful neighbours, had been compelled by similar reasons of national survival to rely on

1. *Salazar Says* (Secretariado de Propaganda Nacional, Lisbon, no date).

their own resources and follow the overall European process of industrialization. But Portugal had learned to live off the proceeds of overseas conquests and the riches of other peoples' land and labour.

In the end Portugal became trapped by its own empire. With far-flung dominions extending along the coast of Africa, around the Cape, to India and other parts of the East, and across the ocean to Brazil, the empire was out of all proportion to Portugal's resources in population, administration and defence. The Portuguese had to be content to 'scuttle along the seashore like so many crabs', unable to evolve in their methods as the world was transformed through industrial and technological advancement.

Having entered into a 'perpetual' alliance with England in 1373 – even before the process of expansion had begun with the conquest of Ceuta in 1415 – Portugal had gradually been so surpassed by its ally that it had long become no more than a satellite of the British super-power. The first empire in India and the prosperous trade with the East had long been taken over by other imperialist rivals – the British, the Dutch and the French – and Portuguese territory was now reduced to Goa and other small enclaves in vast 'British India'. Moreover, Portugal had been overwhelmed by the march of history and had no means to defend the far-flung empire from stronger European rivals.

In order to keep the 'special relationship' with England, which had become the great 'protector' of the overseas colonies, Portuguese rulers accepted the terms of the Methuen Treaty of 1703, irrevocably compromising the country's industrialization. Under the treaty, Portugal had undertaken to accept industrial imports from England, in exchange for exports of wines and agricultural produce, to the detriment of her own fledgling textile and other industry.

This treaty, reinforced by another dating from 1810, had more than precluded Portugal from entering the age of industry, with all the multiple educational and social effects that are bound up with technological advance. As the English were to become the main source of investment in Portugal, and were to control the production and trade of Port wine as well, the treaty set up a colonial type of relationship between the two countries.

Brazil, which had become independent in 1822, under a Portuguese-born emperor, had become a republic in 1889, the year Salazar was born, and was further alienated from Portugal. The profitable slave trade, despite much resistance and prevarication, had petered out. Now it was the turn of the Portuguese to divert masses of emigrants to Brazil and provide cheap labour as well as a better demographic balance between whites and blacks.

In Africa, the dream of building an empire extending from Lourenço Marques to Luanda had been shattered by the English 'ultimatum' of 1890 claiming the lands in central-southern Africa that were deemed vital to fulfil Rhodes's design of a British-ruled empire spanning from the Cape to Cairo. And if Portugal was not able to raise the funds necessary to buy a warship to confront the mighty British fleet, even by public subscription, it certainly would not have enough capital to develop what remained of its neglected African possessions.

Lost in the age of electricity, Portugal had neither the know-how nor the equipment to open up faster maritime connections and the ports and railways that were necessary to provide sea-outlets for the landlocked territories of central Africa, from the gold-rich Rand up to copper-rich Katanga. The British duly provided Angola and Mozambique with railways and ports, owned and controlled by themselves through subsidiary companies.

Moreover, in order to settle their own differences with imperial Germany, 'perfidious Albion' had begun in 1898 the first of a series of secret negotiations with the Germans for an 'amicable partition' of Portuguese colonies between the two Great Powers. This move was accompanied by otherwise justified campaigns in the international press exposing the economic neglect and social abuses perpetrated on the 'natives' by the Portuguese colonial administration and settler populations.

37

Indeed, it appeared as if Portugal's history after nearly seven centuries of independence had now reached its full cycle. After having resisted many invasions from its Iberian neighbours and restored its independence from Spain after sixty years of rule by Spanish kings in the heyday of the Philippine empire, some republican thinkers were now debating the idea of forming a Federation of Iberian Republics. This was seen by many people as implying the eventual extinction of Portugal as a national entity and a surrender of all that successive generations had fought for.

Since Portugal had soon after the fifteenth-century golden age been surpassed even in those navigational and ship-building techniques that had accounted for its initiative in the discovery of maritime routes and uncharted lands and continents, the technical gap between Portugal and the leading industrial nations had widened at an ever-increasing pace. Although the first commercial steam engine had been introduced in England by Watt and Boulton in 1776, there are no references in Portuguese industrial inventories of its use in Portugal until after 1834. Those who wrote the few industrial studies available at the time complained that the Portuguese still did all their work by the strength of human and animal labour, while in other countries men were no longer necessary for the heaviest work and consequently the fruits of industry increased. 'In parts of Europe and the United States the rivers and even the seas are navigated by fire, without masts, sails or oars; and amongst us Portuguese not a single steam engine is established in factories,'[1] as Jose Acurcio Neves observed in a report written in the mid-nineteenth century. The figures tell the same story about the many developments in engineering, chemistry, electricity, which took place in the closing decades of the last century.

Between 1890 and 1900 more than 60 per cent of the Portuguese still worked in agriculture and less than 20 per cent in secondary industries. By 1911, the percentages had only changed to 57·1 per cent and 21·1 per cent, for agriculture and industry respectively. The number of illiterate people between 1890 and

1. Armando de Castro, *A Revolução industrial em Portugal no sec. XIX* (Dom Quixote, Lisbon, 1971), p. 263.

1911, one year after the establishment of the republic, also reflects dramatically the social backwardness and slow pace of development:

	Total percentage	Men	Women
1890	76	67·6	83·5
1900	74·1	65	82·1
1911	69·7	60·8	77·4

Again, those living during the last years of the monarchy complained that while outside Portugal a work day of twelve hours would be considered exceptionally heavy, inside Portugal a work day could last for seventeen hours. Both in the centre and in the north of the country peasants would work on their own pieces of land at night, to make themselves available for work on other peoples' land during the daytime hours. Nor was the situation better in the few incipient industries and public services. Masons and carpenters for instance, would start work in the summer at 4.30 in the morning and leave at 7.30 in the evening; girl telephone operators could be expected to work twelve hours, from 8 a.m. to 8 p.m., including Sundays.[1]

But if, faced with such overwhelming evidence, the left-wing republicans and the right-wing monarchists agreed on the need for a national revolution of some kind, they had almost diametrically opposed views as to the immediate causes of national decline. The traditionalists blamed the libertarian period of the constitutional monarchy, freedom of the press, and all those features of parliamentary government which 'carried the seeds of subversion of established social and religious values'. But the republican leaders, themselves members of the ruling middle classes, also had a vested interest in not delving too deeply into the reasons for Portugal's decadence.

The republican leaders did not see, or want to see, that if the social and economic structure of the monarchy remained intact, it mattered little to replace a king who did not govern by a president who was powerless, or to change the blue and white royal flag for the red and green republican colours, or the anthem of the *Charter* for the *Portuguesa*. As surely as fate, the capitalists

1. Jacinto Baptista Arcadia, *Cinco de outubro* (Lisbon, 1964).

would get richer and the mass of the poor would get poorer.[1]

And indeed, within a few years, there was genuine disillusionment amongst the working class. Rural workers, as so often happened in the past, took to emigration, especially to Brazil, which was now again importing massive numbers of Portuguese labourers. The urban working classes, too, began to demonstrate their discontent within months of the proclamation of the republic. The new régime had restored the right to strike and introduced legislative reforms which favoured the reorganization of trade unions immediately after the fall of the monarchy. But by March 1911, only six months after the Provisional Government had assumed power, the government was faced with yet another large front of opposition.

This is how Alexandre Vieira, one of Portugal's most militant trade unionists and best historians of the trade union movement, summed up the situation:

> Although the trade union movement had not been collectively associated with the preparations for the establishment of the republic, many of its individual militants had actively cooperated with those preparations – and the truth is that it was with justified satisfaction that the working class had welcomed the new political régime, for which a great many workers had fought with weapons in their hands.
>
> The mass of the people were convinced that with the coming of the republic their precarious economic existence would improve. But as up to the end of 1910 no favourable change had been noticed, the impatience of workers had begun to be expressed, and many workforces came out on strike in 1911, notably those of the Lisbon Tramways Co., CP [National Railways] as well as shop assistants, metal workers, gas company workers, ferry-boat operators and stevedores at the Port of Lisbon, and printers. In the town of Setubal the sardine and tuna canning factory workers also went on strike and here, as the police used violence against the strikers, all other trade union organizations in the town came out in their support. The murder of two strikers by the Republican Guard added to public indignation.[2]

1. Cunha Leal, *As Minhas Memorias* (Lisbon, 1966), pp. 184–5.
2. Alexandre Vieira, *Para a historia do sindicalismo em Portugal* (Seara Nova, Lisbon, 1970), p. 42.

The contemporary labour magazine *Terra Livre (Free Land)*, commenting upon the same events, stated that '13 March 1911 is the date that marks the divorce between the republic and the working class'.[1] From then on the trade union movement was to become one of the greatest enemies of the 'bourgeois' republic.

In 1917, Portugal had hardly any heavy or manufacturing industries. Whereas Belgium, a country with a comparable population, had an installed motor capacity with a total of 700,000 h.p., the total for Portugal did not exceed 83,368 h.p., 10 per cent of which was generated by hydraulic, rather than combustion motors.[2] At that time Portugal had an industrial working population of a little over 130,000, out of a total population of six million. Of the total number of workers 35 per cent were women and over 15 per cent were children. Moreover, industrial workers were dispersed in minute manufacturing units, 60 per cent of which were located in or around the most important cities: Lisbon, Oporto, Aveiro, Setubal and Braga. While there were nearly 4,000 factories with less than ten workers, only nineteen factories had between 500 and 1,000 workers, and only six more than 1,000 workers.[3]

Yet the Portuguese working class, throughout the republican period, showed a remarkable degree of organization and was perhaps the most important single group influencing the political development in the country.

Most of the many organized strikes were, predictably enough, concerned with increases in wages, but many also related to demands over working conditions and high issues of principle at the time, notably the establishment of the eight-hour working day, which was finally granted in 1919.

The following table shows the number of strikes during the republican period, their causes and results:

1. *Terra livre* (Lisbon), No. 6, 20 March 1913.
2. Armando de Castro, *Desenvolvimento economico ou estagnação?* (Dom Quixote, Lisbon, 1970).
3. Jose Pacheco Pereira, 'As lutas operarias contra a carestia da vida em Portugal', in *Textos de apoio* (Oporto), No. 2, 1971.

Year	Total no.	Reasons				Outcomes		
		Wages	Support	Working hours	Other	Compromise	Victory	Defeat
1910	85	47	4	17	14	36	36	6
1911	162	64	39	21	41	43	73	21
1912	35	3	12	4	16	13	1	7
1913	19	5	2	4	6	8	5	3
1914	10	2	1	2	5	4	2	1
1915	15	5	2	7	1	9	4	2
1916	7	3	—	3	1	4	3	—
1917	26	12	—	9	4	10	14	2
1918	11	6	1	3	1	4	3	3
1919	21	7	8	2	3	8	7	3
1920	39	19	6	3	11	26	9	4
1921	10	4	2	—	4	4	2	2
1922	22	11	7	3	1	6	10	2
1923	21	7	5	2	7	7	4	3
1924	25	10	4	4	7	11	5	4
1925	10	2	4	3	1	3	4	—
	518	207	97	87	123	196	182	63

Source: *Anuario estatistico de Portugal* (Imprensa Nacional, Lisbon, 1927).

The workers published hundreds of newspapers and magazines, some ephemeral, others linked to the biggest labour organizations. Their names could be so suggestive that even a short random selection will give an indication of their mood and direction: *A Batalha* (*The Battle*), *A Bandeira Vermelha* (*The Red Flag*), *O Comunista* (*The Communist*), *A Conquista do Pão* (*The Conquest of Bread*).

The main workers' organizations had international affiliations and contacts in many European countries, including the newly created Soviet Union. The União Operaria Nacional (Workers' National Union), founded at a Labour Congress in the town of Tomar in 1914, gave place later to the CGT (Confederação Geral do Trabalho – General Confederation of Labour), related to its foreign counterparts. In 1917, following the Russian Revolution, the anarcho-syndicalist Portuguese Maximalist Federation came to the fore, and 1921 saw the emergence of the Partido Comunista Portugues (Portuguese Communist Party). In 1923, following the organization of a separate trade union movement by the communists in Moscow, the Internacional Sindicalista Vermelha (Red International Trades Union) in Portugal had been formed. It appeared as if the downtrodden Portuguese working class was dreaming of its own revolution and was on the way to achieving a fair deal.

Salazar and his friends at the CADC were following these events from Coimbra. The social agitation, and its economic consequences, only served to reinforce their dislike of democratic and parliamentary rule and their aversion to freedom of press and association, which they held to be an open way to indiscipline and subversion. And although their own counter-revolutionary, but rather less successful, Catholic Workers' and Youth Associations were themselves linked to Christian internationalist groups in Italy, France and other countries – not to mention their alleged connections with Heaven – Salazar saw in the free trade union movement a confirmation of the dangers of 'internationalism'.

He had, however, plenty of reasons not to lose heart. The Great Powers, despite the diversions and antagonisms that had culminated in the First World War, were still refraining from giving any comfort or economic aid to the socialist-leaning republic. The Vatican, through its influential connections with Catholic kings and governments and many friends in the international press, was helping to bring discredit upon republican Portugal. Reactionary circles all over Europe worked towards the same end so spontaneously that even the British residents in Portugal, never to be heard in matters of conscience after the right-wing *coup d'état* of May 1926, were adding to the protests. Referring to conditions in several prisons, an improvised Committee of British Residents in Portugal alleged that political prisoners were being brutally treated. In statements published in British papers they described the punishment cells as

places of horror, without air or light, with stone floors, and kept in a filthy condition, overrun with rats and full of vermin ... The infirmary is composed of a single room in a dirty and insanitary condition, where patients suffering from every kind of disease, infectious or otherwise, are placed together; often cotton wool and dressings are used a second time on a different patient, this having led in many cases to blood poisoning.[1]

In the following year, a British National Committee, headed by the Earl of Lytton, Adeline, Duchess of Bedford, and the Hon. Aubrey Herbert, M P, was also fulminating against the republican régime from England, holding public meetings and writing denunciations in the press against the republican tyranny in Portugal.[2] And of course, *The Times* was not happy either.

Salazar himself, although silent on prison conditions, was extremely indignant at the indiscriminate arrests made during the republican period and this might have influenced the coldness and cynicism with which republican opponents and successive generations of political prisoners were to be treated under his rule. Referring to members of various parties which had been victimized by arbitrary arrests, Salazar, in a defence statement during a disciplinary inquiry at the University of Coimbra in 1919, alleged that '. . . in the course of a few years, half the population of Portugal – monarchists, Catholics, democrats, evolutionists, Camachists, syndicalists, socialists, Sidonists, and some with no political views at all – have entered the prisons and fortresses of the republic, sometimes successively, sometimes alternately, and sometimes simultaneously'.[3]

Moreover, inside Portugal, as Catholic resistance was being reorganized at all levels and gaining momentum, mysterious events of religious and political significance began to take place. In the years of the Russian Revolution and the consequent emergence of the first communist and anarcho-syndicalist workers' groups in Portugal, three child shepherds, Lucia de Jesus, aged ten, and her cousins Francisco and Jacinta Marto,

---

1. Report of a Committee of British Residents, in Bragança-Cunha, op. cit., p. 147. See also *Morning Post*, 30 January 1912, *Spectator*, 22 March 1913, and other newspapers of that time.
2. See *Nineteenth Century Review*, May 1913.
3. A. de O. Salazar, *A Minha Resposta*, op. cit., p. 34.

aged eight and seven, all as illiterate and simple-minded as could be expected amongst peasant children at the time, had begun to see apparitions. They claimed they had first been visited by an angel in the spring of 1916 but now, on 13 May 1917 at a point called Cova da Iria, not far from the ancient town of Leiria, the visitor had been a 'beautiful girl of sixteen' standing on an oak tree.

At first, so the story goes, she merely asked that the three should meet in the same spot on the 13th of every month. But on 13 October, in a final appearance before 70,000 people who had gathered to witness the meeting, the visitor is alleged to have identified herself as 'Our Lady of the Rosary' who had come out from Heaven to entrust some divine messages to the three shepherds. To mark the occasion she is alleged to have requested that a church be built on the spot to welcome even more pilgrims. Apparently the celestial visitor had a message of pacifism and hope to deliver and was duly declared worthy of credence by the Bishop of Leiria, who gave sanction for the cult of 'Our Lady of Fatima' in 1930.

The message of pacifism was rather untimely and embarrassing for the Republican government, as Portugal had just entered the war against Germany and the unsophisticated soldiers could become confused and lose their fighting spirit. But although no one, apart from the young shepherds, actually heard anything, and the full message was never made public, the persistent rumour amongst the credulous mass of the Portuguese was that 'Our Lady of Fatima' had chosen Portugal to announce the conversion of Bolshevik Russia to Catholicism, and other events of worldwide interest.

There have been several exposés of the alleged apparitions at Fatima as a fraud, and a book circulating clandestinely in Portugal, by Tomas da Fonseca, *A Verdade sobre Fatima* (*The Truth about Fatima*), explains the economic, political and religious reasons for the emergence of the cult. Many Catholics ignore the cult, however, on the theological grounds that unlike Islam with Mecca, and Judaism with Jerusalem, the concept of a central 'holy place' is alien to Christianity; other Catholics are embarrassed by the conspicuous commercialism pervading the village of Fatima, and the 'branches' of the cult that have been set up in the overseas territories. The Pope, however, visited the shrine on 13 May 1967 to mark the fiftieth anniversary of the alleged apparitions.

That Portugal should have been elected to receive such an important message by a Portuguese-speaking celestial visitor from the top of an oak tree, in a place suitable to build a shrine and sanctuary capable of accommodating hundreds of thousands of pilgrims and vying with Lourdes is one of those natural mysteries that a good Catholic nationalist Portuguese is expected to accept without question. Besides, visitors from Heaven already knew how to find little Portugal in the universe. According to popular belief, Count Afonso Henriques, who seized power from his own mother to become Portugal's first king, had received divine advice in 1139 from none other than Christ himself during an eve-of-battle meeting in the fields of Ourique.

Moreover, according to rumour and anonymous literature distributed at the time amongst peasant people, Our Lady of Fatima had shown great concern in the Portuguese situation during the republic. She had confided to the three shepherds that the country would soon be rescued from the war and from its financial, economic and moral chaos by a 'saviour'. And no doubt, in the irrationally immodest nationalist circles, Salazar was one of the many men who alone knew whom Our Lady had in mind.

Chapter 2
Rich man's steward and dictator

> *'The army has the secret of perpetual
> youth, and like a great and ancient family
> of noble descent it maintains and passes on
> its traditions so unimpaired and alive that
> it always forms one and the same moral
> unity'* –
> SALAZAR

The road to power

Understanding the significance of edifying theological omens, a member of the CADC group launched the first issue of a new periodical called *A Voz de Fatima* (*The Voice of Fatima*). But at their regular meetings the students were discussing other encouraging events taking place in Portugal and abroad. The Portuguese monarchists, who had found asylum and support in King Alfonso XIII's Spain, and had carried out armed incursions and conspiracies almost every year since 1911, were now gaining a new impetus.

In 1919 the monarchy had been restored temporarily at Oporto. Paiva Couceiro, a monarchist officer who had previously invaded northern Portugal from Spain, was proclaimed regent; an attempt to extend the monarchist revolt to Lisbon had been curbed at Monsanto, and eventually, with the defeat of the monarchist forces at Mirandela, the republicans had regained control of the northernmost provinces. But, according to news of meetings between 'integralist' delegates and the exiled King Manuel, in London, 'two more monarchist revolts were planned for later in the same year', and it would be only a matter of time before the monarchists would again rule in Portugal.

But Salazar had many other practical reasons for comfort. As fascism in Italy and Spain were gaining the momentum that led to the dictatorships of Mussolini and Primo de Rivera, in 1922 and

47

1923 respectively, the republican régime was becoming increasingly more vulnerable inside Portugal itself.

The agitation of the Portuguese working class was causing many surprising reactions within the élite of republican leaders and the ranks of middle-class supporters. They were discovering that in the old days, during the monarchy, the antiroyalist struggles had acted as a common denominator of unity. Now the republicans were divided into various factions with different degrees of radicalism and moderation. Put to the test, the socialist leanings of many republicans were revealed as no more than an intellectual posture, which was now overcome by the instinct of defence of the class in which they had been socially and culturally brought up. At first, most republicans had been supporting the veteran Partido Republicano (Republican Party) led by positivist and anti-clerical Afonso Costa. But although the nucleus of revolutionaries around the party had had decades in which to develop their views and aims, within a year there were sharp divergences over many of the basic points of the rather sweeping and ambitious programme of the Provisional Government. Points of contention developed over the question of how to react to the new situation. The basic points of the programme touched all aspects of Portuguese life: the development of education and defence; administrative decentralization and autonomy for the overseas territories; the establishment of fundamental civic rights, guaranteed by an independent judicial system; strengthening credit and finance; increasing production, industrialization and external trade. Moreover, as has been mentioned, the programme included the separation of Church and State; obligatory civil registration; legalization of divorce; limitation of religious orders; expulsion of monks and nuns; and the setting up of lay institutions, including 'lay missions', to speed up education in the overseas territories. The constitution, voted in on 18 August 1911, provided for a parliamentary republic with a constituent assembly, later divided into a senate and a lower house. The president held executive power and appointed the government with ministers selected from the members of the parliamentary majority party.

48

By the time of the first presidential elections the republicans were divided into two factions, each supporting a different candidate – one party, comprising the majority of radicals and progressives, adopted the name of the Democratic Party, still under the leadership of Afonso Costa; the dissident minority, led by Costa's great rival Antonio Jose de Almeida, formed the more right-wing Evolutionist Party, so named to emphasize its non-revolutionary nature and attract a more moderate type of supporter. There were other minor parties, and within a few years time-consuming inter-party feuding was to develop into a labyrinth of parties and coalitions.

To add to the parliamentary agitation and the inter-party antagonisms instigated by different newspapers and magazines, the régime was still threatened by the monarchists and other right-wing forces. The first attempt to re-establish a dictatorship was made by General Pimenta e Castro, but it lasted only for about four months between January and May 1915. Another was led by Major Sidonio Pais in December 1917 and arose partly from the difficulties and divergences caused by Portugal's entry into the First World War.

In such a situation the succession of governments was causing much confusion in diplomatic circles abroad, and further discontent inside the country. The international press, despite the fact that a Portuguese expeditionary force was fighting with the Allies on the front in France, was accusing Portugal of being the only European country too absorbed with its internal problems to be concerned with the war. At home, both the middle-class press as well as the trade union movement were noting that more time was being spent on party politics and parliamentary rhetoric than practical administration.

The widespread dissatisfaction might explain why Sidonio Pais, after his *pronunciamento* (*coup*), was actually elected President with only 513,958 votes cast in his favour – a result which, despite the limitations of the suffrage, gave a warning that a considerable part of the qualifying middle-class and literate electors was showing a desire to return to authoritarian rule.

President Sidonio Pais, seen by many as a precursor of the

dictatorship that was to come in 1926, had his career as a dictator ended when he was shot and fatally wounded at Lisbon's main railway station, Rocio, on 14 December 1918, one year and nine days after his own *coup d'état*. But he was by no means the only man assassinated for political reasons during the period. The republic, which had been born in the aftermath of the murder of the king and his heir, was marked by violence, not only upon ordinary workers on strike or in street demonstrations, but upon well-known public figures as well. In one day alone, 19 October 1919, a group of marines and members of a revolutionary society, the Carbonaria, called on the homes of moderate republican leaders, whom they suspected of pro-monarchist treason, and simply murdered those they found. According to the *Annual Register* for 1921, in the previous year alone Portugal had had 'nine governments, one lasting for twenty-four hours and another for six days'. In fact, the 'Democratic Republic' was to end its sixteen years of rule, from 1910 to the final *coup d'état* in 1926, with a record of nine presidents, forty-four governments, twenty-five uprisings, and three counter-revolutionary dictatorships.

Obviously, as has been shown, most of the violent actions were originated not by the republicans or democrats, but by the forces of reaction converging against them. Republican violence, in its turn, was often either exercised in the course of self-defence or took the form of individual, rather than institutional, acts.

Salazar did not share the libertarian ideals of republicanism, or the somewhat romantic vision of the republic that was to be retained by successive generations of democrats, particularly after the republic had been overthrown by the *coup d'état* of 1926 and institutionalized repression became the order of the day. But if one is to explain Salazar's ideas one must take into account that he always kept fresh in his memory the agitation against the Church, the clergy and ordinary Catholics, in the early days of the republic, followed by the growing divisions and antagonisms between republican factions. In fact, he was to reveal an obsession with 'law and order', and a disturbing ruthlessness in curbing what he called at different times 'the rule of the mob', 'street power' and 'subversion by the masses'. Having been deprived as a child of a youthful and relaxed environment, Salazar was always the opposite of the romantic liberal. For him, 'true liberty can only exist in the spirit of man . . . there can be absolute authority; there can never be absolute liberty; order has always been the true condition of beauty'.[1]

If one takes into account how isolated the small Portuguese republic was internationally, the reactionary pressures to which it was subjected, and the impact of the First World War, which extended over much of the short-lived republican period, one cannot dismiss the republic just as a historical episode of no lasting consequence. The republicans had inherited a humanitarian tradition from the liberals and constitutionalists under the monarchy, who had abolished the death penalty in Portugal as far back as 1867 – long before any of the 'Great Powers' who claim the leadership of progressive enlightenment. Indeed, some of the republic's first laws, abolishing duelling, gambling and prostitution, must have proved embarrassing for those moralist forces of convention who had allowed those institutions to persist. All the major republican legislative acts, from the Law of Separation of Church and State to reforms and expansion of the educational system, had a crucial significance in the backward and obscurantist Portugal of their time. In 1911, after only one year of government, the number of schools had increased by 20 per cent.[2]

And even if most of their achievements – freedom of the press, the right of association, the right to strike, divorce, the secularization of education – were to be reversed after 1926, in some basic social features Portugal was never to look back. The Portuguese, by and large, had rejected the monarchy as a completely surpassed system which embodied an unjust and archaic aristocratic order. The aristocracy might have only been replaced by a middle class which asserted its social ascendancy by having a good business, a high rank in the army or attaining a

1. *Salazar Says* (Secretariado de Propaganda Nacional, Lisbon, no date), p. 31.
2. *Censo da população de Portugal*, No. 1, December 1911, p. 23.

university diploma; the old titles might have only been succeeded by other styles of address, such as *'senhor professor'*, *'senhor doutor'*, *'senhor engenheiro'* (engineer) or, alternatively, *'vossa excelencia'* (your excellency). 'We are now all called *excelentissimos senhores,'* remarked a disillusioned Portuguese of the time to a visiting French writer.[1] But the fact remains that the old and anti-scientific concepts embodied in the hereditary rights of the monarchic system were overcome by the republican assertion of a theoretical equality conditioned by achievement. And in the same way that King Carlos, in the last years of his rule, complained that 'the monarchy was governed by republicans', the monarchists had to resign themselves to sharing the government of a dictatorship under a puppet president after 1926, rather than press too far for the restoration of the monarchy. Salazar himself appeared happy enough with his promotion from *'senhor doutor'* to *'senhor professor doutor'* when he was appointed to a teaching post in Economics and Finance at Coimbra University, though he certainly had his eyes set on even higher targets.

It is now accepted that in the first years of his administration Afonso Costa had been successful in halting the successive deficits of previous monarchist budgets and had managed to achieve even a small surplus. But the trouble was that few people in Portugal had more than a vague notion of political economy. With power traditionally alternating between the military class and the legal profession, the concept of economy was confined to the casual administrative intuition of lawyers and politicians.

In the particular circumstances of such a country as Portugal it is improbable that a political economist would advise a revolutionary overhaul of every institution and proclaim a socialist republic isolated from the economic context in which it was situated. But barring unforeseen factors, the simple manipulation of the budget would not offer a lasting solution either.

Portugal was classified as an 'agricultural country', but it was neither self-sufficient in food production nor capable of pro-

1. See André Maurois, *The Silence of Colonel Bramble* (Bodley Head, 1965).

viding itself with modernized farming equipment or chemical fertilizers. All the coal for its railways, ships and industrial machines was imported from Britain.

Foreign trade earnings were confined to a handful of agricultural and maritime products – wine, cork, sardines, a few minerals, and a few tropical raw materials and foodstuffs from the colonies. But all the capital equipment required to develop the country's infrastructures, as well as industrial raw-materials – iron, steel and other essential metals – had to be imported. Invisible earnings, mostly in the form of remittances from emigrants in Brazil, did not cover the trade deficits and were, furthermore, an unreliable source of income.

As for the empire, such was the neglect and stagnation that most of its component parts were a liability rather than an asset. This mystery, which no doubt baffled the budgetary accountants, was no surprise to political economists. After all, most of the production was in the hands of chartered companies under foreign control; a great deal of the shipping, ports and railway services were owned by British concerns. The true economic picture could perhaps be seen in the companies' books and reports, but the budgets only reflected a partial view. Needless to say, in such circumstances, whether the companies were owned by foreigners or by nationals who spent their profits abroad, the end result was that the net income hardly covered the administrative and military expenses of the sleeping empire.

It is, therefore, only natural that Portugal should have experienced a period of social and economic turbulence now that there was open government and free discussion and that such factors, instead of helping, should have aggravated the situation.

Reading the newspapers and books that have been written about this period, one finds all the features of an irreversible crisis. While the national debt, particularly to Britain, increased, the classical pattern of rising prices – labour unrest, strikes – had been set in motion. The working class, which now demanded the rights that for so long had been denied to it, was the greatest victim in economic terms and suffered most from repressive measures. Between 1914 and 1922, according to estimates based on official statistics, while the average wages for artisans and industrial workers had increased seven times, the average prices for essential foodstuffs had increased twelve times.[1]

The following table shows the increase in the cost of living as compared with the increase in wages during most of the republican period:

Year (July)	Wages Index	Cost of Living Index
1914	100	100
1915	—	111·5
1916	—	137·1
1917	—	162·3
1918	—	292·7
1919	317	316·8
1920	400	551·6
1921	750	816·7
1922	900	1128·0
1923	1650	1719·5
1924	2241	2652·0
1925	2230	2286·4
1926	2096	2147·9
1927	2183	2430·1

Source: *Anuario estatistico de Portugal* (Imprensa Nacional, Lisbon, 1927), p. 269.

It was a situation of which a few could take advantage to the detriment of everyone else. Republican governments had to contend with interest rates of 11 per cent on Treasury Bills, while 20 and 25 per cent rates for private advances were current throughout the country. Many banks showed substantial profits in the midst of a country-wide depression. Virtually every economic indicator tells the same story. The escudo was being devalued with regularity and the government had little hope of halting the spiral. Many finance ministers tried to balance the budget – the great obsession at the time – but the budgetary deficits, when converted into gold at the current rate of exchange for each fiscal year, were accumulating at an annual

1. José Pacheco Pereira, 'As lutas operarias contra a carestia da vida em Portugal', in *Textos de apoio* (Oporto), No. 2, 1971, pp. 178–9.

rate of £5m., which meant that within a few years the accumulated deficit would be greater than the entire budget. Many of the lawyers and army officers who had passed through the republic's forty-four governments had begun to realize that the effort of balancing the national budget was, to quote a Portuguese saying, 'as futile as to try and straighten the shadow of a twisted tree'. But many others within the establishment, whose personal and class interests were bound up with the idea of 'national survival', were claiming that the 'country was sick' and this time choosing freedom and democracy as the scapegoat.

Although the republican period may be regarded as having been dominated by 'civilian power', the military were never far from key positions in the administration, both in Portugal and the overseas territories. In fact, if one balances the brilliant *'senhores doutores'*, mainly lawyers, who animated the republican scene with the military figures of the régime, one finds that their numbers are almost even. Some, like Commander Machado Santos and General Norton de Matos, were genuinely liberal 'republicans'. But others – like General Gomes da Costa, the Portuguese First World War hero who served under the *'senhores doutores'*, always remained identified with a military establishment which lurked behind the scenes of civilian administration.

By 1923 the financial situation had come to a head. The expenses incurred by the wartime coalition government which had called itself the 'Sacred Union' were still unpaid. Britain had only financed the expeditionary force sent to the front in France, but Portugal had had to engage in more immediate defence operations in Mozambique and Angola against the Germans, and its debt to London was £80m. With devaluation of the escudo since the war this was equivalent to 8,000m. escudos by 1924. A further loan was contracted, this time at 13 per cent interest.

Socially Portugal had reached the point described in a popular saying to the effect that 'in a home with no bread, all quarrel and no one is right'. There were strikes in vital industries and services; unrest in the army; even street conflicts between the police and the Republican Guard. Even veteran fighters like Afonso Costa, then living in Paris, had refused to return and attempt to form a government. On 8 November 1925 – in a year that already had seen the fall of four governments – Teixeira Gomes, a refined and sensitive man who was Portugal's representative in London, was elected President of the Republic. But he, too, disgusted with the confusing situation and anxious to be left in peace, resigned within a month of taking office. He was succeeded by Bernardino Machado, a man who, despite his seventy years and bitter experiences during a previous presidential term of office (1915–17) which had been ended by Sidonio Pais's *pronunciamento*, was still prepared to accept the presidency as a matter of civic duty.

In February 1926 a group of army radicals, headed by a civilian leader, Martins Junior, attempted another revolt which was suppressed upon the arrest of the leaders. The next session of parliament, which saw the discussion of an embarrassing and highly controversial proposal for a government takeover of the tobacco industry, was more agitated and bitter than usual.

A famous fraud by a Portuguese businessman, Alves Reis, had brought further international discredit to Portugal. As if to emphasize Portugal's chaotic situation and neglect of the colonies, Alves Reis had decided to set up his own investment bank, the 'Angola & Metropole'. But having no capital, and wanting to spare himself the trouble of printing notes one by one, Reis had departed from the classical pattern of counterfeiting by managing to falsify single-handed an entire set of requisitions, on 'behalf' of the board of directors of the Bank of Portugal, to the London specialist printers Waterlow & Sons, for an entire re-issue of 200,000 notes of 500 escudos denomination. Undetected for a few years he had, indeed, been investing a great deal of 'his' capital in Angola; but now the fraud had been discovered and the Bank of Portugal had to sue the London printers for compensation, bringing the respectable firm of Waterlow near to bankruptcy and banking and administrative security in Portugal into further disrepute.[1]

1. See Murray Teigh Bloom, *The Man who Stole Portugal* (Secker & Warburg, 1967).

Salazar and his disciples at the CADC were not amused by these events and began to make the sign of the cross in a fashion that more and more resembled the 'thumbs-down' sign in the ancient Roman circuses. Both nationally and internationally, there were for him encouraging developments in the 'right' direction, in more senses than one. Mussolini and Primo de Rivera were now established as dictators in Italy and Spain, Hitler, having published *Mein Kampf* and recovered from the failure of the Nazi 'putsch' at Munich, had now reconstituted the Nazi Party. In Britain, after the sensation of the 'Zinoviev Letter', the Labour government had fallen and the Portuguese republicans had lost their only friend in high places – none other than Prime Minister Ramsay MacDonald[1] – and saw the old Tory, Baldwin, back in power.

In Portugal the impact of these events and the teachings of the CADC were echoing in the hearts of many good nationalists. One of the most promising was the young Marcello Caetano, a Lisbon law student and a veteran right-wing militant by the time he was twenty years old. He was the editor of a political magazine named *Ordem Nova* (*New Order*) which had proclaimed in the front page of its inaugural issue a set of principles certainly provocative and perhaps even further to the right than those professed by the CADC: 'An anti-modern, anti-liberal, anti-democratic, anti-bourgeois, and anti-bolshevik magazine; counter-revolutionary and reactionary; Catholic, Apostolic and Roman; monarchist, intolerant and intransigent; showing no solidarity with writers, journalists, or any other professionals in the arts, letters and press.' And while this might be dismissed as youthful ideological enthusiasm, the more mature men of the 'integralist' movement were looking further into the past, perhaps to compete with the Italian and German ultra-nationalists, in their theories of 'Lusitanianism'. According to them neither of Portugal's frontiers – the sea and Spain – were accidental; the modern Portuguese were descended from a pre-Roman tribe, the 'Lusitanians', who resisted Roman occupation under the leadership of the shepherd Viriato, who was, there-

1. See V. de Bragança-Cunha, *Revolutionary Portugal (1910–1936)* (James Clarke, London, 1937), p. 161.

fore, the first known hero of an incipient Portuguese nationality. Such theories were a little too sophisticated for discussion in army barracks and officers' messes but many generals and colonels, Viriato or no Viriato, knew that something had to be done to save the country and with it their social status, manly pride and privileged pay and conditions of work.

Appropriately enough, the military Messiah, when he came, took his inspiration from Braga, a little town in northern Portugal, some twenty miles north of Oporto and in the heart of the original county of Portucale, from which the country had expanded. Braga, the seat of the Archbishop, Primate of All Portugal, a town famous for its seven seminaries, its Academy of Theology and its annual programme of holy festivals and processions, was the point from which the ageing General Gomes da Costa set out for Lisbon at the head of a small army. He met little resistance. Not content with imitating Mussolini's March on Rome, the General even repeated the Duce's words:

> The parliamentary system has outlived its day ... what we need is a real National Government which will enable the State to fulfil its mission on a basis of justice and honour. But only the army can create such a government, only the army can give the citizen liberty – safe and sane liberty of the kind he needs.

A triumvirate junta including General Carmona and Commander Mendes Cabeçadas – leader of an aborted revolt in July 1925 – was formed. General Carmona, a friend of the then ruling Spanish dictator, Primo Rivera, was less idealistic when he explained to a foreign journalist the circumstances of his decision: 'I was at Evora [the small capital town of Upper Alemtejo], my military post, when officers came and told me there had been a revolution, and that there was need of me. I went to Lisbon and joined the government. I was a soldier. I stand for the army ... that is all.'[1]

The seemingly naïve and physically delicate General Carmona was soon to be the only survivor of the triumvirate.

1. William Leon Smyser, 'General Carmona: Dictatorship without a Dictator in Portugal', in *Contemporary Review*, September 1930.

Gomes da Costa, who had become over-enthusiastic and too demanding, was soon deported to the islands of the Azores and duly honoured with the title of Field-Marshal; Commander Mendes Cabeçadas was to withdraw and fall into obscurity. But if Carmona had been shrewd enough to become president, the post he was to hold through successive unopposed elections until he died in 1951, he was at a loss as to how he should govern the country.

He had, however, heard of Senhor Professor Doutor Antonio de Oliveira Salazar of Coimbra University, who was then a comparatively young thirty-seven. The conservative and Catholic press, from as far away as Oporto, was hailing Salazar as 'a great intellectual, one of the most powerful in the new generation'. And by all accounts Salazar certainly was clever. Significantly, during the dictatorship of Sidonio Pais, in 1918, he had been invited to join the Finance Ministry as a secretary; he had politely declined – only four months before that strongman was assassinated and promptly replaced. In 1921 he had been one of three Catholic deputies elected to Parliament; he made one appearance in the Chamber of Deputies and decided to return to Coimbra and Santa Comba to reflect on his own. He had, indeed, kept aloof from the political turmoil of the times.

Like the witchdoctor of a backward tribe, Salazar said much that was impressively spiritualist and obscure.

The modern State which does not profess any allegiance to a Supreme Being and, at the same time, declares that its *raison d'être* is not of itself the will of the people, finds itself in a very awkward position ... A changing will, which expresses and imposes itself in different directions, endangers the State both as regards fundamental principle and constitution. The indispensable stability can be assured only in two ways. Either the State must withdraw itself from the fluctuations of public opinion, and this would be tantamount to a denial of its own position, or it must maintain a public opinion that is stable and consistent so far as the essential part of the doctrine is concerned.

And so on and so forth. He also made some disturbing admissions for someone who lectured on economics, such as 'I owe to Providence the grace of being poor.' But he also uttered many platitudes which the simple-minded, but powerful, establishment found less difficult to read and more comforting: 'Give us these souls transformed by the Christian spirit of obedience, renunciation, and love. The peace of Christ is perfectly compatible with trade unionism, with new methods of labour, new systems of property, and with very different types of organization.'[1]

General Carmona, having heard good recommendations, duly sent for the young Professor of Economics, who, as was to be expected, turned out not to have any miraculous and immediate cure for the evils and debts besetting the country. Appointed Finance Minister, Salazar soon had a disagreement with the then Prime Minister, Colonel Vicente de Freitas, which resulted in the latter's replacement by General Ivens Ferraz and Salazar's own return to Coimbra. Apparently Salazar had imposed stringent conditions for his acceptance of the Finance Ministry, had demanded full powers over expenditure and had talked of long-term solutions and hard work.

In the following year, the new Finance Minister, General Sinel Cordes, put into practice a plan promising faster results. He secured first an agreement with Britain, signed by Winston Churchill, by which the Portuguese debt was scaled down from £28m. to £23m. He then proposed to pledge the State monopoly of tobacco in exchange for a loan. This suggestion was turned down and as a contingency he applied for a loan to the League of Nations in Geneva.

A specially appointed Financial Committee of Inquiry, after a visit to Portugal, approved of a loan of £12m., but on certain conditions. These included a balanced budget in the next few years; a halt to inflation and devaluation; consolidation of the State's debt to the Bank of Portugal; and, eventually, redemption of the League's loan with an international loan. To guarantee payment, however, the League demanded that an international commission should supervise the collection of customs duties.

1. F. C. C. Egerton, *Salazar, Rebuilder of Portugal* (Hodder & Stoughton, 1943), pp. 112–13.

Now, for the first and only time, the points of view of the democratic opposition and those of the frustrated Salazar almost coincided. The democratic opposition, which still included men who had held ministerial and diplomatic posts, made representations abroad pointing out that the granting of the loan, apart from showing a favouritism towards the new régime that had been denied to the republican governments, was a form of aid to an unrepresentative government. Inside Portugal, however, they denounced it as a national humiliation, while Salazar, in an interview with the Lisbon daily newspaper *O Seculo*, made the same point by referring to it as 'alms' – always in keeping with his religious imagery.

After the failure to negotiate the loan the military junta was ready to surrender. They promptly summoned Salazar, apologized for past misunderstandings and accepted the equally humiliating terms imposed by him. These terms are described in an address by Salazar to the Portuguese Cabinet in April 1928, which has since become a public document of historical interest to Portugal and of some curiosity to students of politics. It ran:

I have accepted this office, but please do not offer me your thanks. To me it means such a sacrifice that I could not have undertaken it just for the sake of obliging someone. It is a sacrifice I am willing to make for my country, in serene and calm discharge of a conscientious duty. Nevertheless I could not have undertaken such a heavy task if I had not at least been certain of the usefulness of my action, and if I had not been assured of efficient working conditions.

Your Excellency the Prime Minister has testified here that the Cabinet is unanimous in its views on this matter and has agreed on a form of collaboration with me (the Finance Minister) ... under an arrangement which has been reduced to the following four points:

(a) each government department shall undertake to limit and organize its services within the total amount allotted to it by the Ministry of Finance;

(b) any measures adopted by the various government departments which may directly affect the State's revenue and expenditure shall be discussed beforehand and an agreement arrived at with the Ministry of Finance;

61

(c) the Ministry of Finance shall be entitled to place its veto on all increases of current and ordinary expenditure for development purposes, for which the necessary credit operations shall not be undertaken without the knowledge of the Ministry of Finance;

(d) the Ministry of Finance undertakes to collaborate with the other departments in such measures as may be adopted for the reduction of expenditure or collection of revenue, which will be organized as far as possible on uniform principles . . .

This rigid code, by which our common task will be guided, shows a firm determination to set in order, once and for all, the economic and financial life of the nation.

And he added peremptorily:

I know quite well what I want and where I am going, but let it not be demanded that I reach my goal in a few months. For the rest, let the country study, let it suggest, let it claim, let it discuss, but when the time comes for me to give orders I shall expect it to obey.

Well – Salazar had not, after all, been wasting his time in the 'shade and solitude'. It almost seemed as if the respected Professor of Economics from Coimbra had decided to take seriously a national joke to the effect that the only way of balancing the national budget was simply to eliminate expenditure.

In fact, under his budgetary reform, Salazar was to distribute orders to every department, commanding those responsible to eliminate, within forty-five days, any staff, vehicles, equipment or items of expenditure that might be regarded as superfluous. He himself provided the example, by dressing more grimly than most funeral directors and still using ordinary dip pens long after the fountain pen had been introduced in Portugal. The reasons for his austerity, however, were far more complex than this anecdote would suggest: he was determined to find at this stage a way out through budgetary reforms, rather than adopt any effective and far-reaching social and economic measures, in order to appease and please the *'excelentissimos senhores generais'* and others who had brought him to power. In the last analysis, Salazar's power as a dictator would, as in the cases of all other dictators, be consolidated through subservient cunning and an acrobatic manipulation of the forces nominally under his command.

Since Salazar, to the best of public knowledge, was not getting money from Heaven, the process of bringing the budget from a deficit of some £3m. in 1927–8, to a surplus of £16,000 in the following fiscal year (the first of his office) could be regarded as the work of a talented budget director, heedless of the demands of public services, including education, health, social assistance and so forth. In a speech made on 25 August 1929, Salazar himself admitted: 'The nation has been burdened with more than 360,000m. escudos of taxes. These might have been, in many cases, their misery, their tears, their blood. It remains to be seen, in full conscience of such great sacrifices, whether the Finance Minister has been too zealous in administering public expenditure.'

Salazar's zeal as Minister of Finance was not in question. More questionable was his order of priorities, which revealed his intention to further his political career and accumulation of power. According to a report by the League of Nations for the years 1928–9, and covering six other European countries – the United Kingdom, France, Italy, Czechoslovakia, Romania and Hungary – Portugal was one of the countries with the heaviest defence expenditure. In fact, no less than 23·42 per cent of the entire budget, compared with 10·63 for the United Kingdom, was being spent on defence. If Salazar was to remain an enemy of democratic and parliamentary institutions and methods, it is because he already had his eyes set on governing without vote-catching. His technique 'was to keep the archaic and ruinous military caste happy'[1] and rely on a tacit mutual understanding with it to achieve and retain power. It was a discreet and long-term form of opportunism, in keeping with his obsessions with moral appearances and 'respectability'.

It was from his position as a financial dictator, established by a decree of 14 May 1928 which amongst other measures made it a punishable offence for 'heads of departments to allow the Budget provisions to be exceeded', that Salazar worked his

1. Cunha Leal, *As Minhas Memorias* (Lisbon, 1966), p. 187.

way up to his appointment as Prime Minister (His Excellency, President of the Council of Ministers) in 1932. Since the President of the Republic, General Carmona, was theoretically to retain the power to dismiss and appoint the Prime Minister, Salazar was to become constitutionally a dictator by proxy. In fact, he exercised a dual dictatorship with General Carmona until the latter gradually became a secondary figure, politically superseded by Salazar. Before Marshal Carmona died, still President, in 1951, he was to confide that he was no more than 'a prisoner in a golden cage'.

Salazar was either unaware of his passion for power or consciously concealed it by sponsoring the image of a professor who was involved in politics against his own will. In a speech to the First Eucharistic Congress in Braga, on 4 July 1924, he piously stated that one must not 'aspire to power as a right, but accept it as a duty, considering the State as God's Ministry for the common good'; in the foreword to his *Discursos* (*Speeches*), vol. 2, published in Coimbra in 1939, he pictures himself as the martyr 'who was obliged to abandon the high calling of teaching to tread a more difficult path with a heavier cross'. And several times during his career as Prime Minister–Dictator he hinted at his resignation or reverted to the fatalistic theme of being unwillingly compelled by circumstances to remain in power.

Such claims are entirely inconsistent with his character and, as we have seen, Salazar himself had brusquely declined other political posts before, until certain conditions of absolute power were granted to him as Finance Minister. Moreover, although Salazar had the military and religious establishment solidly behind him, he was given plenty of indications, in the form of a persistent underground opposition, that a considerable number of people, if not the majority, would gladly see him go back to Coimbra or even further away. Instead, he clung to power to the end of his life.

Since Salazar – who was often described as having 'married the country', as a priest marries the Church – led an uneventful life, particularly after he became Prime Minister–Dictator in

1932, his biographers can only study his psychological make-up and political ideas through his carefully elaborated speeches, and the occasional interviews given to Portuguese and foreign journalists. Such writings, which form the main source of doctrine for the régime, are also very revealing of the way Salazar was reacting to the evolution of world events.

Events themselves provide clues to the influences bearing on Salazar's character. In the mid-1930s Mussolini, having consolidated his power in Italy, was already directing a resurgence of Italian expansionism towards North-East Africa and had occupied Abyssinia; Hitler had become Reichsführer and had promised a 'New Order' lasting for 1,000 years; in Spain, where the Fascist Party and the Falange had been founded in 1932, Franco was winning the Civil War and re-awakening the ideals of '*hispanidad*'. The battle in Spain to 'save the land of nobles and *hidalgos*' for Christian civilization was also securing the future of Salazar and Portuguese fascism. Everywhere the old democratic and parliamentary forms of government were under threat. In France the para-fascist Croix de Feu, in Belgium Degrelle's Fascist Party, were expressions of the same aggressive nationalism that was leading Japan into its expansionist wars against China and the signing of the Anti-Comintern Pact of 1936 with Nazi Germany.

These were the times of the bombing of Guernica in Spain; the proclamation of Victor Emmanuel II of Italy as Emperor of Abyssinia; the lifting of sanctions against Italy by the League of Nations; and the fall of the French left-wing parties' Popular Front led by Léon Blum. It is not surprising, therefore, that in the introduction to a book published in London soon after Hitler had assumed the command of the German army and Britain had surrendered to Germany's expansionist designs in the Munich Pact of 1938, Salazar should arrogantly proclaim to his English-speaking readers: 'We are anti-parliamentarian, anti-democratic, anti-liberal, and we are determined to establish a Corporative State.'[1]

The fact that the government established by the military

1. A. de O. Salazar, *Doctrine and Action: Internal and Foreign Policy of the New Portugal, 1928–1939* (Faber & Faber, 1939), p. 29.

junta in 1926 had no doctrine or programme had provided Sal-azar with a unique opportunity to usurp its original short-term intention by introducing his own version of the corporate system. But unlike Mussolini or Hitler, who had the support of organized parties or headed political movements, Salazar, having been invited by force of circumstance to become a dictator, had to create his own movement and adapt Italian and German doctrines and methods to Portuguese condi-tions.

'Unless a *raison d'être* is found', he had said in the early stages of his government career, 'there is nothing to be done but to re-establish the Constitution which has been suspended or violated since 1926.' The threat implied in this statement worked effectively on the ruling and ecclesiastical classes, who were prepared to welcome any measures designed to provide the con-tinuity of an authoritarian régime. Realizing how backward the Portuguese reaction was in the practical adaptation of Italian corporate ideology, Salazar was the first to admit that the government machine was not yet ready to put it into effect, and he set about filling the doctrinal vacuum in gradual stages. The trend of events in the outside world seemed to indicate that since he need no longer worry about free elections he could take his time.

On 30 July 1930, in the presence of all the cabinet ministers, Salazar read the Manifesto of the União Nacional (National Union), which was to be the country's only legal political as-sociation. As it was opposed to the party system, the União Nacional did not acknowledge its own condition as a 'political party'. It was defined as a broad movement of nationalism, a coalition of 'men of good will' who had, in fact, formed them-selves into an unpopular front.

One of the aims of the National Union was that it should, under a subsidiary Centre of Political and Social Studies, pre-sent 'certain convenient and opportune suggestions aiming at the revision of certain judicial aspects [of government] or methods of application'. This situation is very revealing of a com-bination of circumstances whereby the more shrewd and politi-cally minded were taking advantage of an establishment completely destitute of ideological doctrine and whose 'programme' merely was to cling to power.

Salazar was gradually forming his nucleus of collaborators in every field – one of the youngest and most useful being Marcello Caetano who, after a brilliant career as a law student, had become a Professor of Law at Lisbon University in 1933, when he was only twenty-seven. In the late twenties and early thirties he had already served in various capacities at the Ministry of Finance, and was a member of the Council of the Colonial Empire. He had written various books on legal, constitutional, and corporate matters, and is said to have been instrumental in the drafting of the 'Estado Novo's' 1933 constitution approved by a national referendum on a limited suffrage and with abstentions counting as 'yes' votes.

As for the ideas then prevailing amongst his collaborators regarding the future of the 'Nation-State', to totalitarian 'corporativism', the most explicit are to be found in the following passage of a book written at the time by Martinho Nobre de Melo in an essay entitled 'Beyond the Revolution':

'The Mission of the Nation-State had to come into being by various ways and means which are in the interests of the nation and therefore must cover all aspects of national life, from the structural and the static to the spiritual and the dynamic.' After a long first point in which he called for the economic development of the nation through a combination of private enterprise and State intervention, and including the 'creation of new markets through colonization', Nobre de Melo proceeded:

2. To enact all measures and reinvigorate all institutions which may tend to the conservation and reproduction of the species, such as the institution of the family, and to set up and maintain a stable and natural order, through professional corporations.

3. To preserve from deleterious influences and maintain the language, the religion, the social morality and patriotic myths, which are the physiological creation of the race, or national adaptations of the Truth, or inventions prompted by the instinct of self-preservation of the national group.

4. To feed the national spirit through the cult of traditions and glories of the past, through the daring hope of national aggrand-

izement in the future – in short, through the concept of an heroic Nation–State, which embraces countless ideas and institutions, briefly described in this essay.[1]

Salazar himself made the same point in a speech made on 28 April 1934 – the day on which he celebrated his forty-fourth birthday and seventh anniversary as a member of the government, two of these as Prime Minister. 'The New Era', he said, 'was awakening national conscience ... the prestige of Portugal will shine for ever ... Everywhere the pride of being Portuguese will quicken the life-blood of the people and will vouchsafe peace and repose to the ashes of our heroes who are no longer with us. To reach our goal we have experienced a far-reaching revolution in economics, politics, ideas, customs, institutions and in our collective life.'

Salazar turned his National Union into a hierarchically organized party intertwined with a bureaucratic framework of government. Like the Nazi and Fascist Parties, the bulk of the National Union membership were passive adherents, mostly public functionaries, who had answered Salazar's call for men willing to offer allegiance to the New Era. The movement was not run on 'democratic' lines even for the insiders, and many of its leaders were simply appointed by Salazar himself, or by manipulations of the régime's most influential collaborators.

The régime at this time was also introducing in Portugal all the framework of repressive institutions that had been created in Nazi Germany and Fascist Italy. The 'temporary' censorship became a permanent feature regulated by especially appointed censorship boards. A Security Police modelled upon, and initially trained by, the German Gestapo was now in operation with full discretionary powers and a network of agents and informers at all levels of society, including the Church and the army, and covering the whole of Portugal and diplomatic consular delegations abroad.

Moreover, the régime's leaders were importing active ideological methods and organizations from the Axis powers. Curi-

1. Martinho Nobre de Melo, 'Para alem da revolução', in Cunha Leal, op. cit., Vol. 3, p. 98.

ously enough, at about the time of Hitler's purge of Nazi radicals and former friends, such as Röhm and Schleicher, during the so-called 'night of the long knives', Salazar had had to overcome a similar extremist faction in Portugal, the 'Blue Shirts', led by his friend Rolão Preto, who unsuccessfully tried to oppose him. But Salazar, preferring to keep the political leadership in safer hands, had set up his own essentially similar institutions, such as the Legião Portuguesa (Portuguese Legion), an armed militia, and its naval branch the Naval Brigade, whose para-military role was, as in Germany, resented and viewed with suspicion by the regular armed forces.

Aiming at creating its own new generation of nationalists, the régime entrusted the organization of the Portuguese equivalent of the 'Hitler Youth', the Mocidade Portuguesa (MP – Portuguese Youth) to the young Professor Marcello Caetano, who was one of its first national commissars. The MP had its own military structure and hierarchy, its own uniforms, including the nationalist emblem on the pocket over the heart, and a conspicuous 'S' in the buckle of the belt, somewhat appropriately just over the stomach. 'S' stood for '*Servir*' (to serve), and Salazar. At the time, the first generation of primary-school pupils was forcibly enrolled in the MP and had to attend the para-military instruction given by army officers of MP senior graduates. Before classes there was a compulsory ritual, as totalitarian in its implications as those practised by the 'Hitler Youth': both the teacher and the class began the day by standing up and giving the extended arm and open-hand fascist salute. As the teacher asked three times 'Who lives?' and 'Who commands?' the whole class had to shout in unison: 'Portugal! Portugal! Portugal!' 'Salazar! Salazar! Salazar!' before sitting for the day's lesson from the newly introduced textbooks.

The rural and fishing population was to fall under the care of *casas do povo* (people's houses) and *casas dos pescadores* (fishermen's houses) which were set up in every locality and village throughout the country, and supervised by the INT (Instituto Nacional do Trabalho – National Labour Institute). Often referred to by the paternalist establishment as the '*arraia miuda*' – which translates as 'small fry', and means in the

Portuguese context 'mob' or 'riff-raff' – the rural and fishing workers came to look upon the *casas* as centres for government propaganda. And in fact they did have a role of vigilance. Any nonconformist element or any visitor who might enlighten local people or excite their curiosity about political ideas, would be reported as a possible 'subversive agent'.

In the meantime, developing its 'new social order' the régime enacted its first Estatuto Nacional do Trabalho (National Labour Statute) which was to lay the foundations of the vertical *sindicatos* (syndicates) which were to replace all those trade unions and workers' associations that had existed under the 'Democratic Republic' and long since been disbanded. Salazar's utterances on the subject of labour principles embodied in the Estatuto were a reiteration of the spirit, if not of the letter, of one of the key passages in the Italian Charter of Labour: 'Since the private organization of production is a function of national concern ... the employee ... is an active collaborator of the enterprise, while its direction belongs to the employer who also bears responsibility for it.'

The 'Estado Novo', although in practice it reflected an élitist, contemptuous approach to industry and a prejudice against manual labour, was based upon a theory of the State which is basically concerned with workers' rights. The doctrine was an attempt to resurrect the principles behind the ancient *corporaçoes de artes e officios* (crafts and trades' corporations) which prevailed in certain European kingdoms in medieval times. Ignoring the experience of the centuries that had gone by – including the whole of the industrial revolution and the emergence of the technological age – 'corporativism' appealed to Salazar's lack of creative imagination as the kind of solution for which everybody was waiting to stop the 'frightening threat of Bolshevism'.

However, significantly enough, such were the traditions of exploiting the working class in Portugal that even the improvements the régime introduced from time to time in working conditions and wages were in practice often resisted – and in the rural areas often simply ignored by the employers. And although 'corporativism' tried to assert itself in a system of 'syn-

70

dicates' and 'guilds' it never managed to raise any widespread 'moral idealism' except perhaps amongst the employers who most benefited from the system. The 'syndicates' and 'guilds' became the bureaucratic instruments of social discipline having, at most, a purely advisory role. The régime's 'upper house', the Corporative Chamber, whose Chairman ranked in protocol as high as the Prime Minister, never had in fact more than a purely ceremonial function. Despite having hundreds of members representing local and institutional corporate interests – from sport to all branches of industry, the Church and overseas territories – the Corporative Chamber had an even more limited and negative role than the National Assembly. It existed to approve or veto, rather than originate, legislation, and to extend to its individual members the recognition that they were honourable members of the régime.

Since the very belief in 'corporativism' betrays an ignorance of the most elementary notions of the pressures of a modern society and a complete disregard for fundamental civic rights, we could perhaps define it as a form of 'authoritarian capitalism'. In fact, although the ultimate ends may be diametrically opposed to the Communist system, the 'Estado Novo' adopted the same basic principle of the paramountcy of the State over individual interests, though in Portugal, with the régime controlled by the capitalist oligarchy, only the working class had its rights and interests controlled by the State in the name of the nation as a whole.

The discipline imposed upon the working class was the essential foundation of Salazar's plans to achieve what he conceived to be the rebuilding of Portugal. Since Portugal, in the context of the circumstances prevailing in the thirties, could only count on its own resources, Salazar conceived a long-term plan of national reconstruction. This would require the development of Portugal's infrastructure of communications – roads, railways, bridges – hydro-electric dams, irrigation schemes, etc., concurrently with the gradual industrialization of the country by private concerns. It is significant that in the early period of the régime, one of the star ministers was the Minister of 'Public Works', a dynamic technocrat named Duarte Pacheco.

As one would expect of a man who owed to 'Providence the grace of being poor', Salazar was certainly frugal and austere in his administration. Since, tacitly, he was only answerable to the oligarchy of landlords, bankers and industrialists, the army and the Church, provided he kept them on his side he had a free hand and as much time as he might need. He was himself occasionally aware of his own limitations. 'I have always advocated', he said while still Finance Minister, 'an open and simple administration, such as can be carried out by a good housekeeper; a modest and easily understandable policy which consists in knowing how to spend well what one has, and not spend more than one's resources can afford.'[1] With his incredible aptitude for rationalizing situations to suit his own concepts, he could make a virtue of necessity. And since social assistance was expensive he entertained some strange ideas which turned it into a social evil.

An interesting aspect of Salazar's simplistic views relates to the 'colonial question' – as the overseas territories were then known. In 1968, when many people, seeing in the overall development of Angola and Mozambique a confirmation of Salazar's genius, were hailing him as 'the rebuilder of the empire', the former republican statesman Cunha Leal reprinted some personal impressions he had written nearly forty years before, criticizing Salazar's views on colonial matters. The time was 1930 and Salazar had been Finance Minister for the last three years; for Salazar, Cunha Leal wrote,

the colonies were a cancer and a nightmare ... He moans about the loans he has had to advance, and concludes that the brakes must be applied to what he calls administrative extravagance. He insists on not seeing the assets which counterbalance these liabilities, leaving those who talk to him with such a painful impression that one day, as one empties a bucket of cold water, I let drop the following phrase: 'I must conclude, therefore, that if Angola were to be taken away from us, that would be a great service rendered to us.' To which Salazar replied with an indefinable gesture: 'I wouldn't go as far as that!'

It appears that at the time, while still a comparative new-

* Quoted in *Vida mundial* (Lisbon), 31 July 1970.

comer in the government, the young Finance Minister and would-be Dictator had fallen under the influence of an old hand in government affairs, Quirino de Jesus. A few years later, seeing that he had been discarded, de Jesus wrote a book entitled *Nacionalismo portugues* (*Portuguese Nationalism*) where he claimed he had had a hand in the drafting of the Manifesto and Constitution of the National Union and several of the major acts promulgated by Salazar in the early stages of the régime. Cunha Leal, to demonstrate where Salazar had collected his views on the colonial economic situation, quoted the following naïve passage from de Jesus's book:

> The colonies have cost Portugal more than £150m. since 1850, if we take into account the colonies' budgetary deficits – which amount to a third of that total – as well as the expenses we incurred with the Colonial Secretariat and the costs of our intervention in the First World War, which was, anyway, caused by the colonies. In the final balance, of course, we reaped many advantages for the national economy, owing to the employment provided for the functionaries settled in the colonies, and our earnings with trade and shipping. But it is evident that the advantages would have been greater had we applied the same £150m. to the development of Portugal itself.[1]

Since, on the one hand, Cunha Leal provides personal evidence of Salazar's narrow views and, on the other, Salazar was in fact the rebuilder of a neglected and stagnating empire, an apparent contradiction arises, the explanation of which provides another revealing clue to Salazar's character and the nature of his rule. Upon taking a closer look at Portugal's situation Salazar had decided that the country should, according to a well-known slogan of the time, 'produce and save' from its own resources; and as for the colonies, these should be turned into really profitable sources of income for Portugal. Salazar, who never even once in his life visited any of the African colonies, might well have built an empire as a by-product of his concern for finding an economic solution for Portugal.

1. See Cunha Leal, op. cit., Vol. 3, pp. 184–5.

Chapter 3
The rebuilder of the empire

> *'Loads are carried on Negroes' backs and this increases the difficulties of travel because even in ordinary circumstances the Negroes are continually deserting ... We could find no way to avoid this evil, although we tried everything that reason dictated: now mildness and affection, now rigour. Whatever method we used, the end result was the same'* –
> A. C. P. GAMITTO[1]

Empire by decree

The empire, some twenty-two times the size of Portugal and almost as big as Western Europe, gave a sense of purpose and a new dimension to the 'Revolução Nacional' which had emerged from what Salazar himself defined as the 'dictatorship of reason and intelligence'. Schoolchildren, the main target of the grand re-education designs of the régime, were proudly shown by their schoolmasters the map of the empire superimposed over the map of Europe to illustrate the slogan: *'Portugal não e um pais pequeno'* ('Portugal is not a small country'). When one turned to Salazar's analysis of the Portuguese economic situation at the time one sees that he too had been developing his own versions of the theories of expansionism and the need for 'living space' that were a dominant feature of Nazi Germany's 'New Order'.

Addressing the inaugural session of the Economic Conference of the Portuguese Colonial Empire, held in the Corporative Chamber in Lisbon on 8 June 1936, Salazar justified Portugal's need for 'living space' in the following terms:

The Mother Country and her adjacent islands have a population of seven million people, while more than a million have emigrated

1. From *King Kambeze – Diary of a Portuguese Expedition in the Years 1831–32* (Junta Investigações do Ultramar, Lisbon, 1960).

during the last fifty years. After allowing for births and deaths, the annual increase in the population is now over 80,000; at one time it was nearly 90,000, and soon it will be 100,000; that is, one million people every ten years. Consequently, if no untoward circumstances arise, particularly if the Portuguese are not converted to the practice of birth control as advocated by pretended modern civilization, and even if Brazilian preference for the Portuguese emigrant should continue, we shall have to support and maintain within thirty years from now a population of nine to ten million . . . When we reach the figure of nine million, we shall have in Portugal and adjacent islands (Madeira and the Azores) an average of 100 inhabitants per square kilometre, and unless new outlets can be found the Mother Country will not be able to support this figure, except on a progressively lower standard of living.

He then described the grim prospects facing the Portuguese. With the existing population relying heavily on agriculture, uncultivated parts of the country were rare, and in certain areas such as Alemtejo there were none at all. The Portuguese had used all the available land, with the exception of some barren tracts which could be made valuable by irrigation, and the dunes and hills which had not yet been afforested.

The possibility of an increase in production through overall improvement in agricultural methods did not look economically viable because of the time and technical resources needed to re-educate the traditionalist mass of the peasant population. Industrialization was still some time away, needing the development of an adequate infrastructure of public works, and cheap electrical energy. The mineral wealth of the country, though not wholly prospected, could be considered small; this was the case precisely with those minerals that are required in large quantities for modern industry. 'The climate of Portugal', Salazar stated, 'is excellent for living but not for producing. The rivers are an irregular force and the sea is not always generous and friendly.' Therefore the problem of the ever-increasing population which agriculture would be unable to support 'demanded a solution in the immediate future'.

In fact, I cannot see a way out except through emigration to the colonies, or by a more active development of the industries of the country. Through the latter alternative, the surplus population could be absorbed, and it would be possible for dense populations to exist without discomfort; but, in this case, it will be necessary to establish favourable conditions for Portugal's industrial development.

Salazar, with his eyes and administrative instinct firmly turned towards Angola and Mozambique, did not relent here and continued to demonstrate the inevitability of Portugal's colonizing 'vocation'. However fast industrial development may have been in the previous years it was still hampered by lack of markets, inefficiency, defects in organization, technical incompetence, the high cost of fuel and electric power, and conditions obtaining in the supply of raw materials. And he pointedly concluded: 'Under the circumstances the logical solution is for the colonies to produce the raw materials and to send them to the Mother Country in exchange for manufactured goods.'

Salazar must have visualized a self-contained empire developing as fast as meagre national resources and army expenditure would allow. The colonies would absorb the 'excess population' through settlement, and this would stave off the need for an agrarian reform in Portugal. Further, 'the Portuguese by their control of shipping, by giving an impetus to trade, by developing industry, by organizing agriculture, and by establishing themselves on the land, will have shown in an unequivocal manner the essential character of the nation'. Within the empire 'the distribution and the type of work will be governed by the density of population; production will adjust itself to economic conditions, while the mutual interchange of commodities will demonstrate the complementary character of the economy'. In other words, the Portuguese would become the *Herrenvolk* in the colonies, to ensure that there would be a 'division of work' whereby some ten million black 'natives' would produce raw materials necessary for the industrial development of Portugal.

Marxists had long been warning the world of the evils of capitalism with capital, but no one had turned his attention to the still worse evils of capitalism *without* capital. Many people knew of the consequences of 'imperialism as the last stage of capitalism' – but under the rule of an impoverished and archaic country, only a few million Africans really knew, and were to learn further, the consequences of imperialism as an extension of the forms of feudalism which had survived in Portuguese economic methods and social attitudes.

Salazar was not concerned with, or could not grasp, the implications of massive white settlement in Angola and Mozambique, or the practical meaning of a 'division of labour' which ascribed to Africans a role similar to that of slavery. As an echo of Nazi ideas reaching Portugal, in another passage of the same speech he even referred to the Africans as 'inferior races'. In the seclusion of his Prime Minister's office and on his long walks in the family's walled farm in Santa Comba Dão, Salazar saw the future of the empire merely in relation to Portugal.

When one studies the implications and timing of the extensive decree which created the new 'Portuguese Colonial Empire' in May 1930 – when Salazar was still Finance Minister plenipotentiary – one can be in no doubt that the 'Revolução Nacional' he wanted to promote was to find its economic viability largely in colonial exploitation. Referring to the economic plans he had announced and which were embodied in the new decree, Salazar himself pointed out: 'Economic conditions prevailing in the world today are unlikely adversely to affect the carrying out of this programme; in fact, it seems to me that the present moment is an exceptionally favourable one for its execution.' And in this respect, although the course of history was to have unexpected turns, he was not wrong.

The decree of May 1930 introduced many new features in colonial administration. Instead of being known just by a number, in chronological sequence, as all Portuguese decrees and orders normally are, it was named the 'Colonial Act' – after the fashion used in the legislation of British Commonwealth countries and South Africa. This was to emphasize its unique constitutional importance until it was incorporated in the constitution introduced by the régime.

In many ways it was a regression and it caused a stir at the

77

time, particularly in remote Goa, where an educated class of Catholics had long gained social ascendancy in a predominantly Hindu community, and were more aware than any other colonial peoples of the implications of Portuguese laws. Whereas successive previous constitutions, that of 1822 and the Constitutional Charter of 1826, regarded all the overseas possessions as provinces, and the republican constitution made no distinction between the territories and regarded the inhabitants as citizens, the Colonial Act made a new distinction of territorial status. The islands of the Azores and Madeira were integrated into Portugal as adjacent territories. But from the Cape Verde Islands and Guinea-Bissau, down to S. Tome Island and Angola, and around the Cape to Mozambique, Goa, Macau and Timor, all were in future to be regarded as colonies and, as such, parts of the 'Portuguese Colonial Empire'. Both the Act, introduced while Salazar briefly occupied the position of Minister of Colonies, and the subsequent legislation introduced by his successor, the Imperial Organic Charter and the Overseas Administrative Reform Act (both of 1933), emphasized the words 'colonies' and 'Empire'. In the same way that the Head of State, General Carmona, often claimed at the time that Portugal was a 'dictatorship without a dictator', the régime saw no anachronism in having 'an empire without an emperor' ... but with a president.

Needless to say the Colonial Act also had the immediate aim of bringing about a resurgence of Catholicism in the empire. Catholic missions regained a privileged position as an 'instrument of civilization and national influence'. Their status and role were to be further defined in the pact between State and Church – the Concordat – and the Portuguese Missionary Agreement, both enacted in 1940, as well as the Missionary Statute of 1941. These enactments were a model of marriage between spiritual devotion and utilitarian purpose. In order to avoid the duplication of roles between lay teachers and religious missionaries, the missions would be subsidized by the State, which would also pay the salaries of the clergy, including the bishops and the Cardinal of Lourenço Marques (whose salary was equal to that the Governor General). This offered a double guarantee that their mission really complied with the State's designs. Article 68 of the Statute states:

Native education will conform to the doctrinal orientation established by the Political Constitution, will for all purposes be considered official, and will regulate itself to the plans and programmes adopted by the governments of the colonies. These plans and programmes will have in view the perfect assimilation and moral uplift of the natives and the acquisition of habits and aptitudes for work ... it being understood that by moral uplift is meant the abandonment of indolence and the preparation of future rural and industrial workers who produce enough to meet their own necessities and fulfil their social obligations.

As for civil rights, this is how a Goanese writer saw the new Colonial Act:

Former Portuguese constitutions had conceded to the inhabitants of the colonies the same rights and privileges as the inhabitants of Portugal, without any discrimination whatsoever. The situation arising from the new Act would be considered embarrassing in a land where vested interests were regarded as sacred. But in Portugal – where it is easier to withdraw political rights than to grant them – the rights of the inhabitants of the colonies no longer had the character of constitutional rights.

Their rights were now dependent 'on the laws in force for the time being', and the Lisbon government reserved for itself 'the authority to publish decrees having the force of law – a statute bad in itself, and worse still by reason of its incompatibility with the character of rulers whose parasitism poses in vain as imperialistic spirit.'[1]

In fact, the fears expressed by the writer were confirmed. Further legislation, namely the 'Estatuto do Indigenato' ('Native's Statute') applying to Guinea-Bissau, Angola and Mozambique, and making conditions for the attainment of citizenship equivalent to an 'assimilation' test, effectively reduced the then ten million inhabitants of those territories to the status of wards of the administration; unless they were 'assimilated',

1. See V. de Bragança-Cunha, *Revolutionary Portugal (1910–1936)* (James Clarke, London, 1937), p. 234; also his articles on 'The Portuguese Empire', in *New English Review*, December 1934.

they were 'natives'. Unlike citizens, Africans were no longer covered by the normal judicial framework and became directly subject to the administrative authorities in the colonies.

This was the legal status that best suited a situation whereby Africans were summarily disposed of as forced labourers by the local Portuguese administrative officers even if this entailed transporting them thousands of miles away, inside the territories themselves or to the rich, cocoa-producing S. Tome Island, whenever their work was needed. The significance of this law cannot be exaggerated if one is to understand the 'National Revolution'. In practice it meant that the Portuguese, who had for centuries based their colonization on the exploitation of African labour by transporting slaves from trading posts along the West Coast of Africa – and occasionally even Mozambique – to the Americas, were now exploiting them on a massive scale inside the colonies themselves.

The obscurantism of Portugal and the silent and stagnated empire fostered a type of isolationism that shrewd Salazar would anyway have found congenial. The system was, in many respects, even more profitable and convenient than the old system of slavery, which had formally been abolished. There was no need for financial investment in a new fleet of slave ships. Individual ownership of slaves, which still required a certain care to protect the capital outlay, was replaced by collective ownership by the whites of African forced labourers in a pool system, for as long as they were of an active age. Moreover, Portugal had found a source of tropical foodstuffs, such as sugar and coffee, and raw materials that would in time compensate for the loss of Brazil as a colony. And, therefore, while Portugal only occasionally involved itself in European affairs – either as a supporter of Franco's Civil War or as an ambiguous 'neutral' in the Second World War – in the vast and secluded empire, Africans were to work like legions of ants, for as many decades as necessary, for the restoration of Portugal.

In the climate of censorship and police repression, even the best of Portuguese observers failed to see some of the implications of the Act. Cunha Leal, former republican prime minister and himself a man with many interests in Angola, criticized the régime for some of the provisions of the Act, namely Articles 17 and 18, which are seemingly humanitarian:

Art. 17. The labour of natives working for the State or administrative bodies is to be paid for.

Art. 18. The following are forbidden:(1) all practices whereby the State undertakes itself to supply native labourers to economic enterprises; (2) all practices whereby natives residing in any administrative area may be forced to give [enterprises] any work on any account.

Cunha Leal felt that the introduction of these provisions gave the impression that such practices had existed before and this was, of course, an indiscreet and embarrassing admission to make.[1]

Had he been less partisan and nationalistic himself, he would have pointed out that Portuguese legislation, particularly that appertaining to the colonies, was more often than not intended to answer persistent outside criticism. Portugal had been accused with regularity of perpetuating a system of slavery. Germany, for instance, claimed that 'it would gladly introduce and maintain order in the Portuguese colonies based on Christian principles'. Nevinson, Ross, Cadbury and many other writers had written corroborative indictments of Portuguese rule. In this case, with the peculiar parochial shrewdness of Salazar, the Colonial Act had deliberately made an admission which could at one and the same time be taken as an implied criticism of the previous republican régime and as a declaration of administrative regeneration for the future. The phenomenon, observed by Marvin Harris[2] and others, that Portuguese colonial law, when conforming to the letter, does not conform to the spirit, and when conforming to the spirit, does not conform to the letter, falls into this category of legal expediency for international consumption.

With the territories reduced by censorship and administrative secrecy to self-contained 'islands of separateness', few people,

1. Cunha Leal, *As Minhas Memorias* (Lisbon, 1966), Vol. 3, pp. 349–50.
2. Marvin Harris, *Portugal's African 'Wards'* (American Committee on Africa, New York, 1958).

except those who had served in more than one territory, or those who had access to the centralized information held by the higher cadres of the Ministry for the Colonies, knew what was happening outside their own narrow field of experience. In fact no ordinary Portuguese, even those who more closely followed world events, knew exactly what was going on in the empire. At the time of the introduction of the Colonial Act, for instance, the Goanese were the only people to claim that whereas in the past colonial subjects had enjoyed full theoretical rights of citizenship as European Portuguese – and indeed many Indians and some Africans had attained prominent positions – now they were reduced to second-class citizens and barred from military and administrative careers and appointments.

To leave no doubt that the revolution was strictly 'national', i.e. for the benefit of Portugal, Salazar, through the Colonial Act and several other measures, also curbed the separatist and nativist tendencies that had been entertained by white settlers, Angolan-born and Mozambique-born Portuguese, and small *élites* of half-castes and educated blacks. He downgraded the High Commissioners' status to the lesser category of Governors General; in practice he saw to it that no more public figures, comparable to the republican High Commissioners General Norton de Matos and Brito Camacho, would be in charge of colonial governments. He deliberately nominated lesser men from the ranks of his subservient followers for temporary commissions of service as governors. The elected individual members of the legislative councils in each colony were reduced to a minority within a majority of government nominees. With his budgetary obsession, Salazar ensured the strict division of public accounts by 'granting', in the new Act, 'financial autonomy' to each colony. This meant that each colonial government, upon submitting budgetary estimates to the Ministry for the Colonies in Lisbon for approval, should see to it that they were self-balancing. And in another typical touch of his political style, Salazar had the salaries of the colonial officials – from governors to district officers – increased so as to gain their approval of the Colonial Act and ensure their collaboration in bringing it into practice.

No wonder, therefore, that under the spell of Salazar's policies public functionaries should have adopted a new style of rhetoric which became a feature of public addresses given by the régime's men. One of the earliest manifestations of this exalted language is found in the following quotation from a circular addressed to all departments by the first Governor General of Angola appointed by the 'Estado Novo', Filomeno Camara, upon arriving in Luanda:

As I accepted the government of this colony, the most beautiful jewel of the Colonial Empire, created by that great visionary Henry the Navigator, from the Promontory of Sagres, who in a gigantic effort, managed to unravel the secrets of the Ocean, ending once and for all the terrors and legends that surrounded it, I formally pledged myself before the Motherland to the task of achieving the concrete and demystified balance of Angola's budget.[1]

The Spanish Civil War

The ruthless activity of the 'Police for Vigilance and the Defence of the State', later the PIDE, protected by the cloak of censorship, saw to it that no important political events were taking place within Portugal's domestic boundaries. The fate of the régime was being decided outside Portugal, and specifically by the turn of events in neighbouring Spain.

Although the two states which comprise the Iberian Peninsula share the same cultural heritage and similar historical experiences, such as overseas expansion, there are some striking differences between them. Portugal, owing perhaps to its size more than any other factor, became a fairly well integrated country. Although there may be regional variations in socioeconomic development, such as between the Lisbon district and the north-eastern province of Tras-os-Montes, Portuguese society is comparatively free from cultural, as opposed to socioeconomic, antagonisms. But Spain, four times bigger than Portugal, is a mosaic of nations. Catalonia, the Basque country and Galicia are as distinct culturally from Castille, and from each

1. Quoted by Cunha Leal, op. cit., p. 361.

other, as they are from Portugal. Basques and Catalans, who have totally different origins and languages, both inhabit France as well as Spain; Galicians and Portuguese shared a common language and literature for centuries after Portuguese independence, and can still understand each other better today than either can understand Spaniards.

Spain has all the social and economic conflicts that could be expected in a country subject to the lasting violence of feudalism, Inquisition, Catholic obscurantism, military rule and deep class divisions, plus the impact of historical dislocation when it lost its empire and gradually fell from a position of ascendancy into the condition of a colonized and underdeveloped country. The pressure of all these social and economic factors, common to all 'Spain', is made even more complex by Catalan and Basque nationalist desires to separate from the centrifugal and undemocratic rule of Madrid. Paradoxically, the permanent threat of separatism might well be the greatest single factor accounting for the continuation of a unified Spanish State, as Spanish 'nationalists' find in the fear of 'national disintegration' a rallying point of unity and a justification for repressive rule.

All these factors, together with tensions naturally arising under the impact of more immediate political circumstances, such as ideological and partisan rivalries, contributed to a state of polarization by 1936 when Spain, ruled by a left-wing coalition, the Popular Front, and on the way to a socialist revolution, was deeply divided between two factions – the republicans on the one hand, and the nationalists and traditionalists on the other. The situation regarding public instability, anti-clericalism and the impact of revolutionary ideas was essentially similar to that of the Portuguese republic, but naturally on a much larger scale and intensified by the emotional conflicts peculiar to the 'Spanish labyrinth'.

Nationalist generals, including one Francisco Franco, then Military Commander in the Canaries, began to conspire to 'save traditionalist Spain from the dangers of Bolshevism'. At the time, Nazi Germany and Fascist Italy were posing as defenders of Christian and Western civilization, a role similar to that later to be assumed by the United States. Franco turned to them for help against the republican government, and so saw fit to win Spain back to traditionalist nationalism with the aid of foreign divisions – a paradox one would expect nationalists everywhere to find at least a little confusing. The volunteer 'International Brigades' who came to the rescue of the republicans were not regular troops, but groups formed by idealists from many countries and of many creeds, and this was quite consistent with the republicans' concepts of internationalism. Moreover, the republicans were the constitutionally elected government of the day and this should have appealed to Salazar's sense of, shall we say, respectability. But Salazar was not to be dismayed by these scruples; he knew that the survival of the newly born 'Estado Novo', and his own formula of Nation–State–Myself, which alone could carry out his grand designs, depended on the outcome of the Spanish Civil War.

At first sight, from the point of view of Portugal, a small nation which always saw itself threatened by its bigger neighbour, the republicans, with their policy of democratic representation, would appear to be a better proposition. The continuation of republican rule would be bound to lead to the emergence of a Federation of Iberian States, thus dividing Spain into independent units comparable in geographical scale and population size to Portugal itself. But evidently the long-term strategic and political interests of Portugal were not to be confused with those of the 'Estado Novo', and Salazar found it expedient to believe that a stronger 'Red Spain' would eventually invade Portugal to integrate it in a 'Bolshevik bloc'.

How Salazar managed to collaborate with Franco in the face of widespread opposition from abroad is revealing of his capacity for sophistry and prevarication. He was hard pressed to adhere to the 'non-intervention' policy adopted by the League of Nations and, for appearance's sake, he eventually did so, all the while 'reserving the right of freedom of action on the border in case of attack'. But Salazar, who now had virtual control over the slightest movement of a political nature, allowed a special legion to be formed to fight on the side of Franco's Nationalists. The legion, ironically enough named 'Legião de Viriato', after the legendary 'Lusitanian' tribal leader who supposedly led native resistance against Roman invaders in 200 BC, was to invade Spain side by side with the troops of Nazi Germany and Fascist Italy. The final tally revealed that of the 20,000 Portuguese – 'mostly volunteers, but also unwilling conscripts'[1] – nearly half of them died.

One only has to look at the various stages of Franco's offensive, expanding strategically eastwards from the Portuguese border, to grasp the extent of Portugal's contribution to Franco. However, while the war proceeded, a number of blatant prevarications took place, at national and international level. Under the pressure of the Soviet Union at the League of Nations, a Non-Intervention Committee was set up to observe movements along the Portuguese border; Salazar refused an international committee but, with an eye to the alliance with Britain, he proposed instead that a British Mission should come to Portugal. 'His Majesty's Government', said a formal note from Britain, 'much appreciate the confidence shown in them by the Portuguese Government in inviting them to provide officers for the Portuguese–Spanish frontier. They are the more gratified at this invitation because they appreciate that it is a further indication of the close friendship and understanding that exists between the two countries.'[2]

Concerning Portugal's aid to Spain, Salazar himself, in a carefully prepared speech celebrating Franco's victory, showed a capacity for prevarication that even his most loyal spokesmen must have found extremely embarrassing. After indignantly complaining that 'unbridled international publicity ... which scrutinizes every attitude' had given rise to 'a great evil in Europe', he added apologetically:

Contrary to pledges given by the Government for sufficiently obvious political reasons, and as if those pledges ran counter to the thought and inmost feelings of the people, several thousand Portuguese, evading in countless ways the vigilance of the authorities, left their life and interests and ease to fight for Spain, to die for Spain. It

1. Hugh Thomas, *The Spanish Civil War* (Penguin, 1965), p. 794.
2. Quoted in A. de O. Salazar, *Doctrine and Action: Internal and Foreign Policy of the New Portugal, 1928–1939* (Faber & Faber, 1939), p. 333.

is a source of pride to me that they should have died well and that all, the survivors and the dead, should have written yet another heroic page in the history of the Peninsula.

Carried away by the emotions of the moment and feeling strengthened by the nationalist victory in Spain, he continued imperturbably: 'In every sphere in which we had freedom of action we helped, so far as it lay in our power, the cause of Spanish nationalism and Christian civilization ...' As if the survival of the 'Estado Novo', and his own survival, had not been involved, he concluded:

Without dismay, without thought of gain we were from the first, as it was our duty to be, faithful friends of Spain and true sons at heart of the Peninsula. With constant effort, with loss of life, we took our share of risk and suffering; we ask nothing in return, we have no account to present. We won, that is enough.[1]

In the period after the nationalist victory early in 1939, Portugal made the first discreet re-alignment of its foreign policy. In March 1939 Spain had joined the Anti-Comintern Pact with Germany, Italy and Japan; this was followed by a bilateral Treaty of Friendship with Germany, and a Non-Aggression Pact whereby the Franco and Salazar régimes committed themselves to reciprocal assistance in case of external attack and internal 'subversion'. Here again, an analogy with the Iberian position in relation to NATO is most appropriate: owing to the opposition on the part of some of its members, Spain, unlike Portugal, was excluded from NATO; but by a bilateral Military Pact with the United States and by the Iberian Pact, Spain is effectively interlocked with the North Atlantic Alliance.

With Portugal effectively isolated from Western European liberal influences by Spain, it is significant that 1939 marks the period in which Portugal began to intensify its relations with South Africa, then already enjoying the independence of a sovereign state since the Statute of Westminster of 1931. Referring to the forthcoming first visit by the Portuguese Head of State President Carmona to Mozambique and South Africa in 1939, Salazar commented on 22 May, during an extraordinary session

1. Speech made on 22 May 1939 at the National Assembly.

of the National Assembly especially summoned to approve the visit:

> The voyage of the Head of State to our empire in Africa (and I pray that this year's visit be crowned with as much success and reap as many advantages as his visit last year to Angola) is part of the same guiding thought, the same aim, the same spirit of the Colonial Act.
>
> We feel also that to regard Africa as the village common of Europe is no longer in accordance with reality; it may have been so in the past, but it will scarcely be so in the future; and we feel also that for Europe to speak exclusively in the name of Africa likewise belongs to the past. There are interests which it is difficult to discuss in Europe and sovereignties which on the continent of Africa impose themselves with the force and evidence of reality.
>
> A vast and prosperous country, forming part of the British Commonwealth, has grown up on the frontier of our colonies in Africa, and between our colonies and that country there exist understanding, good will and mutual respect which have transformed into cooperation the rivalry, envy and friction that could only have jeopardized peace and common development.

After analysing the Portuguese situation following the Spanish Civil War, he ended his speech with his usual humourless sense of propriety by asking on behalf of the government for the National Assembly to discuss the presidential visit to South Africa: 'It is in this spirit that the government, having given its assent to the voyage of the Head of State, hopes that the National Assembly will also give its assent.' By then, Portugal had already become such a tamed country that the Head of State, President Carmona, did not wait for the debate to begin before he and his committee started packing.

Chapter 4
The economics of neutrality

> *'The man who becomes a nationalist*
> *belongs to no party or school; he makes*
> *use of materials according to their*
> *usefulness for the reconstruction of the*
> *country; his great, his only objective is*
> *that they should serve and become part*
> *of the national system* ...
>   *Like a great family or a great concern,*
> *the nation requires, for the protection of its*
> *common interests and the attainment of its*
> *common aims, a head to control it, a*
> *centre of life and action'* – SALAZAR[1]

The Second World War

The President of the Republic was returning from his visit to the empire and South Africa when the Second World War broke out. On 9 October 1939, Salazar, who had for some time been making allusions to the probability of war, took advantage of another session at the National Assembly to expound Portugal's policy in relation to the European conflict. This address reveals the inward-looking and ethnocentric nature of Salazar's vision of the world, and his approach to peace and neutrality as a means to an end. It reflects Salazar's preoccupation with the empire and his desire to keep Portugal away from the war and European affairs as well as looking detached and in full control of the situation. For Salazar, Europe and the war were far more distant than the empire – an empire which he had managed to visualize with only the help of other people's reports and black-and-white films and photographs which his own imagination coloured. This is how he welcomed the President, exalted the empire, and in passing referred to the war, as if it was an event

1. From *Salazar Says* (Secretariado de Propaganda Nacional, Lisbon, no date).

of secondary interest to Portugal happening in some remote point beyond the Pyrenees:

> We followed with emotion and, for the later moments, with true anxiety the visit of the Head of State to our lands in Africa ... Our claim to them is our self-abnegation and stubbornness in discovery; the seal of our title is conferred by the blood of our soldiers in the battles for occupation; but what is achieved there goes beyond these things – it is the fusion of race and land, the widening, to the limits of the bush, of our narrow frontiers in the Peninsula – the same country, reproduced, blood and soul, like a mother in her children ... The Presidential trip this year was crowned by the visit to the Union of South Africa, where the warm welcome corresponded entirely to the friendship and common interests between our two countries.
>
> In the meantime Europe has been shaken by war ... Germany has made it known to us that she is prepared to respect the integrity of Portugal and its overseas possessions should we keep neutral; England has asked us nothing in the name of the centuries-old Alliance and friendship which would oblige us to enter the conflict; and, apart from common interests which link us with European nations, we have no direct interests of our own to defend in the conflict.[1]

In fact, anyone visiting Portugal in 1940 would hardly have believed that a world war was going on. In Lisbon, covering a large area in Belem district around the Mosteiro dos Jeronimos (Hieronymite Monastery) where national heroes such as Vasco da Gama and Camões are buried, an impressive exhibition, commemorating the eighth centenary of the proclamation of the Kingdom of Portugal (1140) and third centenary of the restoration of independence from Spanish annexation (1640), was being staged. This was still a time when the swastikas, the fasces and the caravels were essentially similar ideological symbols. The exhibition of the 'Portuguese World', as it was called, comprised several pavilions and stands covering various phases of Portuguese history and showing each of the component parts of the empire. It had been organized by one Cap-

1. A. de O. Salazar, *Discursos e notas politicas, 1938–1943* (Editora Coimbra, Coimbra, 1959).

90

tain Henrique Galvão, one of the régime's bright boys and a close friend of Salazar; rumours that the then Director of Colonial Fairs and Exhibitions and National Broadcasting had personally done well out of the exhibition were put down to 'communist invention'. Salazar was said to have been pleased and proud of what was also a grandiose display of modern Portuguese talent. And most ordinary people, grateful for the peace that the National Propaganda Office attributed to Salazar's diplomatic genius and the protection of 'Our Lady of Fatima', were in a mood to enjoy this show of past achievements and confidence in the future. While the nation, 'who was happy enough not to have to choose', lived in carefree innocence, Papa Salazar would take care of Portugal's problems. And Salazar could indeed be trusted to make the best of a delicate situation.

In the speech of 9 October 1939 Salazar had stated that on no account would Portugal take advantage of its position of neutrality to 'make business out of the war'. There is, however, plenty of evidence to suggest that Salazar, with his instinct for budgetary revenue, did not resist the temptation of breaking such a promise at any stage of the war. The régime was then trying to reorganize the army under the leadership of an extremely right-wing and loyal nationalist, a Captain Santos Costa, a bureaucrat of the military administration whom Salazar himself had discovered while Minister of Finance. A good armchair financial strategist and an ideologically reliable officer of the 'new generation', Santos Costa was appointed Under-Secretary for War and given the task of rebuilding the army. This job required more than just ideological zeal, and Portugal had already failed to persuade other powers, in particular Britain, to provide the (in Portugal's terms) massive aid that would be needed. Salazar, having saved as much as he could in such budgetary items as education, social assistance and health services, increased military expenditure in the hope of building the armed forces to a level where they were adequate to defend Portugal and the empire. But all these plans, as Salazar knew better than anyone else, still required money.

Ironically the war was to become the most immediate source

91

of revenue. Portugal became one of Germany's main suppliers of wolfram – the main source of tungsten, and therefore a mineral of great strategic value. This was not only an example of sheer opportunism, but it could be construed as a breach of neutrality. Lisbon became a well-known centre for the interchange of goods and intelligence. More often than not goods were imported from and re-exported to the various belligerent countries by enterprising concerns. After undergoing an incredibly fast process of 'nationalization', which sometimes lasted just the time it took to change trading marks, if any, and transfer the goods from one ship or plane to another, such trade could not be more lucrative. These operations naturally involved bureaucratic cooperation at an official or semi-official level. Even the considerations behind the hospitality to thousands of refugees, mostly Jews assisted by international organizations in the United States and elsewhere, were far from being merely altruistic.

In fact most of Portugal's disagreements in its relations with the belligerent powers concerned trade matters; and after a settlement agreed in 1942, Portugal was selling 75 per cent of its wolfram to the Reich and 25 per cent to the Allies – an estimated 16,000 tons a year bearing an export tax of £300 a ton.[1] Britain herself ended up with a considerable war debt to Portugal which was later to be used by Salazar to pay for the Portuguese take-over of British-owned interests in the colonies, namely the port and railway in Beira, Mozambique.

There were other indications of a pro-Axis bias on the part of Portuguese officialdom, which was perhaps natural considering that the 'Estado Novo', from its salute to its framework of institutions, was modelled on the fascist pattern. At any rate, a strict censorship applied to British and American magazines and newspapers. Articles causing offence to the Axis powers were torn from the issues in circulation; listening to BBC broadcasts was suppressed. On the other hand the Reich was allowed to flood Portugal with the most impressive propaganda and 'Agfacolor' films. In the empire – in Lourenço Marques,

1. Hugh Kay, *Salazar and Modern Portugal* (Eyre & Spottiswoode, 1970), p. 178.

Luanda and elsewhere – the Germans maintained centres for spying on shipping movements, and indeed the ability to do this was one of the factors governing their interest in maintaining Portugal's collaborationist 'neutrality'. But while most of the régime's supporters sided with the Nazis and Fascists, all of its opponents sided with the Allies, often cooperating at great personal risk with British and American intelligence agents and the Resistance groups operating in occupied Europe.

These facts, however, cannot provide a basis for understanding the real problems which were being faced behind the scenes. Salazar had reason to be rather more ambivalent towards the belligerent powers than most people appear to believe. The question of Europe was for him secondary to his nationalist and colonialist calculations and he saw the war above all in relation to the dangers it might bring to the empire. This gave rise to a dilemma which was not new for Portugal, and which stemmed from the Anglo-Portuguese Alliance.

Portugal might be said to owe its survival to the six-centuries-old alliance, but in almost every other respect the British have been the side to extract the most tangible advantages from it. Economically, the Methuen Treaty of 1703 had created a situation whereby Portugal 'gave England a greater trading balance than any other country whatsoever', enough to have 'paid English armies in Spain and Portugal, and to draw ... considerable sums for troops elsewhere, in other parts, without remitting one farthing from England'. In fact the Treaty was one of the main factors leading to England's supremacy over France and eventually in opening up the way to superpower.[1] Salazar himself had once tried to show the advantages of the alliance by quoting the following letter by Lord Palmerston to Lord John Russell:

Those advantages are many, great and obvious; commercial, political, military, and naval, and if we were thus to lose them, some of them would not be mere loss, but would become formidable

1. See A. D. Francis, *The Methuens and Portugal* (Cambridge University Press, 1966).

weapons of attack against us in the hands of a hostile power. For instance, the naval position of the Tagus ought never be in the hands of any power, whether French of Spanish, which might become hostile to England, and it is only by maintaining Portugal in its separate existence, and in its intimate and protected state of alliance with England, that we can be sure of having the Tagus as a friendly instead of being a hostile naval station. Only fancy for a moment Portugal forming a part of Spain, and Spain led away by France into war with England, and what could be our naval condition with all the ports from Calais to Marseilles hostile to us ... and with nothing between us and Malta but Gibraltar ... If, on the contrary, the Tagus were at our command, we should occupy an intermediate position greatly impeding the naval movements of France and Spain.[1]

In the 100 years since those words were written, the strategic importance of Portugal for Britain had, if anything, increased. Salazar reminded his British listeners and readers that whilst the British empire had grown, other forces had come into being; and notwithstanding the great friendship between Great Britain and the United States, Britain had to maintain her communications along the Mediterranean, and to the East via the Cape. Indeed, with strategically placed colonies and islands, such as the Azores, in a dominating position over larger maritime areas, Portugal still offered, in the age of the medium-range plane, a chain of bases vital for war operations.

Salazar, as would be expected from a man holding the position of Prime Minister, politely understated the Portuguese case. After all, while Portugal had lost but a few islands and small possessions to its traditional enemy Spain, Britain had carried out considerable overseas expansion in the East and in Southern Africa at Portugal's expense. Some of the lands of the British empire, such as Bombay, were ceded as dowry for a royal marriage; Central-Southern Africa was surrendered after the 1890 ultimatum. But Portugal, which had entered the alliance to guarantee its independence, was now a prey to its own

1. Evelyn Ashley, *The Life of Henry John Temple, Viscount Palmerston* (London, 1876), Vol. 1, p. 18; see also A. de O. Salazar, *Doctrine and Action* (Faber & Faber, 1939), p. 328.

empire. During the Napoleonic wars the Portuguese rulers had no option but to take sides with Britain; and when the Portuguese king and royal family, leaving for exile in Brazil, were rescued by British ships, Portugal had to declare Brazilian ports open to British trade. During the 1914–18 war, as the introductory remarks of the Colonial Act recalled, 'Portugal had entered the war on account of its overseas possessions.'

Wherever the Portuguese turned in the empire they had the British next door or not very far away. Angola and Mozambique had the Dominion of South Africa, the colonies of Southern and Northern Rhodesia, Nyasaland, the protectorates of Bechuanaland and Swaziland, Tanganyika and South-West Africa, as their neighbours; Goa was but an enclave in massive British India; Macau was close to Shanghai and Hong Kong; Timor comparatively near Australia. There were friendly everyday contacts between the British and Portuguese administrations along the borders of all these territories; and the sporadic shipping connections Portugal had with the most remote parts of the empire were carried out by British ships. Therefore, the relationship with mighty Britain was not so much a question of love-hate, as some amateur psychiatrists of history would have us believe, but a permanent exercise in fear and subjection.

Britain, as Salazar well knew from his study of history, could be a treacherous ally. In 1898 the British had signed a secret agreement with Germany, granting the latter a share of Portugal's African empire. This arrangement had been scotched by the Boer War, and anyway Britain might have thought twice about the desirability of having a strong imperial German presence in Africa. But again in 1914 the thought of appeasing Germany at Portugal's expense crossed the minds of British politicians. So that when in the thirties Germany once more aspired to take her place among the imperial powers, Salazar could be excused if he looked somewhat nervously over his shoulder at the activities of his British ally.

True to form, in 1936 Prime Minister Chamberlain started conducting a series of negotiations with the object of appeasing Hitler. Salazar himself published the following year one of his ambiguous notes for external consumption: 'We will not be party to any collusion, we will not sell, we will not cede, we will not share, we will not rent our colonies . . . No such things are allowed by our constitutional laws, and even if these did not exist, our national conscience would not allow them to take place.'[1]

According to a recent publication by the Portuguese Foreign Ministry, *Ten Years of External Policy, 1936–1947*, reports by the then Ambassador in Britain, Armindo Monteiro – corroborated by the documents now available for consultation in the Public Records Office – showed that Chamberlain had been party to a plan whereby Nazi Germany was to have been offered vast areas of Angola and the Belgian Congo in which to find raw materials, if not 'living space'. It appears that there was no unanimous agreement in Britain over this line of appeasement. According to Portuguese sources, only a wing of the Conservative government – Hoare, Halifax, Macmillan, Butler – approved of the scheme; Eden was apparently opposed to the plan and in fact made a statement in the House of Commons in favour of continuing the Anglo-Portuguese Alliance. On the other hand, South African leaders such as the anti-British Prime Minister Hertzog, and the pro-Nazi Foreign Minister Pirov, apparently indicated that they would welcome having the Germans as neighbours along the lines of the German Colonial League's designs for an African Reich. His Majesty's Government must have hesitated, for the King granted the Order of the Bath to the Portuguese President, General Carmona, who most probably had to ask Salazar what he had done to be given such an honour; and the whole issue was overtaken in 1939 by the new war in Europe.

The Portuguese dilemma, however, persisted in other forms. A Nazi victory would most probably mean the end of Portugal in Africa. Moreover, close collaboration with Nazi Germany or even the materialization of Hitler's plans to invade the Iberian Peninsula could imply immediate British action over all Portuguese overseas territories with imponderable consequences. No

1. Official State note, carried in the daily newspapers on 29 January 1937.

wonder Salazar was instrumental in influencing Franco to remain neutral, and wait, before committing himself further than sending the Spanish Blue Division to fight with the Germans on the Russian front. The Allies themselves had a vested interest in not seeing the war extended to the Iberian Peninsula, where Hitler would have found a more than willing Fifth Column to build up another strategically important dependency of the Third Reich.

The Allies certainly knew of the Führer Conferences on Naval Affairs, for they reprinted the relevant operational plans, such as Directive 18, of 12 November 1940, in the secret staff memoranda printed by the Technical Reproduction of the Admiralty at the time. The directive, from the Führer Headquarters, stated:

2. *Spain and Portugal* – Political measures are to be instigated for the early entry into war of Spain. The object of German intervention in the Iberian Peninsula (code name 'Felix') is to expel the English from the Western Mediterranean; for this –

(a) Gibraltar will be taken and the Straits closed;

(b) the English will be prevented from gaining a foothold in the Iberian Peninsula and in the Atlantic Islands. The Atlantic Islands Canaries and Cape Verde, and Madeira and the Azores are also being considered.

Regarding the Azores, whose mid-Atlantic position was of major importance in controlling a vast maritime area, a large part of the North-West African mainland, and the entrance to the Mediterranean by air, the following was the German position as early as 1940:

The subject of the occupation of the Azores was brought up by the Führer. Judging from an earlier summary of the situation, which has not undergone any change since, it would be possible to carry out the initial occupation of the Azores using combat forces. It is extremely unlikely, however, that the islands could be held and supplies brought up in the face of British, and possibly American, attacks. Moreover, all our combat forces in the area, including submarines, would be necessary to achieve this, and they would therefore have to be withdrawn from all offensive activities in the Battle of the Atlantic; this is intolerable. The Navy must, therefore, reject the idea of occupying the Azores.

The Führer, however, is still in favour of occupying the Azores, in order to be able to operate long-range bombers from there against the United States. The occasion for this might arise by the autumn. In reply to the Commander in Chief of the Navy, the Führer confirmed that the Navy's main task in the summer of 1941 must be the disruption of British supply lines.

German U-boats, in fact, were causing devastating losses to the British fleet out of operational range of the aircraft of the time, and the Americans were aware of the eventual dangers of German occupation of the Azores. Conversely, the Allies were aware of the importance of bringing pressure to bear on Salazar to cede bases in the Azores to the Allies so that they could pursue their counter-offensive plans and gain the initiative.

At Britain's request, at the end of 1941 Salazar entrusted a young major named Humberto Delgado with the task of making a survey of the Azores, in respect of available facilities, including ports, highways, medical services, electricity and water supplies. The survey was carried out in record time and Major Delgado, ostensibly heading a team of Portuguese pilots being sent for training in Britain, opened discussions with British air chiefs. Owing to the ideological divisions within the Portuguese army, particularly since the military command of the Azores had in the meantime been given by Santos Costa to pro-Nazi General Ramires, Major Delgado had to operate under considerable risks – and, indeed, while he was in England a Portuguese typist at the Embassy was arrested as a spy and sentenced to death. Aware of the risks Major Delgado had taken, his British colleagues recommended he be awarded the CBE for 'having staked his whole future on behalf of the Allied cause'.[1]

However, the Portuguese procrastinated over the Azores as long as they could. Describing Salazar's loneliness at the time, Augusto de Castro, editor of one of Portugal's biggest daily newspapers, the pro-régime *Diario de Noticias*, recalled the following events based on a confidential talk he had with Salazar himself:

1. Humberto Delgado, *Memoirs* (Cassell, 1964), pp. 62–7.

On 7 November 1942 at 9.30 p.m., as Salazar was, as usual, having dinner by himself in his residence behind the National Assembly Palace, he received a phone call from the British Ambassador, Sir Ronald Campbell, requesting an immediate interview. Salazar tried to delay it until the following afternoon, but the Ambassador insisted the interview should take place that same night, at 1 a.m. Salazar, who usually went to bed early, was surprised with the uncommon timing, but he had to agree. Minutes later the telephone rang again; this time it was President Carmona who was staying at his summer residence in Cascais informing him that the United States Ambassador had made a similar request for an audience.

Salazar reflected. That double request, the unusual and direct way it had been put, the Ambassador's tone of voice – all seemed to indicate that something exceptionally important had taken place. What could it be? The Prime Minister, who in the last two years had had many worrying and mortifying moments, thought for a moment that Allied troops might have landed in the Azores.

That would have been the ruin of the scheme laboriously and painfully developed. Salazar knew that 'neutrality was a single and indivisible reality'. A break, even accidental, in that system, and unforeseen action by one of the belligerent sides would bring a reaction from the other side – and a wave of disaster would inevitably follow. Salazar left immediately for Cascais, some 30 km. out of Lisbon, to discuss the situation with the President and returned to his home in Lisbon in time for the interview with the British Ambassador.

The Ambassador had called to announce, in the name of the British Government, that Allied forces had begun to land in North Africa; Portuguese neutrality would be respected, and neither Portugal's nor Spain's positions would be affected. 'Salazar breathes with relief. He thanks the Ambassador for the friendly wishes and promises to inform Madrid immediately.'[1]

The Germans, for their part, had long been aware of the ambivalence and expediency which had characterized the twin Iberian régimes, now linked by an Iberian Pact which grew closer with each new ratification. 'Ungrateful' Franco had alleged from the beginning that the Second World War would mean for Spain, not a new war, but a continuation of the three-years-long Civil War from which she had emerged deeply

1. *Diario de Noticias* (Lisbon), 29 July 1970.

wounded and ruined. Salazar had also displayed the same ambivalence between a wider ideological identification and a narrower national interest. To the Nazis, who were now rapidly losing the war, the lesson certainly was that one could never build an internationalist movement on the basis of nationalism.

Two entries from Goebbel's *Diary* epitomize the duplicity the Germans saw in Salazar's policies. In one, Goebbels makes an enigmatic reference to an address by Salazar, delivered to a 'small group' and 'not released for general use'. Aware of its contents, Goebbels was able to conclude that 'as long as Salazar remains in power nothing really hostile to us will be done'. But when the bases in the Azores were finally granted to the Allies, Goebbels summed up the situation in his entry for 13 November 1943 in more explicit terms:

I have received a detailed report about the situation in Portugal. From it the following can be gathered. Salazar is undoubtedly the master of Portugal but he relies on his armed forces. Unfortunately he has lost his faith in us to some extent, and therefore keeps swaying to and fro between the extremes of the pendulum. The same is true of Franco. The dictators would do far better if they openly took sides with us, for if our side does not win they are lost anyway.

Although this gross miscalculation of future political events could be described as peculiarly characteristic of Nazi leaders, Goebbels's views coincided with those widely held at the time by many people particularly in Portugal, where an emotional atmosphere of resistance to oppressive rule had been fermenting for a long time.

But Salazar had not only been praying and clinging to his rosary. He had already been reassessing the international situation, with reference to the survival of his régime, as far back as 1942, even before the deal over the Azores materialized. In a speech made in June 1942 he stated sardonically that 'it was an exaggeration to believe that Great Britain wished to favour the growth of Communism in Europe', and, commenting on the enormous task of reconstruction that would fall to the victors, he added: 'No one can suppose that such a task, which will call

for decades of intensive work, brotherly collaboration and
mutual understanding, both within each nation and without,
can be carried on in the conditions of political, economic and
social disorder into which Europe was thrown as a result of the
previous war.'[1]

In the meantime he continued to sell wolfram to the Reich
for another two years until, with Germany's total economic
disruption reflected in her inability to pay, and the Allies well
supplied from other sources, he published a note dated 7 June
1944 announcing the 'ban on sales of wolfram to all desti-
nations'. One year later, in May 1945, when the appalling nature
of that Hitlerian nightmare stood plainly revealed, Salazar,
always ready to repay material gain with a tangible sentimental
gesture, was to order the national flag to be flown at half-mast
on the death of Hitler – the sign of mournful respect usually
reserved for Heads of State of friendly foreign nations.

Moreover, long before Churchill officially announced it in his
famous Fulton speech the following year, Salazar's instinct, or
perhaps his many friends in high international places, must have
been telling him that an 'Iron Curtain' would soon descend in
Europe. But in the meantime, Salazar was more concerned with
the immediate moves in Portuguese policy. In August 1945,
only three months after Germany's unconditional surrender,
Salazar dispatched another important visitor to South Africa to
greet General Smuts and other South African leaders. The visitor was that young veteran who had edited the magazine *New
Order* in the twenties, and who had since provided the régime
with inestimable services in constitutional, ideological and colonial matters. He was the then Minister of Colonies, Senhor
Professor Doutor Marcello Caetano.

The occasion could not have looked more prosaic. Marcello
Caetano, then one of the great stars of the régime, had just
come for the commemoration ceremonies of the fiftieth anniversary of the inauguration of the Lourenço Marques Railway
to South Africa being held at Pretoria. But, as it happened, the

1. From a broadcast on defence, quoted in Salazar, *Discursos e notas
politicas, 1938–1943*, op. cit., Vol. 2, p. 348.

railway had a deep significance in Portuguese–South African relations.

When, towards 1886, gold was discovered in Witwatersrand, South Africans also discovered – since gold mining is one of the most labour-intensive industries – that they would need a permanent flow of tens of thousands of labourers a year. Slavery had been abolished in 1834 and mineral magnates and legislators alike therefore set out to find the best possible substitute system. Eventually they came out with the idea of migratory labour which could be imported from the vast hinterland formed by neighbouring British protectorates and colonies, and Mozambique. The advantages of the system were obvious: by recruiting each year the required labour on short-term contracts, wages could be kept at the low level for unskilled workers, while avoiding the need to divert local labourers from industries and farming in South Africa. Moreover, the system had the advantage of ensuring that no mine-workers would settle and become part of the South African proletariat. Eventually, in order to avoid competition in payment and working conditions, recruitment was organized through a Native Recruiting Corporation, founded in 1896. Later this was taken over by the Witwatersrand Native Labour Association which was to extend its activities to Mozambique, Malawi and beyond.

A Mozambique Convention was signed in 1909 to regulate the traffic of labourers and goods. This was followed by a Portuguese–South African Convention of 1928, revised and ratified in 1934, 1936 and 1940 by successive Ministers of Colonies of the Salazar régime. The annual numbers of workers involved came to an average of 100,000 – some four million up to 1945, allowing for the smaller averages in the first decades. The Portuguese authorities were allowed to take half the workers' earnings, a 'deferred payment' which was to be paid upon their return to their homes in Mozambique. And although the money had been earned abroad, the Africans had to pay taxes to the Mozambique administration for themselves and their dependants, including the old and infirm in the family. The South Africans paid the Portuguese government a fee of about £2.00 in gold, and allowed the Portuguese to maintain tax collection through their *curadorias*, or administrative agencies, within the Union. Since the recruiting was done by the WNLA, they had their own 'public-relations budget' to distribute amongst Portuguese administrative officials. Moreover, since all travelling and accommodation expenses for the duration of the eighteen-month contract were paid by the South African concerns, the profit made by the Portuguese out of African labour, plus the revenue of the millions of tons of cargo handled by the Ports and Railways Administration in Lourenço Marques, was a net gain. No wonder, therefore, that behind the prosaic façade the visit of Marcello Caetano was really a diplomatic exercise to assess the relationships that were to be further developed between Portugal and South Africa.

Utimately, however, despite all Salazar's attempts to evade the issues, the Second World War inevitably brought the régime into a new phase of its history. The grandiose totalitarian schemes of Hitler and Mussolini had only lasted for some ten or twenty years, instead of the promised 1,000. Like Franco in Spain, Salazar was obliged to become, not the creator of a 'New Order', but a more pragmatic type of nationalist autocrat.

Just after the war the régime began to tone down many of its totalitarian features. Salazar never wanted to create a 'corporate' State, it was said, but a 'corporative' State, whatever the distinction may be; the 'S' in the belts of Portuguese Youth uniforms meant only *'Servir'*, to 'Serve', not 'Salazar' as was previously believed; the fascist salute became far less conspicuous; the portrait of Mussolini which Salazar kept on his working desk disappeared, and was later to be replaced – if only for a series of propaganda photographs – by that of Queen Elizabeth II. In fact Salazar ruled according not to a theory of government but to a pragmatic compromise, developed during the first fifteen years of his government, between the various forces behind him – the National Union, the Church, the army, the para-military party organizations and the all-powerful PIDE (State Security Police) of which he was the real leader.

As for the world outside, the old dangers of imperial rivalries seemed to be temporarily over. But with the agitation for independence in India and in other parts of the British and French colonial empires, with the impact of the victory of the democracies, and the prospect of communist revolution hanging over three quarters of mankind, new dangers for the empire were certainly on the way. The visit of Marcello Caetano to South Africa, where there were so many frustrated pro-Nazis, seemed to be an advisable initiative to take following the pre-war visit by the President. South Africa was, moreover, rapidly returning to Afrikaner control. Salazar had learned of their brand of nationalism, and although their culture was somewhat alien to the Portuguese, there were many features in it which looked familiar. They also believed in putting up a fight against history and, if they did not have caravels as ideological symbols, they certainly had a similar nationalist ideology, complete with epic treks and ox-wagons. Moreover, they had gold and power, and whether one wanted to know them or not, they had become a decisive factor for Mozambique and Angola and, as such, for Portuguese foreign policy.

Chapter 5
Oppression and resistance

'Lawyers, notaries, councillors, guards and prison warders – all these, by virtue of their mission, are looked upon with hatred by those who disbelieve, by the blasphemous and by many other sinners. For this reason it is very just that such men and their families should have arms at their disposal, above all in those places where heretics abound, but even in those places that are suspected of heresy' –
FRANCISCO PENHA[1]

Salazar welcomed the end of the war with immediate references to the strengthening of good relations with 'England and her empire'. Addressing the National Assembly on 8 May 1945, he claimed, with either exaggeration or hypocrisy, that

no one among us ever failed to consider the national interest identified with the position of England and the Commonwealth ... And we see now that, though bleeding from many wounds, England rises again, not only victorious but invincible, and having consolidated her ties with the Commonwealth, she can present herself to the world, and amongst the greatest, as a true educator of peoples, a true mother of nations. Blessed be victory!

But while Salazar's mind was flying high and far towards the intricacies of international politics and the economic promises of the distant empire, average Portuguese were naturally reacting to the more prosaic problems of everyday life and the real consequences of oppressive rule inside Portugal – in their work, in their towns and villages, or in the narrow, walking-distance world they lived in.

For all its impact on Portuguese history, politics and

1. From *Directorium Inquisitorium* (*Manual dos Inquisidores*) (Edições Afrodite, Lisbon, 1972).

economy, and despite its role in the nationalist ideology of the ruling classes, the empire impinged little upon the majority of the Portuguese population. With the economy of the colonies geared to the exploitation of cheap African labour, the Portuguese working class, predominantly agricultural, had no part to play even in those colonies, like Angola and Mozambique, which were suited for settlement. The bulk of Portuguese emigration was directed to Brazil which, for most of the latter part of the nineteenth century and early part of the twentieth, received in one year alone more emigrants than the entire white settler population of Angola and Mozambique. In 1945 less than 100,000 Portuguese had settled in Angola and Mozambique combined; of these, some 20 per cent were public functionaries and technicians on short- and long-term commissions of service, while the remainder formed the *élite* of traders, office clerks, technicians and other professional people working on their own account. The total white settler population for both colonies up to 1945 was little more than 1 per cent of the Portuguese population (eight million) and even then the settlers were almost exclusively from a middle-class background.

Moreover, Salazar's dictatorship was protected by an inheritance of obscurantism at home, and obscurity abroad. In 1945 it could be reliably estimated that of the eight million Portuguese, contrary to the understatements in official statistics, 60 per cent were unable to read or write; only 15 per cent knew how to read; only 20 per cent had had regular schooling up to primary school level; and only 5 per cent could be regarded as being well educated, having secondary courses and university degrees. Of the last category, only a small fraction could afford to travel abroad as tourists or had had the privilege of an occasional professional paid trip.[1] And since, despite what nationalists think, only those who know other nations and cultures can effectively discover and understand their own, few Portuguese were even aware of the importance of the empire as

1. See Edgar Rodrigues and Roberto das Neves, *A Fome em Portugal* (Germinal, Rio de Janeiro, 1959), who quote an address by Prof. Abel Salazar, a democratic opponent of the régime.

a factor in influencing the authoritarian nature of Portuguese rule. Moreover, due to the extreme poverty and neglect of the mass of colonial peoples, and their consequent lack of mobility, there was never any significant number of Africans living in or visiting Portugal. The projection of overseas cultural and political influences amongst the Portuguese was confined to the efforts of groups of students from the empire which had maintained organizations such as the Liga Africana (African League) and the Movimento Nacional Pro-Colonias (Pro-Colonies' Nationalist Movement) which survived the first years of military junta rule after the 1926 *coup d'état*. However, soon after the new order had been established by the Colonial Act in 1930 such organizations were gradually disbanded and by 1945 they had long been forgotten.

The obscurity of Portugal for the outside world, and the casually accepted notion that it was only a small country whose life and significance were overshadowed by neighbouring Spain, suited Salazar's designs. In the aftermath of the war, as Salazar himself had foreseen, most nations were far too involved with their own reconstruction problems and future ideological realignments to devote any particular attention to what might be going on inside the seemingly peaceful, if anachronistic, Portuguese empire.

Little is known inside or outside Portugal of the early resistance to the régime, and how Salazar came to rule for long enough to create a viable system of government. The 'Estado Novo' had a number of reasons for hiding opposition movements from public opinion. Inside the country, under the cloak of censorship, any rebellious actions or strikes were promptly isolated and dealt with before they could reach nationwide proportions. Abroad, once the régime had built its own propaganda around the idea of law and order, and the consequent discrediting of the Republican democratic period for the chronic agitation and rioting that went on, the 'Estado Novo' had a vested interest in appearing in full control of the situation and destroying all traces of opposition.

However, if one tries to piece together the fragmentary information that is available in laconic government notes distributed to the press, or statements made by those involved, a pattern emerges of the nature and development of the 'Estado Novo'.

At first no one thought that the *pronunciamento* of May 1926 would be more than just another short-lived *coup d'état*. Therefore the uprising and attempted *pronunciamentos* that took place immediately after the establishment of the régime were deprived of civilian participation and seemed to be a continuation of the same series of military insurrections that had erupted from time to time during the democratic republic. Later, when Salazar appeared on the scene, many people began to fear that the country was confronted with a new phenomenon. The military junta shared with almost all dictatorships a common claim that the suspension of the constitution was only temporary, and that civil rights and democratic institutions would soon be restored. But Salazar had introduced a constitution which, despite all its principled guarantees, contained a proviso whereby the government had powers to 'regulate' the exercise of fundamental liberties by decree orders and laws, a sophistry designed to ensure the institutionalization of 'temporary' rule. It was only towards the time of the Spanish Civil War, when the socialist and communist organizations that had been outlawed had begun to reorganize clandestinely, that the class antagonisms inherent in the situation in the Iberian Peninsula began to be recognized as the primary factors behind tension and overt acts of rebellion.

Resistance to the régime broke out within the army itself less than one year after the events of May 1926. On 3 February 1927, a *pronunciamento* led from Oporto by General Sousa Dias extended to Lisbon, where the rebel forces were commanded by a young Lieutenant Commander, Agatão Lança. The rebels demanded the 'withdrawal of the government and return to the 1910 Constitution'.

This is how another army officer, Lieutenant Humberto Delgado, then a young nationalist supporter of the régime, saw the events from the side of pro-government troops:

The *largo* (square) now called Praça do Brasil was the scene of much shooting. Still training as a pilot, I volunteered for active service and marched up with thirty airmen and two other officers, one of whom I never saw again until the revolt was over. We manned barricades in a street leading to that ill-fated square. How wild and cruel man can become! A field-gun had been left behind in the square. From the near-by corner the enemy were trying to drag it over to their side by means of a rope. With another officer I ran from door to door as far as the corner and from there, throwing hand grenades at right angles to our left, we wiped out those who had been getting on our nerves with their 'rope tricks'. The whole business was really very cruel ... Near by Lieutenant Henrique Galvão was fighting gallantly. The rebels surrendered after fifty-three hours of fighting.[1]

In his turn Henrique Galvão explained his support of the régime in this vein: 'As an officer in the armed forces, still very young and politically inexperienced, I was one of the men in the revolutionary movement of 28 May 1926 ... Subsequently I was also among the many who believed in ... the Man of Providence.'[2]

After four days of fighting in Oporto and Lisbon, with 120 dead and 650 wounded, the '7th February revolt', as it was to be known, failed, and its leaders surrendered to the government.

Another military uprising, this time led by a former Minister of War, Colonel Jose Mascarenhas, took place on 20 July 1928, but although it engaged the support of several garrisons in Lisbon, it was promptly curbed by government forces, having lasted only twelve hours.

Partly as a consequence of the new status of adjacent islands which Madeira and the Azores had acquired with the enactment of the Colonial Act, rioting broke out in Funchal (Madeira) on 4 April 1931 which extended to the Azores – but again it was defeated when a cruiser was sent from Lisbon, followed by an expeditionary army detachment. Only four months later, on 26 August 1931, an uprising involving air force officers from a base at Alverca, near Lisbon, and an estimated 5,000 civilian

1. Humberto Delgado, *Memoirs* (Cassell, 1964), p. 45.
2. Henrique Galvão, *The Santa Maria – My Crusade for Portugal* (Weidenfeld & Nicolson, 1961), p. 41.

volunteers, was aborted after street fighting between rebels and government troops.

The next major attempted insurrection, combining a general strike with armed action, took place on 18 January 1938. Amongst its leaders was an air force officer, Sarmento Beires, who had become famous in Portugal after a pioneering crossing of the South Atlantic. Judging by the nationwide disruption caused by acts of sabotage and work stoppages, it must have been organized on an unprecedented scale, and this was its downfall. Warned by informers, the régime had had time to plan its repressive action. The government troops regained the control of Marinha Grande, an industrial centre that had come to a halt due to a general strike, and gradually brought the movement to an end. The Minister of the Interior published a note announcing that 'the government in accordance with the statements and pronouncements by the leaders of the movement regards the strike as a revolutionary act . . . and, as such, has sent cable orders to the competent authorities in Southern Angola, to set up immediately at the mouth of the river Cunene a concentration camp to intern those responsible, who will be deported to Angola within a few days'. And many of those sent there were never to return.

The government had embarked on an extensive plan involving both police intimidation and legislative reforms to turn the working class into a disciplined labour force. And in order to relieve the tensions that were mounting amongst urban and rural workers who had seen the reversal of all their achievements in such matters as the rights of association, strike, free labour press and international connections, the government was now trying to impose its alternative system of 'vertical syndicates' more in keeping with the schemes of the corporate State.

While the best-informed working-class leaders could hardly go any further than unmask in clandestine pamphlets the implications of the new system of labour relations, largely modelled on the fascist pattern, other armed rebellions broke out. On 10 September 1935 another attempted uprising led by army officers and a national syndicalist leader, Rolão Preto, was frustrated by the then Policia de Vigilancia e Defesa Social PVDS, later known as PIDE). Curiously enough Rolão Preto was a radical fascist, a former supporter of Salazar whom the latter had come to regard, like Mussolini, as being too 'socialist' minded. This attempted uprising, which aimed at 'the arrest of Prime Minister Salazar and some of his Ministers' involved the cooperation of a wide range of followers including some disgruntled right-wing people who had belonged to the disbanded National Syndicalist Movement and had held positions under the régime. It was not surprising, therefore, that it should have ended with the preventive arrest of some of the leading conspirators who had been denounced even before the uprising. In a note published by the Prime Minister's office it was stated that 'The names of the leaders, meeting places, plans and nominees for a new government were all known to the PIDE.' And by the time their two delegates, one an army officer and the other a civilian, were calling at the President's residence in Cascais, to invite him to accept 'the movement as the expression of the people's will', the PIDE had acted and arrested most of the would-be rebels.

The most serious attempt, because of its implications and consequences, was the mutiny on board two warships, the *Dão* and the *Afonso de Albuquerque*, which occurred in September 1936. Another ship, the *Bartolomeu Dias,* was also involved and preparing to join the others. The aim this time was to head the warships towards Valencia and join the Spanish republican fleet which was engaged in fighting Franco's forces. On the evening of 9 September the then Director of the PIDE, Agostinho Lourenço, whose name was dreaded throughout Portugal, was informed of strange happenings around the ships which were anchored in the Tagus. He alerted several land forces strategically situated on both banks of the Tagus estuary and, as the ships prepared to leave Lisbon, they were placed under heavy fire. There was no option but surrender. Those arrested were 'to be sent immediately to a penal colony and tried in due time'. They were in fact sent to a concentration camp, known as Tarrafal, in the remote islands of Cape Verde, together with other prisoners, mostly Communist Party militants. They were tried summarily in absentia on 14 and 15 October and eighty-two of them sentenced to long terms of internment. Those who survived remained there through all the years of the Spanish Civil War and the Second World War, i.e. from 1936 to 1945; and a few remained after that date and were joined by others until the camp was temporarily closed, following worldwide protests, in 1954.

A pamphlet, written anonymously by a militant of the clandestine Communist Party – *Tarrafal – Camp of Slow Death* – gave a disturbing eye-witness account of the conditions meted out to internees.

Aljube, Caxias, Peniche, Angra [in the Azores] . . . prisons which would form a guide-book of violence and horrors . . . But further away is the worst unit in that machine of tortures and death, the Tarrafal . . . It is there, in the Cape Verde island of Santiago, where Africans die without bread because the land and the droughts refuse to give it to them; where the natives die of devastating tropical fevers because the climate is hostile to all human life, that they have incarcerated 300 brave Portuguese who rose against Fascist Salazarism . . .

The Tarrafal Camp, according to his description, was a rectangular-shaped field, 300 metres in length and 50 metres wide, surrounded by a ditch 4 metres wide and 3 metres deep. It was located on a small plain surrounded on the east by the shark-infested sea and on the north, south and west by hilly, arid lands. It was 3 kilometres away from a small locality, called Tarrafal, from which it derived its name.

At some distance there was a cemetery, shared by Africans and prisoners. The writer of the pamphlet recalled how 'Africans accompanied their dead to the cemetery playing sad tunes on primitive instruments which struck the note of misfortune that had befallen them'. Around all the camp on a 3-metres-high ramp, African troops patrolled the barracks and court-yards day and night. At each corner there was a guard with a machine-gun. A small wooden bridge, forming an entrance dominated by two towers with armed guards, was 'the only passage between the camp and life'. Many had never been tried, others, if tried, had only been sentenced to short terms of imprisonment and arbitrarily sent to the camp where they remained without any hope of appeal or justice. Amongst the prisoners there was the Communist Party General Secretary, Bento Gonçalves, a much-respected working-class man with an outstanding intelligence and wide knowledge. 'But most of us were peasants, workers, soldiers, the sailors from the *Dão*, *Afonso de Albuquerque* and *Bartolomeu Dias*, students, intellectuals, sons of the people who fought for the happiness of our country.'

The writer's account, corroborated by many of the survivors, continues:

For three years our barracks had no light; the food could not be eaten and sometimes we had to put bits of bread in our nostrils to avoid the smell ... The dishes remained on the ground, covered in dust as there was no water to wash them. We worked on near-by stone quarries, under a burning sun, water was rationed and not available for washing; disease was widespread. Eventually from February 1937 a doctor was sent to see us from time to time. He was himself a trusted nationalist and his neglect caused the death of many of us. Discipline was imposed by punishing transgressors or protestors in a block made of concrete, 7 metres high and 3½ metres wide, where light and air only penetrated through three little holes made in the heavy iron door and a little square in the roof. Those under punishment were kept in one of the two cells in the block of concrete on 'little bread and little water' – and, although the block looked like a sinister tomb for the living, the punishment cells were as hot as furnaces. They were in fact bitterly known as *'frigideiras'* – 'frying pans'.

Over the years more than forty prisoners, many of them never having been brought to trial or whose sentences had long since ended, died. Amongst them was Bento Gonçalves, one of the many martyrs the Communist Party has given to the cause of Portuguese democracy.[1]

Tarrafal Camp inflicted a brutal punishment on the enemies

1. *A Resistencia em Portugal: Cronicas* (Editora Felman Rego, São Paulo, 1962). This book was originally published anonymously; later editions were attributed to the sculptor Dias Coelho, an underground Communist Party activist shot by the PIDE in a Lisbon street in December 1961.

113

of the State, but it also acted as an intimidating deterrent to the average Portuguese at home. In those years, according to many eye-witness accounts, Portugal, for the average working man, was itself like a vast concentration camp.

When we talk about politics in the street we first look around in all directions, to make sure there is no spy within earshot. Such is the terror that grips Portugal. In the cafés, public squares, factories, workshops, everywhere, there is the fear planted by the Inquisition of Salazar and [Lisbon's Patriarch Cardinal] Cerejeira. Peoples are so frightened they are afraid they will be denounced to the police by their own fingers. And the truth is hardly different. How many citizens have been arrested, tortured and deported just because they were reading newspapers to a group of workers at the door of the workshop or at the table of the coffee-bar? How many people had their radios seized only because they listened to the BBC in its broadcasts to Portugal? How many illiterate people were maimed in their arms and legs, or contracted TB or trachoma in prison, just because they picked up pamphlets in the street – pamphlets which they, being illiterate, could not even read?[1]

In such circumstances it is not surprising that Salazar should have become the target of much hatred. There was an attempted assassination on 4 July 1937. When Salazar arrived for Sunday mass in the home of one of his wealthy friends in a Lisbon avenue, a bomb exploded in an underground refuse collector near his car. Despite the fact that the bomb had been well placed, fused and timed, it seems that for some technical reason requiring a knowledge of physics beyond the grasp of the conspirators, the bomb exploded along the collector in the wrong direction, causing a vast hole in the direction of the avenue, rather than the residence of Salazar's friend. Salazar escaped, having taken the opportunity, in that particular mass, to give thanks for his survival.

Still, just in case the prayers went unheard, the PIDE immediately started their investigations. An amusing story began to circulate at the time. Apparently one of the suspects seen in the neighbourhood had a wooden leg; before anyone had taken the trouble to ask whether it was the right or left leg, everyone

1. See Rodrigues and Neves, op. cit., p. 168.

within a radius of 200 miles from Lisbon who had a wooden leg was detained for investigation. Eventually the police charged a number of men, all allegedly belonging to the 'Red Legion', a splinter group from the Communist Party which preferred direct action methods. But rumours filtered out of army and official circles to the effect that the PIDE, which had not brought any charges until 22 August, had decided to fabricate charges against those arrested because they were regarded as 'dangerous elements' anyway.

Resistance against the régime in Portugal went on even in the war years, and many strikes and riots were caused directly by the fact that in sending foodstuffs to the Germans – wheat, maize, olive oil, etc. – the régime was creating shortages in Portugal and imposing severe rationing. At the time there were 'hunger marches' in protest against the injustices of a situation when rationing and deprivation coexisted with rampant profiteering and corruption. Despite the particularly rigid discipline of wartime, there were several extensive strikes, particularly in October–November 1942 and July–August 1943, the latter involving more than 50,000 workers in Lisbon and in the industrial centre along the south bank of the Tagus. Again on 8 and 9 May 1944 tens of thousands of workers, industrial as well as agricultural, went on strike, and a combined force of Republican Guards (rural police), ordinary Public Police, PIDE and troops was used to bring them into submission. Thousands of workers were confined in bull-rings which in the 'best' of Iberian traditions, are often used as centres of detention in case of riots and demonstrations involving masses of people.

All over the world the period up to 1945 was marked by violent ideological wars, civil and international. Brutality is an everyday fact in war, and many people have tried to apologize for the Salazar régime on the grounds that it was not as bad as others. However, contrary to widespread belief both inside and outside Portugal, the régime enacted its most repressive legislation after the war. After 1945, as soon as the régime felt sure of its survival and of its new alliances, it passed from the arbitrary, but casual, stage of repression, to the development of a

115

scientific system which in its basic laws and operative methods was tantamount to a Neo-Inquisition. Indeed, perhaps in anticipation of certain legal reforms which were being planned or were already in the drafting stages, the government issued a number of decrees early in 1945, which were a forewarning of a systematic tightening of the vice.

The occasion was provided by a spontaneous civil movement whereby, soon after the war, citizens were requested to sign a national petition to the President calling for free elections, revision of the electoral rolls, the abolition of the Tarrafal Concentration Camp, the return of deportees in colonies as far away as Timor, and an amnesty to political prisoners and exiles. With the cooperation of cinemas and halls in private clubs and institutions, sessions were held to collect signatures and addresses, and at one stage the movement assumed nationwide proportions. But although there was nothing illegal, as such, in the movement, it was to have disastrous consequences for hundreds of people. The régime, after so many years of censorship and repression, had lost track of public opinion and, except for a minority of militant activists known to the PIDE, could not possibly know how many people were still opposed to it. The authorities gained possession of the lists of signatures which had been collected by the president of the improvised citizens' committee, a veteran opponent of the régime and a lawyer, Lima Alves. They were turned into a census of old democratic opponents, as well as the new ones that in the meantime had joined their ranks. As people were gradually persecuted and dismissed from government employment, the opposition was driven underground and a Movimento de Unidade Democratica (Movement of Democratic Unity) organized in clandestine conditions. It was a broad front, largely dominated by the Communists, and its groups and 'cells' extended to the settler population in the overseas territories.

One can well imagine the psychological impact that such measures must have had at the time throughout the country. Many people during the war had believed in the propaganda put out by the Allies which proclaimed Nazism and Fascism to be the scourges of mankind; they had listened to Roosevelt's

116

messages declaring that the United States would be on the side of small peoples who wanted to live under democratic rule or attain self-government. Throughout the war ordinary Portuguese had expressed their ideological sympathies and hopes by extending such warm hospitality to British and American troops passing through Portugal as to leave them with unforgettable experiences of human solidarity and kindness. Such hospitality had also been a way of registering their scorn for the government. These demonstrations had followed the Yalta and Potsdam Conferences and the defeat of the wartime coalition government in Britain which, despite the personal prestige of its leader Winston Churchill, had been replaced by a Labour government under a man suitably plebeian called Attlee. But now, in Portugal, under the pretext of wartime and neutralist security, police rule was to be given legal status.

On 30 April 1945 – nine days before the final surrender of Nazi Germany – an ambiguous decree, No. 34553, established the principle that 'preventive measures against crime' could be taken by a special court against vagrants and other 'persistent anti-social delinquents'. On 13 October 1945 the political police were once again renamed and given special powers. The change of name and the strengthening of powers were obviously related and, in the best tradition of Salazar's sophistry, had the double purpose of misleading public opinion and disguising the true practical implications of the laws.

Originally the political police had been known as Police of Social Vigilance and Defence, and later as Police of Security and Defence of the State – PVIDE. But now, however, with an eye on public opinion abroad and the reorganization of the policing of foreign visitors, it was expedient to name it simply as Policia Internacional e de Defesa do Estado (International and State Defence Police) – better known as the PIDE, after the initials of its Portuguese name. One of its founding leaders, the dreaded Captain Agostinho Lourenço, was soon to be appointed as the Director General of Interpol in Paris – another sign of the times which made many Portuguese opponents of the régime wary of the claimed apolitical integrity of that international police organization covering most Western nations.

117

But while the substitution of the words 'vigilance' and 'security' by 'international' had a nicer connotation about it, the PIDE was to be given powers which made it 'a State within the State'. On 13 October 1945 the PIDE was empowered to arrest and detain anyone suspected of political activities for 45 days without charge and given discretionary powers regarding the initiation of legal proceedings and the release of suspects. There was no mention of it being answerable for wrongful arrest or responsible for any indemnity or compensation in case of loss to those individuals detained. Some mistake must have occurred for seven days later a new decree no. 35042 of 20 October extended the period of detention to 90 days 'in case of need'. Later this was extended to 180 days.

'From then on the threats and insecurity implied in dictatorial rule were legalized and affected one and all,' wrote Manuel Sertorio, a socialist lawyer living in exile in Algiers. 'There is an hour, usually six o'clock in the morning, when any opponent of the régime can hear a knock on the door and be arrested – it is what we call "the milkman's time".'

Many people had already suffered the effects of the new law when another military revolt broke out in the following year, at Oporto. Significantly, since the regular army, under the reorganization of Army Under-Secretary Santos Costa, was now a disciplined political institution, the revolt known as the 'Revolt of the Mealhada' – after the village where it came to a halt – was led by a group of young NCOs and officers, none of them with a rank higher than lieutenant. Their leader was an imaginative lieutenant, Fernando Queiroga, and the idea of the officers involved was to create the impression that the entire Oporto military garrison had joined the uprising, in the hope that troops from other regiments throughout the country would 'adhere' to the revolution. Instead, at Mealhada, approaching Coimbra on their 'march' to Lisbon, they were met by troops sent from Coimbra, Aveiro and Figueira da Foz who forced their surrender.

The officers involved were tried later in the year. Lieutenant Queiroga, who received the heaviest sentence as the man responsible for the frustrated uprising, was to write a book giving an account of his experiences in jail and a description of the treatment meted out to those, more innocent than himself, whom he met there and who fell prey to the régime's laws. In this book, his first complaints arose from what he saw as 'the degradation of the army'. It appears that the class system in Portugal operated even in prison; prisoners from the middle class and the professions could afford to buy better facilities, including better cells and rooms, and deference, from guards; the military class were outside P I D E control in matters of interrogation and detention and had their own privileges in the form of special prisons, such as the Fort of Trafaria. 'The army', complained Queiroga,

now has no personality; it is transformed into an 'official army' with all the former links of solidarity between officers broken ... Where are the expressive gestures of solidarity, such as the 'movement of the swords' which had symbolized their unity and comradeship in the past? ... How can one understand the permission given to the P I D E by the Commander of the Third Military Region to enter the military barracks of a battalion in Coimbra to arrest a group of sergeants, force them to put on civilian clothes, take them to Oporto, where, at P I D E headquarters, they were ordered to get undressed and beaten up with strips of rubber tyres, clubs and other instruments of torture in a bloody orgy? ... How can we describe the indifference of the army before humiliations and sufferings of all kinds inflicted even upon officers who aim to redeem our institutions and end the Salazar régime?[1]

If members of the middle class, often protected by family influence and by professional organizations such as the Order of Lawyers or the Order of Doctors of Medicine, or the army, could undergo so many forms of physical and psychological torture, one can imagine the treatment meted out to workers who belonged to the clandestine Communist Party and had often lost all social contacts while operating illegally. In fact, among the many men who died under torture at the hands of the P I D E, there are some who were never satisfactorily identified. Such men are, as it were, the unsung heroes, the

1. Fernando Queiroga, *Portugal oprimido* (Germinal, Rio de Janeiro, 1958).

'unknown soldiers' of Portugal's long struggle for freedom and a place in the modern world.

Salazar was perhaps the only Prime Minister in the world to have gone on record as admitting that he approved of strong political police action. In an interview with the nationalist journalist Antonio Ferro, who was later to become a diplomat, Salazar declared: 'We came to the conclusion that the ill-treated prisoners were always, or almost always, fearful terrorists, who resisted all attempts by the police to make them confess where they had hidden their criminal and deadly weapons. Only after being subjected to those violent methods did they decide to tell the truth.'[1] In fact, the innocent – whose existence, by implication, Salazar himself admits – were more often than not those who suffered most. The innocent, no matter what pain they sustained, would die without being able to reveal where they had hidden their non-existent 'criminal and deadly weapons'. In some cases they were saved only by later information arising in the course of police action. Moreover, the relations between police and prisoners were not those between professional policemen and accused men 'who were to be regarded as innocent until proved guilty' in a normal court of law. By the very nature of their jobs, PIDE inspectors and agents were recruited from the ranks of government supporters; in fact many of them are known to have been enlisted after having proved themselves as informers, or having been involved in some common offence for which they had not been prosecuted in exchange for services rendered or to be rendered. Moreover, PIDE inspectors and other officials were more often than not enemies anxious to settle scores with those they arrested. There is an impressive array of written statements collected through the years, from different people, at different times and places, by men of various nationalities and a wide spectrum of political and religious affiliations, which together amount to massive corroborative evidence of psychological and physical torture inflicted by the PIDE upon successive generations of opponents of the régime.

Around the time of the 'Mealhada' march, and responding to

1. Antonio Ferro, *Salazar: Portugal and her Leader* (Faber, 1939).

the same moral pressures that had led the group of young soldiers to attempt a revolution, many prominent people in Portugal were anxious to overthrow Salazar. President Carmona himself, according to various accounts originating with his wife, who entertained a strong temperamental dislike for misogynist Salazar, began to call a few of his remaining trusted friends to the Presidential Palace, where he complained to them that Salazar had gradually and insidiously isolated him. A military junta was formed to elaborate extensive plans for a change in the government. Since the President, under the 1933 constitution, retained the power to dismiss or appoint the Prime Minister, President Carmona wanted to make sure he could count on extensive support and that at least a provisional programme for a transitional government was arrived at.

The programme included the proclamation of a Supreme Council of National Liberation; the dismissal of Salazar; the repeal of the 1933 constitution and the Colonial Act; the dissolution of the Council of State, National Assembly and Corporative Chamber, Portuguese Legion, Portuguese Youth, the PIDE. Other points called for the arrest of those responsible for dictatorial rule, including ministers and PIDE officials and heads of institutions, and suspension of political rights to those who had held executive positions in the National Union Party. In keeping with the demands made by the nationwide petition of 1945, there would be free elections, abolition of censorship, and a general amnesty to political prisoners and exiles, including the immediate closure of the Tarrafal Concentration Camp.

However, on the day the large-scale military operation was due to begin some generals raised objections over tactical questions, and the military junta decided to postpone the movement. Inevitably, the PIDE and Salazar eventually came to know of the conspiracy and had in their possession some of the documents and plans of the conspirators. It is said that Salazar, realizing that the PIDE could not hope to curb such a vast conspiracy, and that so many people in the army were against him, decided to take refuge in a loyal army barracks, from where he organized the defence of the régime. His counter-

121

attack came, not in the form of a major trial, which would have been difficult since the movement had the assent of the President and was therefore essentially constitutional, but in the form of a purge.

On 1 June 1947 an official note appeared in all Portuguese newspapers recalling that by Decree No. 25317 of 13 May 1945 – the day of the anniversary of the first apparition of Our Lady of Fatima – the government had given itself powers (a) to dismiss officers of the armed forces who failed in their duties to the established institutions, thereby betraying their obligations towards public authorities and those who were responsible for them; (b) to dismiss all those individuals who had taken a prominent part in acts of sedition, or had shown evidence of active opposition to the Political Constitution in force and who, consequently, gave no guarantees of cooperation in carrying out the high aims of the State, especially in such sensitive sectors as teaching at all levels of education.

In the same note, the government announced that 'The Council of Ministers shall not hesitate to ensure that persistent agitators leave the country or to order them to reside in any part of national territory (including the overseas territories) even when they are not subject to fixed residence by judicial order.'

By government order several prominent people, former ministers, generals and admirals, were compulsorily retired or were dismissed if they were not of retirement age. Eleven high-ranking army and navy officers were treated in this way, including Vice-Admiral Cabeçadas, who had been a member of the original three-man Revolutionary Junta of May 1926, of which General Carmona was the only one still in office. Also sacked were fifteen professors of Lisbon, Oporto and Coimbra Universities, including some of the country's best scientists, mathematicians, surgeons and professors of medicine, and eight young and promising university assistant professors and lecturers, including economists, historians and doctors of engineering. Regarded as 'professional conspirators' and 'traitors' in the press, without any possibility of replying, they could not obtain employment elsewhere – and, except for surgeons and doctors who went into private practice, the others had no alternative but to leave the country where, in most cases, they followed distinguished academic careers.

The insecure Salazar now relied more than ever on Santos Costa, who was himself aspiring to the Ministry of Defence and the role of Salazar's strong-arm man. Santos Costa took the opportunity to promote younger officers of his choice to high-ranking positions which had fallen vacant, and proceeded with an overall purge of lower ranks, dismissing and transferring many who did not offer 'guarantees of loyalty'. In fact, a scandal broke out at the time involving the strange circumstances surrounding the death of General Marques Godinho – one of the conspirators – whose widow tried to sue the then Lieutenant-Colonel Santos Costa for manslaughter. High-ranking officers asked for an inquiry, but none was ever to take place. Salazar himself intervened, 'ordering the police to arrest the poor widow (as if her grief was not enough!), the young lawyer whom she had hired for the case, and her only civilian son, a medical doctor, on grounds that the whole issue was "a state secret". Moreover, in his own dispatch on the case, Salazar ordered "the apprehension of all the documents, which should be filed, after the officials involved are sworn to secrecy".'[1]

Eventually in 1948 Santos Costa, as War (later Defence) Minister, did order a trial of the officers involved in the nationwide conspiracy. This trial, which took place in April and May 1948, after some of the accused had been in jail for over a year, become officially known as the 'National Liberation Board Movement trial'.

The defendants made such allegations and produced such an impressive array of witnesses that the trial became a major political event in itself. Moreover the case branched out into new incidents and it was to acquire an even greater historical significance as some of the accused developed their careers as opposition leaders. Among those arrested at the time, for instance, were the ageing Dr João Soares, former Minister and head of a well-known Lisbon college, the 'Colegio Moderno', and his young son Mario Soares, who was to become a prominent social democratic leader; another was a young air-force

1. Queiroga, op. cit., p. 188.

technician, Herminio da Palma Inacio, who had almost single-handed destroyed half of the Portuguese air fleet at the time of the insurrection in an act of sabotage at the Sintra air base near Lisbon. Sentenced to eight years in jail, he later made a daring escape, and began a career which led to the leadership of LUAR (League of Unity for Revolutionary Action), the urban guerrilla group.

The full extent of the conspiracy was never uncovered and the government itself lost interest in pursuing the case. Eventually, Vice-Admiral Cabeçadas, who had been imprisoned for a year, was sentenced to a token one year in jail, and immediately released.

With the turn of international events, however, the situation began to change for the régime. Churchill's 1946 'Iron Curtain' speech in Fulton made the extreme right all over the world rejoice, in an 'I told you so' mood; by 1948, even Oswald Mosley felt encouraged enough to try and revive the British Fascist Party. In the same year, the South African government formally adopted 'apartheid' as a national policy. Moreover, with the Soviet blockade of West Berlin, the Azores bases, now under American control by an extended agreement with the régime, became a vital link in the allied 'air lift' and acquired a new strategic significance for the United States. And in the following year Portugal, mainly due to the influence of the United States and Britain, became one of the founding members of NATO.

Salazar then joined in with the Western right-wing circles who were making all the appropriate protests about the exclusion of Spain, in order to distract attention from the implications of Portugal's own incongruous integration into an allied bloc ostensibly set up 'to defend democracy' and 'fundamental civil rights'.

Nevertheless, as both Spain's and Portugal's admission into the United Nations Organization was still being resisted by many countries, both inside and outside the Communist bloc, which had been the most immediate victims of Nazi aggression, Salazar still saw the need to adjust to the new diplomatic situation. Accordingly, for the first time since the establishment of the régime, he felt the need to respect the régime's own constitution of 1933 which provided for presidential elections every seven years, and elections for the 120 seats of the National Assembly every four years. These elections were to be by direct suffrage, and would provide the opposition with a periodical opportunity to test the régime before the country and international public opinion.

From then on, resistance to the régime was to crystallize into two types of opposition: one legal, comprising a broad association of individuals, mostly lawyers, who periodically improvised themselves into civil committees to sponsor independent candidates, thus taking advantage of the one month's relaxation of censorship allowed for electoral campaigning; and the other clandestine, comprising the activities of a network of militants who put out stencilled and printed newspapers and periodicals or organized industrial and civil protest action. At both levels, the illegal Communist Party, led by lawyer Alvaro Cunhal first in clandestinity, later from jail and afterwards from exile, was to be the dominant, but by no means the only force, that kept Portuguese democratic resistance alive for the next ten years, until 1958 when General Delgado shook the country as contestant for the Presidency.

Chapter 6
The Neo-Inquisition

I live in fear
I write and speak in fear
I fear what I say to myself alone
In fear I care
In fear I hold my tongue . . .
ANTONIO FERREIRA (1528–69)

There is a striking affinity between the 'Estado Novo' and the Holy Inquisition in the methods of repression used, and also in the subterfuges used by those oppressed to keep resistance alive. This has been noted by various writers who have written books on historical themes which show the realities of Portugal's past while indirectly exposing the analogies with its present.

The well-known historian Antonio Jose Saraiva devoted two penetrating books to the Inquisition itself, and one of them – *A inquisição portuguesa,* which described the censorship on books imposed by the Inquisitors – was itself banned by the régime's censor. More recently a number of well-known writers, lawyers and clergy cooperated in producing a modern edition of a classic, the *Inquisitors' Handbook.*

These books made no direct reference to the Salazar régime, but the techniques they described were closely analagous to those used by the PIDE. To a greater or lesser degree, of course, experiences of torture at the hands of police organizations almost anywhere in the world correspond with each other; but in Portugal these similarities derive from the continuity of a single tradition of oppressive and obscurantist rule. The self-sufficiency of this tradition points to the persistent identification in Portugal of religious dogma with nationalist ideology and class interests, and underlines also just how little colonial policies such as 'assimilation' have changed over the centuries.

The work of the Inquisition, as of the PIDE, relied upon a system of denunciations extracted from each detainee who had in his turn been uncovered as suspect by informers. The PIDE, however, was also closely linked with all other police organizations and paramilitary bodies, such as the Judicial Police, the Republican Guard, etc., through a coordinating Council of National Security headed by the Minister of the Interior. Since this coordination applied to all local and administrative authorities, who were appointed by the government, the PIDE directly or indirectly covered all Portugal and the overseas territories. Any politically incriminating evidence uncovered by other police departments in the course of their normal duties was immediately passed on to the PIDE.

Physical torture of political prisoners was regularly used, though the *Inquisitors' Handbook* contains allusions to it being counter-productive and only to be used on those who showed themselves to be 'negative and stubborn'. Nevertheless, even in the cases where extreme brutality and torture were practised in the fifties – against such leading opponents of the régime as Alvaro Cunhal – the PIDE, like the Inquisition, required as much time as possible to carry out their work at headquarters, where they had all the facilities necessary for their work. The headquarters were like vast 'investigation laboratories', and physical torture was mostly incidental to the main purpose of achieving the breakdown and manipulation of the minds of prisoners.

Under the 'Estado Novo' a series of separate, but interacting, decrees, comprising both censorship and repressive penalization, was established. The circumstances in which the main body of repressive legislation came to be passed are very revealing of the sophistry of Salazar's methods.

They can be best understood by recalling that the original military dictatorship of President Carmona, upon suspending the republican-democratic constitution in May 1926, had to rule by means of temporary decree-orders. The constitution, as we have seen, was fairly liberal, and well within the most advanced principles adopted by international conventions and institutions at the time. As the régime consolidated its rule this constitution had to be replaced. Salazar wanted a constitution which did not unduly offend public opinion. However, in order to ensure the continuity of arbitrary rule, it would have to contain enough catches to accommodate such adjustments as might prove necessary in the light of political developments.

Therefore, contrary to what might be believed abroad, the 1933 'Estado Novo' constitution contained amongst others the following guarantees concerning civil rights:

(a) that no man shall be deprived of his personal liberty or held without formal charge, except in cases foreseen by paragraphs 3 and 4 (dealing with serious criminal offences, such as murder, armed robbery, etc.);

(b) that no man can be sentenced for a criminal offence if the said offence is not covered by a law already in force which renders the act punishable;

(c) defence instructions must be admitted, giving to the accused, both before and after the formulation of charges, the necessary guarantee for defence;

(d) that no man must undergo either perpetual imprisonment or the death penalty (Art. 8, clauses 8 and 11).

But behind this constitutional façade the reality was quite different. Contrary to what happens under genuinely representative parliamentary systems, the so-called National Assembly could only propose certain laws. It was the government which legislated by means of decree-orders or decree-laws (corresponding to Acts), both having the force of Bills. The catch introduced in the constitution, therefore, was that despite all the guarantees so solemnly inscribed in the text of the constitution, the government had the power to promulgate decree-laws of an 'administrative character' which were outside effective judicial control.

It was in the exercise of these powers that the government came to pass successive decree-laws and decree-orders establishing the prior censorship of the press, both in Portugal and the colonies; and the laws dealing with arbitrary detention without charge for successive and renewable periods of 180 days; the establishment of special political courts – *tribunais plenarios* (plenary tribunals) – at Lisbon and Oporto dealing with major security cases; and the laws sanctioning the application of 'security measures' of imprisonment for successive and renewable

128

terms of from six months to three years. In addition there was also special legislation whereby the government had self-attributed powers to order the summary deportation or banishment to a designated place of anyone regarded as politically undesirable.

The purpose of the various decrees which 'regulated' the rights established in the constitution was to isolate the working classes from a minority of educated people who extended their concern in politics beyond the issues more directly involving themselves. Indeed, despite all claims to equality and 'integration', the vigilance exercised by the PIDE in Angola and Mozambique covered social contacts between whites and blacks and led to a form of apartheid.

There are also issues of some international concern arising from these decrees. Foreign governments, international institutions or well-known individuals who supported the régime, often alleged that the 'Estado Novo' was a 'mild' dictatorship, dismissing widespread accusations of physical and mental torture as 'unproved'. Such denials or dismissals were, more often than not, partisan or diplomatic oversimplifications intended to save embarrassment. 'After all,' partisans or supporters of the régime would often say, 'those involved in PIDE persecution are mostly communists and the situation in communist countries is no better.' The point, however, is that the Salazar régime made much more claim to 'Christianity' and by its membership of NATO was supposed to be defending the 'free world'.

Where denials were sincere, they were often based upon long-held misconceptions of a medical and legalistic nature. For instance the PIDE had many months in which to 'work on a prisoner' so that by the time he or she was available to be seen by relatives or independent witnesses, there might be no trace or evidence of torture. But equally valid in a court of law is the principle of corroborative evidence. In Portugal, where so many former prisoners and lawyers can be found, massive documentary evidence has accumulated through the years. In many other countries, where there are humanitarian organizations such as Amnesty International, many sworn statements have been collected and are available for inspection upon application. In Britain, where the weekly *New Statesman* was sued in 1959 for defamation by officials of the PIDE, there are also other voluntary depositions by former Portuguese prisoners living abroad. This mass of corroborative evidence provided by the individual statements of literally hundreds of men and women, of all ages and walks of life and various political affiliations, who were arrested at different times and places, and interviewed by independent individuals, certainly would have a considerable weight as evidence in a court of law. The indictment against the régime could be no other than the systematic use of mental and physical torture.

The second misconception is of a medical character. Not only can the most painful and effective forms of torture be applied without leaving any visible marks, but the use of mental torture is also likely to lead to a breakdown of lasting duration.

In many instances, prolonged imprisonment at Peniche and Caxias resulted in various conditions of a neurotic and psychotic nature, associated with institutionalization as well as continuing psychological pressure on the part of PIDE-trained warders. Indeed, there are inmates in mental institutions who became incurably deranged after being held by the PIDE for some time. Moreover, there are many relatives and friends of individuals who died while in the custody of PIDE, who can bear witness to the mysterious circumstances of their deaths, officially ascribed to 'suicide'.

Equally disturbing, however, is the evidence provided by the letter and implications of the decrees themselves which were recorded in the government's *Diario do Governo*. The combination of laws providing for preventive arrest for investigation, the functioning of special courts, summary deportation without trial, and security measures interacting with the further repressive acts providing for censorship and denying fundamental civil rights of association, etc. were tantamount to a system of inquisition. Indeed, one could say that the government acted less severely than its laws, under which anyone could be detained at the discretion of the régime, allowed. But the system, like a permanent state of emergency or martial law, was always there, victimizing successive generations of opponents of the régime, and hanging as a threat and a deterrent over all Portuguese and African subjects. It has conditioned the whole behaviour of millions of people and shaped the mind of each individual. What could be said to the foreign governments and international institutions, such as NATO, which were associated with Portugal, as well as to those prominent individuals who put about the régime's apologias and propaganda abroad, is that the average Portuguese, Guinean, Angolan and Mozambican paid too heavy a price in repression for their share of 'Western freedom'.

Arrest for investigation

If, as we have seen, Portuguese repressive legislation was in conflict with the régime's own constitutional provisions, it is significant that most of the inquisitorial laws were passed after 1949 when Portugal had already joined NATO. Decree No. 35042 of 20 October 1945, giving the PIDE powers to detain anyone for 90 days without charge, was reinforced by Decree No. 39749 increasing the time limit to 180 days and containing an article. No. 19, with the following provision:

> The functions which the law ascribes to the judges, during the preparation of proceedings, regarding bail or detention of the accused and the application of 'security measures', will be exercised by the Director, Senior Inspector or Sub-Director of PIDE, in all cases where a process is being prepared by this body.

Under the cloak of censorship there was not much Portuguese progressive and liberal lawyers could do to protest against these laws or indeed explain their implications to a public which had long lost any notion of having rights. Salgado Zenha resorted to publishing a series of books where, in conformity with laws governing publishing and copyright, he transcribed legal documents or juxtaposed suitable quotes to make a point. In one of his books, *Quatro Causas*,[1] comparing British and Portuguese legal principles and procedures, he took the following quotation from Lord Denning:

1. Salgado Zenha, *Quatro Causas* (Morais, Lisbon, 1969).

The writ of habeas corpus is available, not only where the original detention is unlawful, but also when a man, who has been lawfully arrested on a criminal charge, is held in prison without trial. The police have no right to hold him on their own authority for more than a day. He must be brought before a magistrate within 24 hours, and it is then for the magistrate to decide whether he shall be further detained pending a trial or let out on bail ... So long as the judges hold the balance there will be no police state ...[1]

In order to emphasize that habeas corpus in Portugal did not apply to political cases Salgado Zenha then succinctly explained his text: 'But the decrees which regulate the PIDE confer upon it powers to apply security measures of internment of six months, so that there is in practice the possibility of detainees being imprisoned for twelve months at the discretion of this police force (six months as detention for investigation plus six months as a provisory "security measure" of internment).'

Since Portuguese laws, as and when applicable, were extended to the overseas territories it follows that in Guinea-Bissau, Mozambique and Angola the long and discretionary detention of political suspects was in force some fifteen years before South Africa was to institutionalize the same measures in 1963 (ninety days) and in 1965 (180 days). Moreover, once colonial Africans, by a special Native Statute, had been defined as wards of the administration, they could be held indefinitely by the authorities.

In the European context, the comparison between Portuguese law and those of other countries is also revealing. Britain, West Germany, Belgium, France and other countries set the time-limit for 'police detention' at twenty-four hours; even in neighbouring Spain, which justifiably enjoys a reputation for repressive rule, the limit is seventy-two hours.

Many people, particularly Spaniards, used to say that Portuguese prisoners probably fared relatively well because the PIDE, having so much time on its hands, was less likely to resort to brutal physical methods for extracting 'spontaneous confessions'. This was not the case. The PIDE's methods varied

1. Lord Denning, *Freedom under the Law* (Stevens & Sons, London, 1949), pp. 8, 9, 31.

according to the type of offence. In cases involving armed action, for instance, the PIDE was so ruthless in its 'detecting' methods that the first suspects caught were tortured just as brutally as in Spain, though they might have had only a minor role in the case; those mainly responsible, if caught after the case had been 'clarified', might even escape torture. In other words, despite the 180-days' detention without charge, Portuguese were subject to the same risks that are involved in an investigation by the Directorate General of Security, or the army, in Spain. And in cases where an individual might be innocent or involved in a fairly innocuous offence that did not justify further proceedings, Portuguese suspects had to endure a term of detention which was even worse than an equivalent term of imprisonment, in so far as the detainee was guarded by the police investigators themselves and was being subjected to interrogation.

Since the aim of detention was to extract a 'confession' involving the denunciation of other people, it had an arbitrary nature which in itself could be extremely demoralizing. 'Reasons of State' overruled 'reasons of right', and indeed even minor PIDE officials were indoctrinated to believe that a political suspect was worse than a criminal because wider consequences could arise from his activities. Portuguese clandestine literature of the time, as well as the hundreds of first-hand accounts by former detainees collected through the years, compel one to believe that the methods of the PIDE were not much different from those used by the Inquisition, especially if one takes into account the different standards obtaining in morals and human relations at the time of the Inquisition.

Since a large proportion of Portuguese were illiterate and had not attained a degree of education sufficient to articulate their emotional resentment of social inequity, the main targets of the PIDE in the 1950s were the hard core of Communist activists, operating underground, certain identifiable opponents of the régime, and politically militant students. On receiving a denunciation or circumstantial evidence on a given individual, PIDE agents would keep watch on his house. The method and timing of the arrest obviously depended on the habits and circumstances of each case. Normally PIDE agents would wait until the morning, not out of respect for civil rights, but because it was bound to make less noise and attract less attention in the neighbourhood. Preferably they would wait for as many people as possible to leave for work or for the children to leave the house to go to school; but their main concern was to isolate the suspect from any contact immediately they entered the house. Then, in his own house, the suspect would be detained for as long as it took the PIDE to carry out an exhaustive search for incriminating evidence – weapons, correspondence, books, printing materials, etc. Such searches could last for hours; if the wife and other relatives or friends were present, or called in, they could also be detained or prevented from using a telephone or coming into contact with anyone.

In the first years of the régime the glaring differences in education between the classes were very noticeable in PIDE work. While the inspectors could even be *'senhores doutores'* with an honours degree in humanities, the PIDE operatives were often semi-literate. There are many stories of agents suddenly pushing a suspect against a wall and, gun pointed at his chin, demanding that he confess where he had hidden the 'cell' – no doubt thinking it might be an instrument or a living biological specimen kept in a flask. In one case, tired and frustrated after a long search in a private library, an agent suddenly shouted triumphantly: *'Larousse Encyclopédie!* And you said you had no books on Russia!' In another case, after PIDE inspectors back at headquarters had lectured agents that they should bear in mind that democrats kept books in foreign languages, someone had the bright idea of suggesting that not only books ending in the Portuguese 'ismo' but also those ending in 'isme' or in 'ism' should be brought in for inspection. The result is that many a medical student was deprived, just before exams, of books on 'metabolism', 'Parkinsonism', 'rheumatism', etc. In an extreme example of zeal, a group of agents turned up at headquarters with all a student's foreign books on psychiatry, including studies on 'behaviour therapy', 'acute neurosis' and 'premature ejaculation'.

Later the PIDE, to avoid making itself the laughing stock of the educated classes in the country, changed tactics and unless teams sent out on arrest-search tasks were accompanied by a qualified official the ordinary agents were strongly recommended not to use their discretion. And in time the quality of PIDE officials improved to such a point that eventually many a senior inspector was so knowledgeable that he would have been able to correct Karl Marx or Lenin themselves for an occasional lapse of memory, had either of them been brought in for questioning.

The main inquisitorial centres were at Lisbon, Oporto and Coimbra. In Oporto the PIDE headquarters, rather ironically, adjoined one of the city's main cemeteries, Prado do Repouso. Many opponents of the régime swore that if they had been allowed to make a search, they would not have had to look very far to clarify the mystery of the sudden disappearance of certain prisoners.

In Lisbon, for more than thirty-five years – until better premises were built in a special prison complex in the suburb of Caxias – the PIDE operative headquarters were fairly central. These consisted of the premises at Rua Antonio Maria Cardoso, and the old and dirty jail at the Aljube, some five miles away in another part of the city. In normal times and with average cases, according to information based upon first-hand accounts, the treatment meted out to those arrested followed a fixed routine. Upon arrival at PIDE headquarters prisoners were kept in cells measuring on average 10 feet by 5 feet, without natural light, and often without furniture, even a chair. When not undergoing round-the-clock interrogation prisoners commuted every day from the Aljube Prison to PIDE headquarters for questioning.

The form of torture known as the 'statue' was the most commonly used. This apparently 'passive' method, which consists in keeping the prisoner standing, and without sleep for days and nights, is extremely effective and has agonizing consequences – swelling of the legs is the least of the trouble. However, since detainees were not previously submitted to medical examination, extensive 'statue' treatment for periods up to fourteen

135

consecutive days and nights often led to heart complaints, hallucinatory states and insanity, phlebitis, etc.

The prisoner was urged to confess for his own good. The blame for the treatment he received or the prolongation of his imprisonment was thus passed on to him for his stubbornness. If he complained that his wife and family would be worried not knowing where he was, he would be told that it was his own fault for not cooperating with the authorities. All manner of expedients were used – changes of style of interrogation between inspectors, changes of mood in the same interrogator, ranging from the persuasive to the brutal. 'The law does not come up to the third floor,' agents would say, referring to the upper-floor rooms where interrogations were carried out at PIDE headquarters in central Lisbon. To extract a full confession, including names of individuals with whom the accused had been involved, some inspectors would use physical torture; others preferred psychological pressures in the form of threats to arrest other members of the family or innuendos as to the behaviour of the suspect's husband or wife.

At some stage prisoners were transferred to Caxias, some ten miles away from Lisbon. Then prisoners would be allowed half an hour's exercise every day and half an hour's daily visit from their close relatives. Since most people could not afford the time to travel to Caxias, and leave their jobs or small children, this meant that many prisoners could not avail themselves of the concession. Moreover, during visits prisoners were separated from visitors by a double glass wall, topped by a grill, and warders were always near by ready to interrupt conversations on sensitive subjects. To understand the situation it is enough to say that many visitors often collapsed under the strain, and others gave up the opportunity of visiting because of the frustration and impossibility of holding any conversation.

As for those imprisoned for the first time, the whole experience could have a lasting effect. During the 180-day terms of investigation, since the police instruction was secret, no judicial control of the activities of the PIDE was permitted. Nor was any contact allowed, either personal or by correspondence, between the prisoner and his lawyer. The odds against an individual who had no previous experience of PIDE methods could be devastating. Some of those who conducted the interrogation had many years of experience; they worked in teams, either by rotation at interrogation sessions or by listening in adjoining rooms to the questions and answers. Except for a hard core of clandestine Communist militants, in almost every case where a group of students, or otherwise intelligent and courageous professional men, were arrested, the PIDE managed to split them, to turn one against the other, leaving mutual suspicions of betrayal. Many, after a period at the hands of the PIDE, were cowed into submission to the end of their lives.

The opposition groups were therefore entirely at the mercy of the PIDE. Since the PIDE could, at the end of 180 days, extend the detention for another 180-day term, many individuals, one way or the other, signed statements, or unconsciously provided clues for further investigation. All details, even those relating to people's personal lives, went into the comprehensive PIDE files.

Therefore, in addition to the official statistics relating to the movement of political prisoners in Portugal, one must include one's own estimate of the number of people who passed through the scrutiny of the PIDE, either as detainees, families, friends, witnesses, etc., every year. In fact, the PIDE had an interest in its reputation for brutality and one of the most sinister features of the PIDE powers was the insidious deterrent effect it had upon the average man and woman for whom politics became too dangerous a proposition to tempt them.

As for the *'negativos e pertinazes'* ('negative and stubborn'), they met with treatment comparable with the worst one reads about concerning other totalitarian régimes. In the handling of routine cases the armchair modern-day inquisitors could spot a 'negative and stubborn' person by his refusal to talk, by the nature of his answers, or merely through experience acquired in dealing with earlier arrests. Such prisoners were, more often than not, men and women functionaries of the 'clandestine organization called portuguese communist party [*sic*]' as the PIDE officially defined them. After a period of intensive questioning they passed on to the stage of solitary confinement –

which, contrary to legal rules, could last for one year or more. When eventually brought to trial they faced a sentence which could be surprisingly light at first sight. However it might contain another of Salazar's typical catches – the application of 'security measures' as provided in Decree No. 40550, of 12 March 1956, and subsequent legislation.

Decree No. 40550, which is a development of that somewhat ambiguous Decree No. 34553 of April 1945, establishing the principle of 'preventive means against criminality' to be applied to vagrants and other 'persistent delinquents', has many infamous implications. International lawyers with a sense of gallows humour would find it worthwhile to learn Portuguese in order fully to appreciate the immense contribution made by official 'Estado Novo' legislators to the sophisticated terminology and phrasing peculiar to autocratic régimes. The main implications of this decree are in conflict with the moral tenets of such long-established religions as Judaism, Christianity, Buddhism, Islam and others, let alone the modern concepts of the rights of man.

The following is a rendering, made as comprehensible as possible, of parts of this decree. In translation it is bound to lose some of the twists of style peculiar to Portuguese legislation, but Articles 7 and 8, duly signed by the President of the Republic, the Prime Minister Salazar and the entire Portuguese cabinet of the time, would be deeply ambiguous in any language. They read as follows:

Article 7: (i) Those [individuals] who form associations, movements or groups of a communist character, with the object of exercising subversive activities, or aiming at committing crimes against the security of the State; or using terrorism as a means of action; as well as those who may adhere to such associations, movements or groups, who may collaborate with them or follow their instructions with or without previous agreement;

(ii) those who consciously facilitate such subversive activities either by providing the place for meetings, or by subsidizing [these activities] or permitting their propaganda are *subject to security measures of internment in an adequate establishment for an indefinite period of time, from six months to three years, renewable*

138

for successive terms of three years, should they continue to reveal themselves dangerous.

Article 8: Should the accused be charged with crimes against the security of the State, the security measures referred to in the previous articles will be applied even if the accusation is not proceeded with.

The first point that needs to be emphasized is that these articles were contrary to the principles specified in the 4th, 11th and 14th paragraphs of Article 8 of the constitution (which recognized respectively freedom of expression, freedom to hold political meetings, and freedom to form, and implicitly belong to, political associations, specifically forbidding life imprisonment).

There was never any public discussion in Portugal over the implications of this decree, since the Censorship Board, which was charged with the 'regulation' of freedom of the press, precluded it. Outside Portugal it seldom, if ever, caught the attention of those legal experts who seem to know all about the intricacies of legislation and police methods in the Soviet Union and other countries. Both the '180-day no-charge detention law' and the three-year 'security measures' of internment, both renewable and consecutive, are also in conflict with several at least of the articles of the Declaration of Human Rights, recognized by the UNO. Article 5 of the Declaration clearly states that 'no one shall be subjected to torture or to cruel, inhuman and degrading treatment or punishment'; Article 9 states that 'no one shall be subjected to arbitrary arrest, detention or exile'; Article 10 states that 'everyone is entitled in full equality to a fair and public hearing by an independent and impartial tribunal'; finally Articles 18, 19 and 20 provide for 'freedom of thought, conscience and religion', freedom of 'opinion and expression', and 'freedom of peaceful assembly or association'.

As we have seen, the decree is full of words and phrases with many and varying connotations (e.g. 'communist character', 'subversive activities', 'crimes against the security of the State', 'associations, movements or groups', 'dangerous', 'subsidizing', 'with or without previous agreement', etc.). A further qualification of some of these phrases and words will help to understand the real aim of this decree, which was to intimidate the average Portuguese citizen, while leaving those victimized under it at the mercy of verbal interpretations by the government's own PIDE and plenary courts.

'Communist character', for instance, could apply not only to the clandestine Communist Party but to all associations (without specification as to the number of people who may be regarded as a group) which adopted Marxist or socialist doctrines, although not necessarily those of the Communist Party, or who might be critical of the system embodied by the régime. With such a vague term it becomes unnecessary to ascertain the ideological identity of the accused. Moreover, with the abolition of the legal right of free political association, all Portuguese political activity was of necessity clandestine and aimed at constitutional change, and so was, in this sense, 'subversive'. A simple pamphlet, comprising no more than a stencilled sheet denouncing, say, the connections between the State, the Church, the army and private companies, or calling for the independence of an 'overseas province', could be regarded as a 'crime against the security of the State'. A few escudos' casual contribution to help to buy stationery for a 'political group' could be regarded as a 'subsidy' – and indeed a Portuguese doctor, Julieta Gandara, who was working in Luanda in the 1950s was once charged with subsidizing an African nationalist movement, the MPLA, then still only operating underground inside Angola, because a payment of 500 escudos (about £7) was traced to her. Moreover, there could hardly be a more sinister ambiguity than the expression 'with or without previous agreement' applied to the casual adherence or sympathy towards a 'subversive' or African nationalist group.

Again, one finds affinities with the provisions of the *Inquisitors' Handbook* when one examines further implications of Decree No. 40550. Indeed this decree could be regarded as an updating of the medieval manual for a more scientific age.

According to Article 9, the Director of the PIDE had powers to apply security measures on a provisional basis (presumably for a first term of six months), and to submit to the special plenary courts, through the directors of the internment establishments (both judges and prison governors. being appointed by the government), proposals for a further application of security measures or imposition of further terms of internment.

In a clandestine study, *A destruição sistematica de seres humanos (The Systematic Destruction of Human Beings)*, dated September 1969, a list is given of nineteen men who had already been in prison for eleven years each, on average, and who between them had still another eighty-seven years to go, or another 139 (more than seven years each on average) if 'security measures' were applied. There was one woman, Sofia Ferreira, who had been in jail for twelve years, another, Corelia Fernandes, for more than ten years, and another two, Maria Alda Nogueira and Fernanda Paiva Tomas, for more than nine years. When one sees the conditions in which they lived in prison, and the restrictions they had to endure in such matters as books and information, one realizes that the régime was well advanced in the new techniques of institutionalized confinement for 'stubborn' opponents. But even when a prisoner decided to cooperate he needed a very good lawyer and considerable influence to be able to escape the PIDE.

In the book mentioned earlier, *Quatro Causas,* Salgado Zenha reproduces, without comment, the self-explanatory documents of a case in which a decision to extend 'security measures' was disputed by a lawyer, Humberto Lopes, who would have completed six years in prison in July 1963. In his first hearing by the PIDE on 27 April 1963 he stated that, if released, 'he would only wish to live for his family and his work' and that 'he would not promote any further demonstrations or acts which might disturb law and order'. Two days later the then Sub-Director of the PIDE, Jose Sachetti, stated that the answers of Lopes still revealed his 'dangerous nature, and that he was still faithful to and linked with the

secret and subversive organization called the 'portuguese communist party' and is still secretly and stubbornly obeying its instructions ... he still does not show himself expurgated of the factors of probable future delinquency, rooted in the delinquent himself, which will inexorably drag him towards committing crimes of the same nature, should he be returned to society. I do not think he is fit for the terms of conditional freedom.

The PIDE then pointed out in a report that Radio Moscow and Radio 'Free Portugal' had referred to the prisoner and that this was evidence that he was still held in high regard by the party. They further alleged that in the past six months Lopes's behaviour in jail had not been satisfactory and that he had caused a scene during visiting time, perhaps under the influence of his wife who often incited other visitors to make protests.

As his lawyer, Salgado Zenha, in an extensive defence, pointed out that although Lopes had been in jail for six years the PIDE only alleged misconduct in the last six months; moreover Lopes could not be held responsible for statements made in foreign broadcasts he had not even heard. And, just in case, Salgado Zenha collected no less than thirty character witnesses, mostly lawyers and former colleagues of Lopes. The depositions of these witnesses provided a vision of contemporary Portugal. All of them vouched for the integrity and reliability of Lopes; some stated their belief that Lopes had abjured his ideals; most pleaded for compassion on account of Lopes's state of health. A doctor and former inmate at Peniche described how Lopes had refused to join another eleven prisoners who had escaped from Peniche in 1960. One of the witnesses, Judge E. Soares, who declared himself apolitical, gave a moving account of an interview he had had with Lopes while on an official visit to Peniche where he happened to go to hear another case involving a criminal offence. Knowing Lopes was a prisoner at Peniche he had requested the Governor's permission to talk with his former colleague. Zenha quotes the judge's testimony as follows:

For about one hour and a half we just reminisced about our student days, but at one point Lopes began to cry when he reflected that it would soon be twenty years since we had graduated. Seeing him prematurely old, revealing serious physical strain, made me feel extremely sad, though I tried to maintain a certain appearance of vivacity. Lopes, however, could not even do that, as tears kept rolling down his face. It was in these conditions, and without any prompting, that he repeatedly stated that once he was restored to conditional liberty, no matter what restrictions might be imposed, he had no fear, 'because I will never again engage in political activities'.

Another lawyer, Artur Cunha Leal, the son of the former republican statesman, after stating that he did not know Lopes personally, disclosed that about the time the PIDE had alleged that Lopes had caused a scene in the visitors' room, he had given a lift to Lisbon to a man who happened to work at Peniche prison. The man had told him during the journey that the prison governor had caused considerable ill-feeling amongst prisoners by refusing to allow visits from prisoners' families at Christmas. The suggestion here was that the prisoners, and particularly those who were soon to qualify for 'conditional freedom' (parole), had been provoked into 'misconduct'.

Six months after the hearing had begun, and after much pleading from witnesses and apostasy from the prisoner, the plenary court, in one of its rare decisions against the PIDE, ordered Lopes's release. But as one can see from the identity of the thirty witnesses, social status clearly had been influential in the outcome of his case. Moreover, since he was a well-known lawyer in a small town – Santarem, not far from Lisbon – the PIDE was never in a position to undermine the fidelity of his friends and colleagues with false allegations of 'trips to the Soviet Union', or 'sinister' innuendo of that kind. Working-class Communists, peasants or workers who rebelled, or Africans who were suspected of nationalist activities, had no hope of justice or even of elementary politeness on the part of PIDE officials.

A good example of the social discrimination used by the PIDE is provided by the outcome of a similar case concerning a woman, Maria Piedade Gomes dos Santos. Both she and her husband Joaquim Gomes had passed into *clandestinidade* – they had joined the ranks of full-time Communist Party militants in 1952. They were both arrested after the PIDE raided their home in 1958. She was not tried until 1961, two and a half years after her arrest. As she was about to qualify for parole her husband succeeded in escaping from Peniche Fortress, together with other leading Communists, on January 1961. Since 'dangerous' circumstances remained, she was kept in prison. When the first period of 'security measures' expired in 1964 the PIDE applied for a further extension. She was heard by the PIDE in January 1964 and, according to the records, committed herself to be of good behaviour.

Asked whether she was still bound to the principles which directed the activities of the secret and subversive organization known as the 'p.c.p.' she replied that she did not intend to engage in further political activities in the future ...

Asked whether she knew where her husband was or what sort of life he was leading, she said she had nothing to declare, or rather nothing to say on the subject.

Asked to make clear whether it was her unshakeable desire not to return to living in clandestinity, even if her husband were to be very insistent that she should, she stated that she was prepared not to engage in any further political activities.

Despite this statement the conclusions drawn by the PIDE in a submission to the plenary tribunal were:

A reading of this report makes it possible to deduce that Maria da Piedade Gomes dos Santos had in no way become less dangerous and that if she were freed she would not fail to return to her underground life ... It does not appear that the punishment inflicted on her has so far had the slightest intimidating effect, and her own statements are sufficient grounds for believing that she would make use of her freedom to continue the practice of crime. In view of her character I consider it more advisable to ... prolong the imprisonment under 'security measures'.[1]

On 16 January the Director of the PIDE, Silva Pais, objecting to parole, stated: 'It would not only be to her advantage, but primarily to the advantage of society, which must be protected against elements threatening its security.' However, in view of the legal weakness of their case, and fearing publicity, the PIDE relented, and Silva Pais added, 'admitting, however, that the degree of danger which she represents is not legally significant, if she is conditionally released I suggest a surety payment of not less than 50,000 escudos [£625 at the time]

1. *Portugal: Women in Prison* (British Committee for Portuguese Amnesty, 1964).

which would at least delay her return to clandestinity'. And eventually Maria Piedade dos Santos was released but, in another curious twist of Portuguese legal history, her lawyer Arnaldo Mesquita was, in his turn, arrested – perhaps because he had proved to be too efficient and embarrassing for the PIDE.

After the April 1974 *coup* many documents were found showing that the PIDE was receiving subsidies directly from private companies, in exchange for information on staff applicants or control of attempted strikes. Many concerns employed PIDE agents, not only for detective work inside their offices and factories, but as a means to support the overall activities of the political police. The interconnection between the régime, the PIDE and big business, in the exploitation of workers, could not have been more intimate.

Chapter 7
Exiles within their own country

'When he left Portugal and heard other people talk, his greatest task had been to forget all he had learned, so that he could understand things well and speak with purpose' –
LUIZ VERNEY (1713–90)[1]

A characteristic of dictatorships, shared by the Salazar régime, is the cynicism with which their supporters dismiss the freedom of expression enjoyed by countries under parliamentarian and multi-party systems as a political fiction not worth having. According to those who see no objection in plutocratic rule in their own countries, the system of private ownership and editorial control in democratic countries abroad in the end results in a form of private-enterprise censorship.

Truly, one can feel sorry for writers and artists in any society who have never felt restricted in their freedom, for that is a sign that they have nothing new of their own to say. Even in those countries in the West where institutionalized censorship does not exist, there is a daily struggle going on, inside each newspaper, television or broadcasting house, between the functionaries of conformity and those who believe that a writer can no more turn his face away from controversial issues than a doctor refuse assistance because a case appears to be too difficult. In the mass media, each time one sees an article which is embarrassing to powerful interests, one can be sure that those of inquiring and independent minds have won a battle with the mercenaries of the intellect who sit behind so many editorial desks.

The point, though, is that such struggle can go on, and that the very competition between newspapers ensures that they interact to remain in a position to criticize the elected govern-

1. From *Verdadeiro metodo de estudar* (Classicos Sa da Costa, Lisbon, 1952).

ment of the day. Moreover, if the same situation of tacit pressures applies to those who have their eyes set on an academic career, the historical fact is that it has been and still is possible in the West to produce works which are sceptical about, or opposed to, governments or the prevailing system.

But under dictatorships all those tacit and universal obstacles to freedom are reinforced by the institutionalized suppression of criticism, combined with the active promotion of an official line of thinking. Under totalitarian and authoritarian régimes of whatever ideology, with ideas programmed from above, with the control of education, with systematic censorship, Party vigilance and other repressive devices, the creative mind has to resort to subtler methods of indicating doubts and criticisms so that it may survive. The bureaucracy of repression has, irrespective of ideological intentions, had the same unhappy effect upon thought and creativeness. Indeed, totalitarian rule even in countries with a history of brilliant achievements has had the consequence of driving writers and artists into exile, while reducing entire nations to mediocrity and sterility.

In Portugal, where the introduction of the printing press coincided with the ecclesiastical monopoly of learning and the period of the Inquisition, creative ideas, more often than not by their nature rebellious, did not even have to be printed to lead a man to the torture chamber and the stake. More than in most countries in Western Europe Portuguese art is almost exclusively devoted to the glory of the Church, the Kings and the Empire. All the great classical writers, from Gil Vicente to Camões, had their works mutilated by Inquisitorial censorship; and if there were any equivalents of Shakespeare the fear of persecution would have been enough to reduce them to 'Portuguese size'.

Writers and thinkers who had, through contact with other European cultures, discovered the obscurantism of their own, were to be known in Portuguese history as the '*estrangeirados*' – the 'foreignized', or those influenced by, or imitative of, foreigners. To this day they are the target of the hatred of the régime's 'ultras' who regard them as 'the dogmatic masters

147

of denationalization',[1] the precursors of liberalism and republicanism. Bearing in mind that the golden age of Portugal's discoveries and navigational achievements was partly a result of cosmopolitan efforts, involving together with the Portuguese, Arabs, Jews, and others, such feelings on the part of ultra-nationalists can only be based upon an ignorance or misreading of Portuguese history. But there is no doubt, however, that such men were the pioneers of the so-called 'denationalized' or 'detribalized' of today.

The official and institutional ban on political and humanitarian thinking in Portugal was re-imposed after the advent of the military dictatorship in 1926 and the gradual assertion of Salazar's 'National Revolution'. Through a series of numbered decrees enacted by the absolutist government of the 'Estado Novo', Portugal was to revert to a system of inquisitorial censorship that strengthened a tradition as old as the history of culture in Portugal itself.

The Portuguese writer Cardoso Pires summed up the situation in the following passage from an essay published in London:

In the five centuries of its publishing history, Portugal has experienced 420 years of censorship. In statistical terms, therefore, publishing in Portugal is a cultural activity which has been carried out at a 'rate of repression' of 84 per cent. For generation after generation while political régimes and scientific and cultural movements have succeeded one another, a slow procession of martyrs has wound its way along the thousands of miles which would be covered by the texts thrown on bonfires and relegated to dusty archives. Resistance has become a historical reality, constantly renewed by the subterfuges devised to evade the watchful eyes of the authorities. And the tradition of repression has been increasingly refined, culminating in the clearly defined technical unity which it achieved under Salazar.[2]

To complete a system of repression based upon the absolute role of the State security police, the régime created a virtually

1. Manuel Murias, *Retrato de Salazar – In Memoriam* (Lisbon, 1971).
2. A. Cardoso Pires, 'Changing a Nation's Way of Thinking', in *Index*, No. 1, Spring 1972.

impregnable institution of censorship that, both in its methods as well as its purposes, evokes a twentieth-century Inquisition. One wonders whether even many of the men who collaborated with the régime have any idea of what was involved.

The chronological order of censorship legislation allows one to grasp how a temporary régime was gradually usurped by the personal views of Salazar turned into a nationalistic doctrine. 'We will not discuss God; we will not discuss the country; we will not discuss authority; we will not discuss the family' – thus spoke Salazar at about the time he promulgated Decree No. 22469 of 11 April 1933. This decree, according to Article 3, established censorship 'to prevent the perversion of public opinion as a social force; it should be carried out in such a way as to defend public opinion from all factors that may misguide it against truth, justice, morality, efficient administration and the common good, and to prevent any attack on the basic principles of the organization of society'. The definitions of all these words were Salazar's own.

The same decree provided for the establishment of censorship boards whose functionaries could be remunerated and who were to have their own offices. The boards were to function under the supervision of the Ministry of the Interior, which also took central control of the PIDE. From time to time the censors, operating wherever a newspaper was published or a printing press functioned, were given practical instructions on the criteria which were to be used in their routine work of reading any printed matter, from leaflets to literary magazines.

Such 'executive rulings' were supposed to be guides as to what was to fall into the four categories: Censored or Deleted, Suspended (pending further decision), Authorized, or Authorized with Cuts.

Newspapers or periodicals were required to send 'readers' proofs', as opposed to typescripts or manuscripts, partly to force journalists and editors to exercise a preliminary self-censorship before incurring the expense of setting copy into type. The rulings as to content were vague enough to compel the censors, usually army officers trying to make extra money, to be over-zealous. Here is a sample of what should *not* be published: attacks or criticism of the State, the government, its personalities and institutions; irreverent references to the authorities or public services; news that might cause alarm or public disquiet; writings which might offend creeds and religious practices; details of suicides and murders, as well as infanticides, when not followed by the news of the arrest of delinquents or their punishment by the courts; articles or local reports or advertisements concerning astrologers, witches or clairvoyants; issues that might prejudice diplomatic relations with foreign countries. Article 11 provided that 'the intervention of censorship may aim at the intention, even if not expressed, in a writing, an image, captions or subtitles, the type of composition or the placing of the item in the page'.[1]

Even more disturbing is Decree No. 23203 of 6 November 1933. This describes as 'crimes of rebellion committed by the press' the following '*atentados*' (attacks or outrages): those against the territorial integrity of the nation (including the empire); those against the form of government; those against the President of the Republic or the Ministers. *But* – according to paragraph 2, the word '*atentado*' covered all *executed acts*; acts of preparation were, for the purposes of this law, equal to executed acts.

Other punishable crimes included: any offence, by any means, against the prestige of the State or against the honour or regard for its president or the government; incitement or propaganda encouraging social indiscipline and subversion; incitement or counselling to the non-fulfilment of duties of public functionaries and military personnel, or disregard of authorities and laws; incitement to the closing of factories or workshops or the suspension of work; the circulation of rumours which might disturb law and order or prejudice public credit; any offence against the national flag or the national anthem. The penalties included deportation to the colonies for periods up to twelve years, fines and jail sentences.

These decrees were extended to the colonies with slight

1. Alberto Arons Carvalho and A. Monteiro Cardoso, *Liberdade de Imprensa* (Meridiano, Lisbon, 1971), p. 519.

changes in the attribution of powers. Decree No. 23229 of this period extended to the governors of the colonies the authority to order the seizure of 'obscene publications or those that contain attacks upon Portuguese sovereignty or give offence to the government or its representatives or might provoke crime or incite rebellion and disorder'. Paragraph 4 lays down that 'such publications shall be destroyed by fire'. This provision alone acted as a powerful deterrent, and bookshops naturally became reluctant to import books which might incur the government's displeasure.

Decree No. 23241 made it a crime of rebellion peculiar to the colonies to advocate the disintegration or separation of any component part of the 'Portuguese Colonial Empire'. It gave powers to the governors to ban from their respective territories the editors of newspapers as well as those individuals 'whose presence may be thought to be undesirable from the point of view of security and public order'.

These decree-laws were complemented by several decree-orders (*portarias*) which combined to cover all possible loopholes that suggested themselves through the years. All publications had to retain a minimum deposit in money as a guarantee for the payment of fines; editors had to be university graduates; no newspaper which did not support the régime was entitled to advertisements from public services, including notices from courts. In order to deal with cable, telex and telephone communications, a special law provided for *prior* censorship of all cables and phone-calls sent by foreign news agents, as well as the *repressive* censorship that was applicable to news sent from abroad, or magazines and newspapers sent for distribution in Portugal. Reading all the decrees one sees that no one involved in publishing escaped the censorship machine. Editors, journalists, printers – all could meet with summary suspension or closing of their businesses, and even individual persecution, irrespective of whether the censors had approved the publication of any item or not.

Decades of life under such a system produced some disturbing phenomena which were perhaps Portugal's major contribution to sociology or the study of politics. The overall aim of censorship was to present an image of a country with no national or local problems, functioning under the guidance of an infallible, wise and benevolent ruler. The public conscience was directed towards events taking place thousands of miles away, and preferably in the negative 'communist world'. In the positive Portuguese empire the well-fed were spared the embarrassment of hearing about the starving; nothing could disturb the routine of Portugal's civilizing mission, least of all in the colonies, those mainstays of Portugal's metaphysical imperialism. Since censorship is also a form of psychological pressure, the censors eventually only had to deal with copy that had already been self-censored by even more experienced veteran editors. The editors in their turn knew that the reporters themselves had taken care to avoid a fact or a name that might be temporarily or permanently 'unmentionable'. Owing to the pressure of time to meet production schedules, in case of doubt all suspect passages or references were deleted before the statutory three copies of printers' proofs were submitted to the censors. Prohibition or suspension of a whole article, just because of a phrase or a paragraph, could cause delays or financial losses.

Any collection of censors' decisions makes one feel as if one has entered the world of the absurd. In Portugal, when the Censorship Board was under the direction of Salvação Barreto, a man who had close associations with the world of sport, even reports of soccer matches or referees' decisions could be subject to deletion or distortion. In Mozambique a censor replaced the word 'blue' for 'muddy' in a sentence reading, 'the South African fleet had arrived in the muddy waters of the bay on a courtesy visit to Lourenço Marques'.

On starting their shifts, journalists would inquire who was the censor on duty in order to adapt the content and style of their reports or articles to the individual censor involved. It was widely known, for instance, that aspiring censors would begin by working as replacements for senior censors on leave, and would often be even more zealous than the regulars.

A well-known Lisbon newspaper editor described how relations between censors and pressmen became casual, 'even cordial, with good manners and explanations on both sides ... like the prisoner who gets used to his cell and his guards and jailers and who talks to them with familiarity. And we must not forget that for most Portuguese journalists there has never been any other professional environment but the "prison" of censorship.'[1]

However amusing individual stories of the censorship system may be, in the long run the effect is to make one shudder in disgust. Anyone in other countries who might be thinking of adopting or pursuing the single-party and censorship systems might have a lesson to learn from Portugal. As a form of government, totalitarianism defeats its own purpose. All that newspapers and periodicals say acquires an officially approved character, so that comments, whether on internal issues or on foreign affairs, are dull and predictable. For example, if an attack was made on a country represented in Portugal, diplomats usually complained directly to the government; if a campaign against alleged permissiveness in Britain or racialism in the United States was then allowed to continue observers could infer that those countries had incurred the Portuguese government's displeasure.

Political culture becomes clandestine and takes a word-of-mouth form; what it may lose in factual knowledge and sophistication, it gains in arguments against the prevailing system. It is not ignorance of facts and events that deters men and women from rebelling; it is rather the knowledge that censorship is only a part of a system operating from the barrel of a gun. Precisely because censorship is there to remind one of the political and ideological implications of government, the proportion of people politically aware, mainly amongst the younger generation, is perhaps higher in Portugal than in many other, freer countries in the West.

The Portuguese could see the parochialism and intellectual 'colonialization' of their entire nation. Instead of buying newspapers many people preferred to rely on the oral tradition that had developed to compensate for the censorship of the written

1. Raul Rego, 'A Censura previa administrativa: Teses e documentos', in *II Congresso republicano de Aveiro* (Seara Nova, Lisbon, 1969), Vol. 2.

word. Others learned to read between the lines, by a process of inverting the meaning of what they read. The more publicity given in the pro-régime press to an individual, an event or a fact, the more he, she or it became discredited. Conversely, all criticism of certain individuals, countries or ideas, became a recommendation. All the biggest newspapers, in their coverage of elections in the United States, Britain, France or Germany, could always be relied upon to favour the most reactionary party, thus providing clues in reverse as to the real situation.

Another long-term consequence of censorship was that the style of language became elliptical and cryptic: official notes and pronouncements, articles by political or religious commentators, often appeared to be denying statements or rumours which no one had ever heard of. Entire polemics, especially on ideological and religious matters, were carried out in jargon that only the authors and their circle of friends could really follow.

Those who spread a fog also lose themselves in it. A good example of the self-defeating effects of censorship is given by the recurrence of rumours discrediting ministers or government institutions. The PIDE was known to interfere with correspondence; indeed, by law, the mail of all detainees was opened as part of the investigatory process. In the late fifties a scandal broke out in certain circles when it was discovered that some agents on duty in key post offices were taking advantage of their position to 'confiscate' money and other valuables from the correspondence of one and all, including the régime's own power *élite*. Such incidents could not be reported and rumours kept recurring which continually cast doubts on the reliability of the postal services.

Moreover, in their predictability and subservience even the biggest newspapers such as Lisbon's *Diario de Noticias* lost their influence not only amongst the public but also amongst those in power. With evident contempt for 'local' newspapers, Salazar often gave interviews to sympathetic newspapers in the United States, France, Germany and Italy in the certainty that they would promptly be translated and reproduced in newspapers in Portugal and the empire, with added prestige. And in the end, there could hardly be a more sadly ironic and thought-provoking sight that to read Portuguese newspapers, marked 'Passed by the Censorship' or 'Passed by the Board of Censors', with a front-page story about the persecution of intellectuals or the existence of censorship in the Soviet Union, Hungary or Czechoslovakia.

The Editors' and Booksellers' Guilds issued confidential circulars giving lists of authors and titles which were included in the régime's 'Index'. In addition to all books by Marx, Lenin, Trotsky, Mao Tse-tung and the better-known socialist authors, all, or some, of the books of Tolstoy, Gogol, Gorky, Zola, Bernanos, Malraux, Camus, Faulkner, Steinbeck, John dos Passos and Bertrand Russell were 'indexed'. The 'Index' was far more implacable towards Portuguese authors and at one stage more than sixty writers in Portugal had one or more books banned. Castro Soromenho, widely recognized as the best novelist who wrote realistically and critically on colonial life, was a favourite target of the censor. Studies on social questions, such as Raul Proença's *Analysis of Portuguese Life*, or on scientific issue, such as *Sexual Life* by the Nobel-Prize-winning neurosurgeon Egas Moniz, were also banned. Books published in Brazil, either by Brazilian writers like Castro Alves, Graciliano Ramos and Jorge Amado, or by Portuguese exiles such as anti-clerical Tomas da Fonseca, were either confiscated or, as in the case of Fonseca's *Fatima: History of a Great Fraud*, returned by the Post Office with the indication: 'Import forbidden in Portugal. Return to sender.' Moreover, authors themselves, whether they were aware of it or not, re-frained from dealing with the most controversial themes. The predicament of scientists and writers was summed up by Prof. Egas Moniz, who complained that he felt like 'an exile in his own country', and the novelist Alves Redol, who wrote as he lay dying in a Lisbon hospital: 'I am one more writer who will die in intellectual solitary confinement. They never allowed me to write down what I wanted to say.'

While the censorship boards muffled writers, sterilized artists, or suppressed the free flow of news and ideas, the régime tried to fill the ideological vacuum by fostering its own ideals and

155

propaganda, both inside and outside Portugal. The barrister Antonio Borges Coutinho, in a study of censorship laws, observed that Portugal was faced with more than an institutionalized and politically orientated censorship:

The relevance the present régime ascribes to censorship goès to the extreme of having given the Director of the Censorship Services an important role in the education of youth; according to the statute of the National Education Board, the Director of the Censorshtp Board, as a member of the civic and moral section of the Education Board, is empowered to examine the textbooks to be adopted in the teaching of moral and civic education, as well as family education.[1]

The ideological indoctrination of the first generation educated under the régime started in the first years of primary school. The propaganda of 'Salazar's work' and the teachings of the Catholic Church, with particular emphasis on Our Lady of Fatima, remained a permanent feature of school programmes. If the book for the first-year class contained no less than thirty-eight lessons on Catholicism, the book for the second year went up to forty. Para-military training and further indoctrination was provided by the Youth Movement, as well as by the 'Moral Lessons' introduced in secondary schools as a discipline.

The National Propaganda Office, modelled after the Nazi and Fascist patterns after exchange visits by officials of the countries concerned, catered for adults through such institutions as the FNAT (National Foundation for Joy in Work), the 'people's houses' and the 'fishermen's houses', as well as the 'houses of Portugal' which operated for a time in the colonies. The Propaganda Office was directly answerable to the Prime Minister's office and had powers to supervise the output of the régime's National Broadcasting Service and television, as well as to licence newspapers and radio stations, issue professional licence cards to Portuguese and foreign journalists, and control cinemas and theatres. Through a network abroad, it promoted exports and tourism, as well as political propaganda through

1. Borges Coutinho, 'Breve Comparação dos regimes juridicos da imprensa em Portugal', in *II Congresso republicano de Aveiro*, op. cit., Vol. 2.

supplements in newspapers such as the London *Financial Times* as well as other well-known periodicals. To make the most of their investment, articles published in the supplements would be used again in Portugal, and presented as translations of independent views. The Propaganda Office also had powers to enforce the publication of government statements in any Portuguese newspaper or periodical; in the colonies the governors could by law compel newspapers and periodicals to publish government notes 'within two days of receipt, it being sufficient that an order written and signed by the Governor be given to "publish them on such and such a page".'[1] The control of news services within Portugal and the empire was held by two agencies – ANI and Lusitania – both patronized by the régime.

To complete the system of censorship and control of news and opinion, Article 149 of the Penal Code provided for a sentence of between two to eight years for 'attacks against the prestige of the country abroad'. This double-edged law was intended for authors residing in Portugal who might want to publish a book abroad, as well as for silencing Portuguese exiles and visitors to foreign countries. In fact this law proved to be an effective form of exercising remote control over Portuguese abroad since, owing to family, social and professional connections, few of them were prepared to risk losing their passports or being prosecuted upon return to Portugal.

Salazar had a vested interest in the opacity of Portugal to foreign observers and for a long time even sympathetic reports were discouraged for fear of provoking critical letters to the editors. In the fifties, after decades of relentless repression, Portuguese political life had been reduced to dull routine. For lack of news, newspapers developed their own techniques of space-filling. Every time a government official was appointed, or left even for a short journey to the overseas territories or abroad, all the names and long Portuguese surnames of those attending the inaugural ceremony or 'present at the airport' were reported in detail. Most journalists were by now so trained in the techniques of censorship that many censors wondered if

1. *Regulamento dos serviços de saude* (Imprensa Nacional, Lisbon, 1937).

157

they were still needed at all; even the political prisons had fewer and fewer inmates and the PIDE inspectors and agents, in order to save embarrassment and justify their salaries, exaggerated the importance of the few cases they came across.

Salazar had succeeded in imposing the kind of discipline at home that he needed if he was to continue his 'national revolution' and develop his colonial and foreign policies.

Chapter 8
The economics of class oppression

'*King D. Luiz, on a sea trip, came to meet some boatmen, and asked them if they were Portuguese. "We here? No, Sire," they replied, "we are fishermen"'* –
ANTONIO SERGIO[1]

'*In accepting the assimilated African, the Portuguese are merely receiving back what they pumped into him. In other words, they are really accepting themselves and not the African . . . The* assimilado *system is a Portuguese refusal to accept the African as he is*' –
AN UNNAMED MOZAMBICAN TALKING TO N. SITHOLE[2]

When in Lisbon Salazar liked to take time off in his seaside residence at S. João do Estoril, on the coastal road which leads from Lisbon to the fashionable tourist and residential areas of Estoril and Cascais. His house was a converted fort, decorated with suitably inspiring mosaics of quotations from *The Lusiads* on the epic discoveries, and with stone parapets overlooking the ocean. In such a setting Salazar could well identify himself with the romantic figure of Henry the Navigator pondering destiny at the Promontory of Sagres.

Old-fashioned people in Portugal are often described as being '*bota de elastico*' ('elastic-sided boots'), and Salazar really wore them. He liked those in government to follow his example in dressing with propriety and sobriety and more than once insisted that a newly appointed junior minister or high-ranking official wore a hat. During the war he praised visiting British government representatives, whom he met on official business, for the simplicity and austerity of their suits. He preferred to

1. From 'Tentativa de interpretação da historia de Portugal', in *Edições Tempo* (Lisbon), No. 6. King D. Luiz reigned from 1861 to 1889.
2. From *African Nationalism* (Oxford University Press, 1968).

159

write his own reflective speeches in longhand rather than dictate them to secretaries. He frequently spent holidays at the family home in Santa Comba Dão, where he liked to observe the seasonal work of the farmland. He would occasionally plant trees, tend flowers, or distribute wine to the day labourers on the farm adjoining his family's modest one-storey house in the style of *'uma porta e uma janela'* ('one door and one window') which is typical of the standards of Portuguese rural architecture. According to many of his friends Salazar used to study government papers or reflect on major projects while at Santa Comba Dão, and the journalist Antonio Ferro suggests that Salazar might have learned more during his secluded holidays in Santa Comba Dão than if he had attended an international conference in London.[1] Salazar's demeanour and idiosyncracies evoked an image of a lonely and singularly dedicated man.

However, for all his intimate knowledge of things Portuguese, Salazar was remarkably pessimistic about Portugal's economic resources. He undoubtedly adhered to the view that Portugal was not only backward, but a 'naturally poor country', a favourite cliché of the middle classes who try to disguise the historical and structural factors which account for Portugal's position as one of the less-developed European countries.

Alvaro Cunhal, the exiled Secretary of the Portuguese Communist Party, in a notable study of Portugal's agrarian problems, disposed of this myth by comparing Portugal with other European countries of the same size:

> With nine million hectares for nine million inhabitants Portugal is a small country. But in Western Europe Austria, Ireland, Denmark, Switzerland, the Netherlands, Belgium and Luxemburg have a small area, the five last mentioned having less than half of Portugal's size. As for population, if the Netherlands and Belgium have more than Portugal, all the others, plus Greece, Sweden and Norway, have even less.
> However, almost all these countries have fairly well developed industries and are comparatively well off economically, while Portugal is placed among the poor and backward countries, with only incipient industry. The difference is the more striking as the

1. Antonio Ferro, *Salazar: Portugal and her Leader* (Faber, 1939).

bourgeois class of Portugal, contrary to the case of the majority of those countries, has a permanent source of wealth in the exploitation of the colonies as well as immigrants who send savings to Portugal amounting to even more than the receipts from tourism.[1]

Cunhal then proceeded to demonstrate that while no adequate economic survey of Portugal's resources had been made, even existing official studies showed that Portugal had far more agricultural and industrial potential than Salazar appeared to believe. And Cunhal draws a convincing picture of a country where widespread poverty and all its consequences – malnutrition, slum-housing, illiteracy, high incidence of TB and certain other illness, high mortality rate – stemmed from human and political neglect rather than natural factors.

But even official planning studies could underestimate the results of Salazar's slow but steady economic policies. Cunhal, for instance, points out that in 1950 Portugal occupied the last place in Europe in electricity output, with only 942 million kWh., of which only 437 million kWh. were hydroelectric. 'Even if the total output were to triple by 1960, which even the most optimistic plans do not foresee,' says Cunhal, 'Portugal would not raise its place in the European table, although the untapped water that runs to the seas could produce 10,000 million kWh. – more than ten times national production (in 1950), both thermal and hydroelectric.'[2]

In fact, in 1960, as a result of production from new dams, and contrary to the forecasts to which Cunhal alludes, hydroelectric output in Portugal had exceeded 3,100 million kWh., that is, some six times more than in 1950. This had been achieved partly by pressing the Caixa Geral dos Depositos, Credito e Previdencia (Assistance and Pensions Funds), the *sindicatos*, and other State-controlled institutions to invest in the extensive programme of dam-building which took place over a period of some fifteen years. With the new dams built at various points along the rivers Tagus, Cavado, Zezere and Douro hydro-

1. Alvaro Cunhal, *A Questão agraria em Portugal* (Civilização Brazileira, Rio de Janeiro, 1968).
2. ibid., p. 4.

electric output was expected to increase to very nearly 10,000 million kWh., by 1970. The largest of the dam schemes, part of a joint Portuguese–Spanish project for the hydroelectric resources of the Douro river and one of the biggest hydroelectric complexes in Western Europe, was linked to developing rich iron ore resources as well as permitting irrigation of some 275,000 acres of land in the Douro basin.

Salazar's concept of nation and nationalism, whether he was aware of this or not, was confined to the élitist values of the upper and middle classes; his economic policies clearly placed the majority working class and the peoples of the colonies at the service of a plutocracy. The Portuguese middle classes could hardly have found a better administrator. The priority given by Salazar to the development of the infrastructure, and above all hydroelectric power, was a way to open up conditions for the establishment of private industries and can be seen as a form of public financing in aid of private enterprise.

Seen in historical perspective, the economic development of Portugal under Salazar can be divided into fairly well-defined periods. Between 1928 and 1934, by adopting stringent measures in the allocation of funds for educational and social purposes, the 'mystic of finance' concentrated his efforts on balancing the budget, paying off the floating debt and restoring financial 'respectability' through the stabilization of the escudo. A Law of Economic Reconstruction covering 1935–50 was passed which permitted various programmes as finances became available. Such programmes included expansion and modernization of the railway and road network, hydroelectric power schemes, and irrigation, afforestation and industrialization projects.

The second period, starting at the time of the launching of the First Development plan, was characterized by an increasing trend towards the economic 'integration' of the colonies in an overall policy of national recovery.

Salazar's main concern was to create conditions for the accumulation of 'national' capital, at the expense of the working class of Portugal and the African peoples in the colonies, without recourse to foreign investments. Indeed the most remarkable feature of the laws establishing the roles of capital and labour on one hand, and the laws all but barring foreign investments on the other, is the way they interact to promote national aggrandizement and the enrichment of one class by exploiting the mass of the working population.

In fact, right at the beginning the régime instituted a *'tabela de preços e salarios minimos'* (a scheme of minimum prices and wages) which was equivalent to a 'freeze' of a permanent character, regulated and adjusted from time to time by the Ministry of the Economy. The sophistry here was that by fixing 'minimum salaries', in a situation where workers were deprived of the rights of free association and strike, the régime ensured that even a small amount paid above the minimum was a generous concession on the part of employers. The aim of such social discipline was to guarantee that private companies had enough profits to provide capitalists with a surplus for capital accumulation. Eduardo Guerra, a well-known Portuguese economist, describing the first stages of the régime's economic policy, points out that

the working classes feel completely alienated from the process of economic development, once they cannot act upon it except in suffering its consequences. As evidence for this statement one needs only to recall the stagnation and minimal improvement in the standard of living in contrast with the impressive accumulation of wealth in the hands of a small group of big landowners and capitalists.[1]

A study of the Portuguese social and economic situation in the fifties, after more than twenty-five years of Salazar's rule, revealed that his 'good housekeeping' concepts of economics had only produced a richer State and a richer *élite* in a poor country. He had not been able to reverse or halt a process whereby, despite apparent statistical increases in the gross national product and the rigid control of prices, the cost of living had consistently increased at a higher rate than wages and salaries, with the consequence that the majority of the working

1. Eduardo Guerra, *Evolução da economia portuguesa* (Seara Nova, Lisbon, 1967).

rural and industrial population had to face a progressively lower standard of living.

In this first period up to the early fifties, in place of an agrarian reform and progressive ideals the régime tried to rally support by combining the tenets of a Corporate State with what could be defined as a 'pastoral ideology'. This ideology was based on a romanticized vision of the rural way of life, medieval simplicity, freedom of Catholic belief and the love of the land which characterizes the instinct of property peculiar to peasant culture. The régime organized nationwide competitions to find the *'aldeia mais portuguesa de Portugal'* ('the most Portuguese village of Portugal') and even the choice of Monsanto, in Beira Baixa – a rugged, harsh and almost inaccessible village which had often been besieged but never captured – served to emphasize the virtues of nationalism, tenacity and hard work. A grand *'campanha do trigo'* ('wheat campaign'), along the lines of similar promotions carried out in Fascist Italy and Nazi Germany, was presented as 'another stage in the crusade for national reconstruction'.

While rural Portugal was being moulded to Salazar's way of thinking, new generations were being awakened to the tasks that awaited them in the overseas empire. Schoolchildren were now taught the glories of Portugal's past, the feats of the empire-builders and the names of the heroes who had brought 'peace' to the colonies. Schoolteachers had to adopt the role of political indoctrinators and lived in fear that innocent comments by children outside the school on half-remembered lessons might be taken as an indication of lack of nationalist zeal.

In practice the role of the colonies in the national reconstruction schemes was defined in various decrees, the most explicit being Decree No. 26509 of 11 April 1936, which gave the right to sanction the establishment of industries in the colonies to the Minister for Colonies in Lisbon. In its introduction the decree explained the reasons why the colonies, apart from semi-processing raw materials and foodstuffs for the export trade to Portugal and foreign countries, could only be allowed to develop certain industries. 'The colonies', says the decree, 'as a general rule do not have specialized manpower, and the technicians are Europeans who demand much higher payment for their services than in Portugal, thus causing products to be dearer.'

The decree, signed by Salazar as well as the then Minister for the Colonies, Vieira Machado – later the Chairman of one of the central issuing banks for the colonies, the Banco Nacional Ultramarino – adds a few comments revealing the colonial concepts informing Portuguese policy at the time. Assuming that the consumer market in the colonies was practically confined to the white settler minority, the next comments describe examples of the types of industries that were to be granted to the colonies:

[I]ndustrial development implies a population density which the colonies as yet do not have. It is, therefore, logical that for the time being the colonies should produce the raw materials required for the Portuguese industry in Europe, and only be granted permission to install those industries which can produce goods at the right price and with guaranteed local consumption. The order of priority for the granting of industrial licences in the colonies must be the following:

(a) Those industries that use local raw materials for local consumption. The typical example of this in Angola is wheat milling; the colony produces wheat which it could not easily sell in Portugal now that we do not need to import this cereal and, moreover, Angola has had to import flour from abroad.

(b) Those industries that use local raw materials for which there is a market in other colonies or abroad. The typical example of this is fish meal produced in Moçamedes, Angola.

(c) Industries which may use raw materials not produced in the ⌐olonies but which find a guaranteed local demand such as the beer industry in Mozambique. Although in this case the colony practically only supplies the water, and all other raw materials have to come from outside, the colony consumes the beer which is produced locally.

Although the implications of these provisions are obvious, it is interesting to note that the only industry that did not use local raw materials 'except water' but which could be allowed to operate in the colonies – beer – is an extreme case of a product which does not lend itself to shipment from Portugal in

165

adequate economic and technical conditions; those industries using local raw materials, by and large of a tropical nature, seldom came into competition with Portugal's industries. Moreover Article 4 of the same decree could not be more explicit:

> Permission will be refused to establish or reopen in any given colony any industry, where there are in Portugal, or any other colony, industrial establishments engaged in manufacturing the same products.

The subordination of the colonies to Portugal's own development schemes is also evident in other administrative policies. Salazar was suspicious of foreign aid and investment to the point of dispensing with American aid under the Marshall Plan. All his legislation was designed to keep foreign capital away, particularly from the colonies, where any large-scale foreign investment would be disproportionate to the comparatively small Portuguese investment and therefore a possible threat to Portugal's sovereignty. It should be noted that the provisions of Decree No. 26509, requiring approval by the Ministry for the Colonies for the establishment of industries, applied equally to foreign investors' and to local settlers' capital.

Moreover, the corporate system and the principles of 'national integration' which were embodied in the constitutional amendment of 1951 (renaming the colonies 'provinces') were remarkably suitable for imposing an autocratic structure of controls intended to keep the colonies as a preserve for Portuguese business interests, and harmonized well with the aim of eventually creating a common 'Portuguese Escudo Zone'. Portuguese companies based in Lisbon were entitled to enter bids for major development projects and the supply of equipment for public works and services on a par with locally represented concerns.

With most of the import business in the hands of Portuguese agents, the control of trade was ensured in many other ways. The Cotton Export Board, the various producers' guilds and the so-called Export Regulating Boards were entrusted to officials appointed by the government and likely, therefore, to agree to whatever prices and conditions importers in Portugal offered for a wide range of raw materials. In many instances, particularly in the case of cotton, the largest concessionaries were associated with the textile manufacturers in Portugal.

Another 'body of economic coordination' dealing with imports, the Import Regulating Commission, was there to see that no goods were imported in Angola and Mozambique from foreign countries if they could be imported from Portugal. In addition to issuing import licences according to quotas and other, undisclosed criteria, the Import Regulating Board's licences were still subject to exchange control by the Exchange Councils.

Despite the fact that by Article 148 of the constitution the territories had financial autonomy in their budgets and currencies, they could not contract loans in foreign countries. There were two central issuing banks – the Bank of Angola and the Banco Nacional Ultramarino, both based in Lisbon – but exchange control was firmly in the hands of the Bank of Portugal. Like all the other economic coordinating boards, the Exchange Councils were agencies of Portugal's own interests, although their own operational budgets were financed by each colony. There was a common 'Exchange Fund', the idea of which was that the colonies deposited all their foreign-currency earnings in a central fund controlled by the Bank of Portugal. This fund was then distributed according to the essential needs of each territory. The role of the Exchange Councils, therefore, was to regulate the distribution of funds allocated to each territory, according to applications from government departments, firms and private individuals. Every transfer of money outside the colonies was subject to 'exchange control', and the rules governing the priorities for transfers were designed to give Portugal a stranglehold over the economy of each territory in furtherance of its own profits and interests. According to Decree No. 40483 of 31 December 1955, concerning Angola, the first priority was intergovernmental payments, followed by the payment of profits, interest on loans and capital earnings, the payment of freight and travelling charges, insurance and banking charges and the payment of 'other imports' authorized by the regulating bodies. There was a similar decree relating to Mozambique.

167

Since most of the business, including shipping to and from Portugal, insurance, banking, etc. was in the hands of Lisbon-based concerns, obviously the exchange controls were geared in their favour. Priority was given to those products which were by no means essential, but happened to be available in Portugal for export. By Decree No. 37084 priority was also given to transfers in payment for 'syrups, common wines and other national beverages, liquors and brandies of national origin'. In the case of common wine, local consumption on the part of millions of Africans was also ensured in other ways. In both Angola and Mozambique local government *portarias* (decree orders) prohibited the making of local beverages from native wild fruits, on the grounds that they were harmful to health. Sales of Portuguese wines were protected and promoted until Africans eventually acquired a taste for what is popularly known as *'agua de Lisboa'* ('Lisbon water'), perhaps as an ironic allusion to the well-known fact that the wine is diluted by fraudulent additions of water all the way from the producer in Portugal to the local canteens in Africa. The principle involved, one can safely assume, was that the money Africans spent on wine went directly to Portugal instead of being used for household effects, bicycles and other industrial goods which Portugal did not produce. In fact, analysis of the composition of the import trade by commodities and values revealed the most glaring contrasts between the consumption of luxuries by little more than 180,000 white settlers and tourists in Mozambique and Angola, and the consumption of essential goods by millions of Africans. When compared with the foreign trade of other colonies ruled by Britain or France it showed an extreme degree of exploitation which resulted from the fact that Portugal, impoverished and industrially backward, was trying to correct, at the expense of Africans, economic and administrative errors accumulated over centuries.

South Africa, far more advanced industrially than Portugal and with the advantages of proximity and modern road and railway connections with Mozambique, and later Angola, was the most feared foreign competitor. But other countries saw

The economics of class oppression

themselves affected as well. An American Consul General, writing about the 1950–60 period, commented:

Nearly all consumer goods – passenger cars, for example – are considered non-essential and their import from the United States is allowed only in exceptional cases. In its own purchases both in Angola and Mozambique the Portuguese government is leaning increasingly to European countries, owing, among other reasons, to dollar-shortage problems and because of European regional arrangements. While dollar shortage and monetary controls are formidable barriers, there are others which include Portuguese Africa's traditionally large trade with Portugal, a pattern in which provincial tariff structures have granted Portuguese-manufactured or Portuguese-assembled goods preferential treatment. In most instances the duties for Portugal's goods are half those for similar foreign goods. With the activation of the 'Escudo Zone' free trade area, which has been under consideration for some time, goods manufactured or assembled in any Portuguese territory will enjoy overwhelming advantages in any other Portuguese territory. Mozambique and Angola licensing controls also grant preferences.[1]

The trend towards further economic integration between Portugal and the colonies can be seen in the major development schemes being undertaken in Portugal, Angola and Mozambique. While still wanting to keep private foreign investors from increasing the imbalance between Portuguese and foreign interests in the colonies, the régime began to depart from its policy of self-reliance and negotiated its first large-scale credit, for $455m., with the Economic Cooperation Administration in 1951. At about this time the first of a series of six-year development plans, covering the period 1953–8, was announced. The total investment budget reached 7,500 million escudos in Portugal and 6,000 million escudos in the overseas territories. Included in the plan were projects concerning the increase in electrical power, oil refining, manufacture of fertilizers, cellulose paper and iron and steel mills for Portugal, and dams,

1. Paul F. Canney, 'Special Report on African Sales Frontiers for United States Business', in *International Commerce* (Washington, DC), 1959, Supplement.

169

roads and railway extensions, port modernization and land-settlement schemes for Angola and Mozambique.

The idea involved in such schemes was that some 8,000 families (2,000 in Cela and 6,000 in Guija) were each to be given a house, livestock, seeds and over 100 acres of farming and grazing land repayable to the State after a fairly long period. It was partly influenced by the writings of a colonial administrator, Vicente Ferreira, who advocated the mass settlement of the colonies along the lines of Fascist settlement schemes in Africa. While the fact that the schemes were to take place simultaneously in Angola and Mozambique served to emphasize the policy of 'national integration', the implication of racialism was denied by pointing out that white farms were to be mixed with plots given to African families. Moreover, white farmers were not to be allowed to employ African labour.

However, by the time the white peasant families were settled in their 're-created' environment the cost per immigrant reached nearly £5,000, a figure which could perhaps have been better spent on education and welfare for the neglected and oppressed African population. In fact the Africans who were to farm in the area were not given housing or other facilities and continued to live in their 'native' condition.

The Limpopo scheme, which included the building of a railway line, provides another illustration of Salazar's administrative style and the increasing cooperation with neighbouring Southern Rhodesia, then the leading partner in a federation including Northern Rhodesia (now Zambia) and Nyasaland (now Malawi) which seemed at that time to ensure white supremacy in the area.

Until then nearly 90 per cent of the total imports and exports of the Federation of Rhodesia and Nyasaland were handled through the port of Beira. But both the port and the Beira–Umtali railway line were frequently congested, despite the efforts of the proud Portuguese administration who had taken over the services from the British after nationalization. Seeing the reciprocal economic and political interests in settling as many whites as possible in Southern Africa, both the Portuguese and the white Rhodesians agreed that the line should be brought up to the Rhodesian border and linked up with the Rhodesian railway system, thus providing an alternative route to the sea for the Federation's trade. Significantly, the increasing cordiality between the Portuguese and the Britons-cum-Rhodesians was marked by naming the last station in Rhodesia Vila Salazar, and the last station in Mozambique Malvernia, after Lord Malvern, the Federation's Prime Minister. And, accordingly, the Limpopo Railway, in addition to making Guija a viable white settlement scheme, became another important source of revenue for the State administration of Mozambique.

These colonization schemes were by no means the only projects covered by the first development plan, and many other public works, including hydroelectric schemes, bridges, airport and dock facilities at all the major ports of Angola and Mozambique were carried out during the period.

The development plan for 1959–64, envisaging an expenditure of 30,000 million escudos, of which 9,000 million escudos were to be spent in Angola (51 per cent) and Mozambique (37 per cent), showed the continued trend towards increased expenditure to widen the scope of the colonies' infrastructure, and prepare conditions for the further development of industry, mining and agriculture.

With the successive development plans carried out in Portugal itself, with increased industrialization, the complete renewal and expansion of the merchant fleet and the establishment of a modern Portuguese international airline, the 'Portuguese Economic Space' began to be more of a proposition for investment by the biggest financial groups. Certain groups which experienced unprecedented expansion came to control, between them, hundreds of subsidiary companies and in one way or another, extend their activities through most of the 'Portuguese whole'. In addition a new industrial and colonialist class emerged which left its mark mainly in speculative buildings in the Avenidas Novas and the Arieiro districts of Lisbon. Likewise, Luanda and Lourenço Marques, as well as other towns in Angola and Mozambique, went through a remarkable building expansion that came to place them among the most

171

intensively urbanized white colonial centres anywhere in Africa. In the period 1950–60, even though the decade was marked by development projects which could only begin to show full results at a later stage, the average annual rate of growth in the gross domestic product, at 4·5 per cent, was almost equal to that obtained in the OECD group as a whole (4·6 per cent). In the period 1957–61, with an average of 5·7 per cent, Portugal accelerated its growth even further when compared with the OECD group average for the same period which had decreased to 4.4 per cent.[1]

However, despite these touches of administrative foresight on the part of the determined Salazar and the apparent economic prosperity revealed by statistical indices, neither the mass of African peoples nor the majority of the Portuguese population could be said to be better off, even when compared with the agitated republican period.

In the colonies, with the extension of Portuguese activity from the coastal towns to the interior, the social situation of Africans had, if anything, deteriorated, as Portuguese interference with the traditional subsistence economy increased. Again the system of exploitation was based upon a combination of laws and practices in some cases devised, in other cases adapted, by the 'Estado Novo'. One of the main instruments of oppression was the 'assimilation' system instituted by the Statute of the Natives of Guinea, Angola and Mozambique, in 1954, which was related to similar colonial principles adopted by the French and the Belgians in their respective colonies. Theoretically the *assimilado* system guaranteed Africans full citizenship provided they went through a process of 'evolution' or conversion from their ancestral ways to a fluent knowledge of Portuguese and adoption of the 'habits and customs presupposed for the application of Portuguese common law'.

In the fifty years since the original law of 1917, this concession never applied to more than a token number of Africans – less than 1 per cent of the combined populations of Angola and Mozambique. In practice the Statute became the legal

1. See Xavier Pintado, *Structure and Growth of the Portuguese Economy* (EFTA Publications, 1964).

instrument which kept Africans in a state of serfdom. According to the law 'all the individuals of the Negro race and their descendants who were born and habitually resided in the said Provinces and who do not yet possess the learning and social and individual habits presupposed for the integral application of the public and private law of Portuguese citizens are considered to be *indigenas* (natives)'. Thus the *'indigenato'*, like the Federation's ideals of 'partnership', or South Africa's 'apartheid', appears as just another aspect of colonial mythology to institutionalize the condition of Africans as wards of the administration.

Within Portugal itself, reliable information on the situation in the colonies was virtually nonexistent. There had only been one serious attempt to raise these issues. In 1948, Captain Henrique Galvão delivered a report to the National Assembly on the real status of the Africans, but he was forced to resign as Colonial Inspector.[1] The task of exposing the bestiality of Portuguese colonial rule then fell to British and American writers who were immune to retaliation by the régime. The British writer Basil Davidson, and the American professors James Duffy and Marvin Harris, who visited Angola and Mozambique during the fifties, left important reports on various features of the workings of the *'indigenato* system', or forced labour. Cynical nationalist Portuguese called Basil Davidson a 'typical British humanitarian busybody' while the Americans were known locally as the *'avançados'* ('advance guard') in an allusion to the observers the Portuguese used to send ahead of their colonizing forces during the peak period of imperialist expansion. But other Portuguese, as soon as the presence of these visitors was known, formed themselves into groups and assisted them with research and reports. Basil Davidson was to become known internationally as an historian and expert on African affairs; he maintained a correspondence with Galvão himself while the latter was imprisoned in Lisbon Penitentiary. In later years Davidson often received in London reports sent anonymously from Angola by members of the Portuguese democratic resistance. Duffy, who wrote two of the most valuable and compre-

1. This episode is more fully described in Chapter 9, pp. 190–92.

hensive books ever written on Portuguese Africa, was also assisted by many local people in his visits to Mozambique, Angola and Portugal. The young Marvin Harris, who was then launched on a career which was to lead to the publication of many scholarly books, acknowledged the cooperation he had received while in Mozambique in the preface of his report published in 1958:

> In the course of my work I came to depend upon a number of people, both Portuguese and African, for information and assistance. To these people I became more than a social anthropologist and even more than a friend. Many of them risked their jobs and their personal safety to tell me about the conditions under which they were forced to live, even though in their own minds they could never be entirely certain that I had not been sent to spy on them. They took these risks more out of desperation than out of confidence. For they realized that I might possibly have the opportunity to help them. They knew that if I wanted to I could at least 'tell the world'.[1]

The 'forced-labour system' operated on two levels – one was labour under 'contract' to the public services, ports and railways, plantations and public works; the other was labour assigned to 'compulsory crops'. Under the first system, all those whites who needed Africans, including domestic servants, merely contacted the local administration. The Portuguese administrative officials would then order the African 'sepoys' to round up the required number of natives. In the case of plantations it was a common occurrence to pay between 500 and 1,000 escudos per 'living tool' to the obliging administrative official. The sepoys, unable to get into the 'white business circle', would in their turn exploit the 'natives' by letting themselves be bribed with chickens, food or household articles to let individual Africans go 'unnoticed' or 'volunteer' for recruitment by some other concern. Over a large area of Mozambique the Africans recruited by the Witwatersrand Native Labour Association for hard work in the South African mines were, in most cases, refugees from Portuguese colonial rule.

1. Marvin Harris, *Portugal's African 'Wards'* (American Committee on Africa, New York, 1958).

According to the law, workers had the right to a rest for a period of six months upon returning to their homesteads after the 'regular' twelve-month labour 'contract'. But Africans were so completely at the mercy of the administrative circumstances that they could be 'recruited' right on the first night of their return. Public works, often including those in the residences of the administrative officials, did not require payment, particularly if the Africans involved had not paid their taxes. Even in the most 'white civilized' cities of Luanda and Lourenço Marques any white employers, including housewives, were entitled to send 'their' servants for punishment at the hands of the 'administration'. This normally consisted of beatings with the *palmatoria* (something like a ping-pong bat), carried out by sepoys in front of white officials, the policy being that the white official should appear detached and the hatred projected by prisoners should be confined amongst the Africans.

In their walking-distance world, for Africans forced to turn their backs on the tribal witchdoctor and listen to the Catholic *missionarios* in white cassocks, there was virtually no hope. Even the priests, under the terms of the Missionary Statute which provided for the teaching of 'habits of work', made money out of schoolchildren, too poor to pay any fees, who had to work on farms adjoining the 'mission'. The framework of European technological civilization was in itself enough to intimidate the Africans.

While 'contract labour' covered the men, and 'missionary training' took care of the children, the system of 'compulsory crops', mainly cotton, involved the women who were left behind and traditionally had the tasks of routine farming while the men did the harder work of clearing the land. Aquino de Bragança summed up the results of the system in Mozambique by recalling that before the 'Estado Novo' the Portuguese textile industry imported its raw materials from the United States and Brazil. When Salazar came to power Mozambique only produced some 800 tons of cotton annually, while Portuguese requirements were in the order of 18,000 tons. With the introduction of the 'compulsory crops' system, Africans produced cotton, paid taxes and bought goods of Portuguese origin.

Portugal: fifty years of dictatorship

The neglect of subsistence crops might have cost the lives of thousands of men, women and children, but the production of cotton increased six times between 1932 and 1937. By 1946 it had reached 65 per cent of Portugal's requirements. By 1953 cotton production in Angola and Mozambique was beginning to exceed Portuguese requirements; and by 1955, in addition to supplying domestic industry, Portugal was actually re-exporting cotton to other countries. By 1960, Mozambique alone was producing nearly 140,000 tons.[1]

The official statistics also showed another side of the Portuguese administration. Out of $10\frac{1}{2}$ million people (Angola 4,500,000; Mozambique 6,000,000) over 99 per cent were illiterate. Less than 4 per cent in Mozambique and less than 8 per cent in Angola knew how to speak Portuguese at all. Less than 5 per cent in Mozambique and less than 10 per cent in Angola lived in or around the white men's towns, the only centres where some development had been achieved by the natural process of social contact.

While even by the standards that obtained in the mid-twentieth-century African colonial context black people in Portuguese-ruled territories were subject to the most extreme degree of exploitation, Portugal itself remained one of the most backward and oppressed nations in Western Europe. In Portugal nearly half of the entire working population, in contrast with most of modern Europe, was still engaged in agriculture. According to official statistics the figure for agricultural workers was 47 per cent, as compared with less than 26·7 per cent in services and 25 per cent in industries (including fishing). Given that in Catholic Portugal the proletariat tends to have larger families than the average middle-class family one can safely conclude that nearly 65 per cent of the entire population was made up of families who depended on agricultural and fishing labour for their livelihood.

In the sixties the average weekly salary for men in industry was 180 escudos for a six-day week; the average for men and women was 25 escudos a day, 150 escudos a week. The average for agricultural workers, both men and women, was 19 escudos a day, 114 escudos a week.

1. Aquino de Bragança, article in *Africasie*, No. 15.

Throughout rural Portugal over one third of the population still lived at subsistence level. In certain regions, mainly in the north-east, there existed an ancestral system of economic relations, 'a closed economy, where labour is paid in kind and produce is bartered without circulation of money'.[1]

Portuguese agriculture had one of the lowest yields per acre and per capita in all Europe. Methods and standards had hardly improved in living memory. In most of the country donkeys, Roman ox-carts, or mule-carts were still the most common means of transport used in local farming. Methods of producing wine by treading the grapes with bare feet were used which could be traced to Roman times. Wheat grain was still separated from the chaff, as in Phoenician times, beneath the hooves of cattle or under the weight of a sledge fitted with prongs of flint or iron. Entire hamlets and villages were made up of stone houses and less than 10 per cent had electricity. Olive-oil lamps and wood fires provided the only means of light and heat in many households. Women worked on the land just like men and they had none of the few opportunities available to boys, such as the seminary or the armed forces, the Republican Guard or the police, to further their education and standards. Children were made to work from a very early age, and often the compulsory primary-school attendance was resisted by extremely poor or exploitative parents.

Land distribution still reflected the system of property that had evolved with the Christian reconquest – fragmentation of holdings in the northern half of the country, and extensive farmlands in the Alemtejo which had been seized by the invading class of warriors. Referring to the structure of property, one of the régime's better-informed economists, Xavier Pintado, commented:

In most parts of the country farms are too small, and made up of too many non-contiguous holdings, to allow integrated farming and rational rotations, while in the south the system of *latifundia* prevents more intensive cultivation. Half the number of farms existing in continental Portugal have an area of less than one hectare, and

1. *Inquerito a habitação rural* (Imprensa Nacional, Lisbon), Vol. 1, p. 91.

almost nine tenths of them fall in the categories below five hectares.[1]

According to *Estatística Agrícola*, in 1954 50 per cent of Portuguese holdings were of less than 1 hectare; 38 per cent between 1 and 5 hectares; 7 per cent between 5 to 10 hectares; 3 per cent more than 20 hectares; 1 per cent between 20 and 50 hectares; 1 per cent more than 50 hectares and only 0.3 per cent more than 200 hectares. Included in this minute 0·3 per cent, however, were the properties of the four greatest landlords in the country – Poser de Andrade, Santos Jorge, the Duke of Cadaval and the Duke of Palmela – who between them owned 235,000 acres, the same amount of land that is held by 50,400 farmers.[2]

In the thirty-two ports and fishing centres along the 530 miles of the Portuguese coast, some 150,000 people or more than 15 per cent of the population lived from fishing. Medieval rowing boats were still in common use. The biggest boats carried about thirty men each, taking turns in handling the nets or rowing, 'bent over their oars like galley-slaves of old'. Without modern boats or harbour installations, the number of accidents during storms was appalling. The dramatic scenes that occurred on the beaches when fishermen's waiting wives and families desperately cried during nights of vigil for their return, have been the theme of plays and folk art.[3]

Many fishermen's families lived in wooden huts. In certain areas some cultivated small plots of land; others, attracted by higher wages, joined in seasonal work such as the 'cod-fish campaigns': fleets of motorized sailing vessels carried groups of fishermen to distant areas in the North Atlantic, around Greenland. There each man fished in individual dinghies, using the vessel as a base. The cod-fish, one of Portugal's staple foods, was then brought back to Portugal to the shipowners' installations where it was treated by a salting and sun-drying method of preservation that had not changed for centuries. In

1. Pintado, op. cit., p. 62.
2. Peter Fryer and Patricia Pinheiro, *Our Oldest Ally* (Dobson, 1961).
3. Raul Brandão, *Os Pescadores* (Lisbon, 1923).

the Azores there survived an even more dangerous fishing profession whereby the sperm whale was hunted in small open boats, with only oars, sails and paddles; the whales were captured and killed with hand harpoons.[1] Less has been written about the fishing communities than about any other Portuguese social group – fishing is a hereditary craft and only the occasional outsider has shown any interest in studying the problems of a class which is so much a part of the surroundings that it goes unnoticed.

If one looks at Portuguese socio-economic statistics one finds even closer analogies with the situation in the African territories than some proud believers in the 'Portuguese civilizing mission' liked to admit. While, for instance, the national rate of illiteracy in Portugal during the period 1950–60 was nearly 45 per cent, it exceeded 60 per cent when the rural population was surveyed separately. Moreover, with the index of illiteracy for Africans in both Angola and Mozambique running at over 98 per cent, international comparisons and tables showing the expenditure on education, the number of schools, the number of classes, the number of teachers, in total and per capita, becomes an exercise in statistical sadism.

The essential point is that education was not a first priority or an end in itself, a liberating force dignifying man and making him understand, at least, the causes and implications of his social and economic condition. Education, on the contrary, had retained many of its feudal characteristics as an instrument of privilege and discrimination. In fact illiterates, whether white or black, did not qualify for the vote; unaware of their rights, while Africans were the 'wards' of the administration, rural Portuguese, in legal and written matters, were equally at the mercy of the learned judicial class. Consistent with Salazar's identification of nationalism with class, the 'Portuguese Empire', the 'Portuguese World', the 'Portuguese Economic Space', or whatever one chooses to call it, was in the grip of a political system whereby a comparatively small bourgeois white minority – comprising much less than one million people –

1. Barnard Venables, *Baleia! The Whalers of the Azores* (Bodley Head, 1968).

managed by force and deceit to rule over seven million whites and fourteen million black subjects. At its best Salazar's 'nation' was simply *dominated* by the upper middle class; at worst, the 'nation' *was* the élitist middle class.

Emigration

About 3 million Portuguese, or one in three, are dispersed throughout the world. So pervasive is the phenomenon of emigration in Portuguese life that Salazar described the need to reverse this chronic trend as one of his main tasks. His failure to do so is one of the most dramatic indications of the bankruptcy of his policies.

Over the centuries, successive generations of sailors, soldiers, traders, settlers and convicts left Portugal for the empire, forsaking their mothers, wives and children in the hope of making a living abroad. In recent times, settlers made their way predominantly to Brazil: more than 1 million emigrated from Portugal to Brazil in the fifty years before Salazar came to power. Overall, between 1886 and 1926, 1,300,000 people left Portugal, out of a population that rose during the same period from 3·5 million to 6 million. This represents a yearly average of nearly 33,000 emigrants.

After the advent of the 'Estado Novo', the pattern scarcely changed. In the first forty years up to 1966, the total was again in the region of 1,300,000. Since the overall population rose from 6 million to 8.5 million between the middle twenties and the middle sixties, it might seem that there had been a proportionate decline in the rate of emigration attributable to more effective government by the régime. But what actually happened was that during the thirties and forties the rate of emigration declined, obviously as a result of international factors such as the Depression and the Second World War, which restricted or prevented the normal flow of emigrants; but by 1951 emigration began to acquire a new momentum, and accelerated continuously until the collapse of the régime. The economic boom in the northern countries of Europe created a demand for cheap labour to satisfy an expanding industry and to replace indigenous labour in the less desirable sectors of the economy. By the early 1970s Portugal had contributed some 12 per cent of the estimated 10 million workers from Southern Europe employed in the EEC countries – 1·2 million Portuguese had made the trek north in a decade.

Portugal was becoming increasingly outdistanced in the age of technology, and the Salazar régime could do nothing about the drain on population this caused. Attempts to stem the tide were made by restricting the number of passports issued; but these only had the effect of producing a staggering increase in the number of illegal emigrants, at the same time concealing the true extent of the problem. Since for many years the periodical bulletins of the Junta de Emigração (Emigration Board) omitted to mention illegal emigration at all, it is difficult to acquire reliable figures on the problem; but one can get an approximate idea by consulting the statistics published by host countries.

According to figures published by the French Office National d'Immigration, from 1963/4 onwards, illegal immigration represented an average of 75 per cent of all immigrants entering France each year. The French authorities were clearly conniving at an irregular situation. From their point of view, illegal immigration had its desirable aspects: French industry was provided with cheap labour on a massive scale, while at the same time demands on housing and social services were minimized, and the chances of illegal immigrants involving themselves in militant trade union or political activity were virtually nonexistent.

For the Portuguese régime, however, the extent of illegal emigration had some rather alarming consequences. General population censuses are taken every ten years. In most countries it is possible, by taking into account the net inflow or outflow of population each year, to get a good idea of the overall size of the population at any time. But since the Portuguese Emigration Board was not keeping track of illegal emigration, no one really had any idea what had been happening to the population since the 1960 census. According to various projections based on published statistics and the ratio of births to deaths, the Portuguese population was expected to have increased from 8.8 million to 9.6 million between 1960 and 1970. However, when the 1970 census was eventually published it was discovered that the population had actually *decreased* by more than 180,000.

Moreover, as there had been an influx into Lisbon and other industrial centres such as Setubal, Aveiro and Braga during this period, the impact of emigration upon rural Portugal was far greater than these figures suggested. Beja, Guarda and Bragança had lost as much as 25 per cent of their population; Evora, Portalegre and Castelo Branco 20 per cent. Alarming as these statistics were, and despite attempts to reduce the flow of emigration by agreement with the EEC countries concerned, the annual average of emigrants continued to increase after 1970. By 1974 there were over 1 million Portuguese working in France alone.

Family correspondence with relatives abroad and verbal reports by emigrants returning to Portugal on holiday were a major source of information on the better life outside Portugal, and since the late fifties even the government-controlled TV, with its inevitable display of the values of the consumer society, also had a tantalizing effect upon the impoverished masses. Moreover, the expansion of tourism and the sight of so many ordinary foreign workers motoring through Portugal emphasized the contrast between Portuguese conditions and those obtaining in industrial countries beyond the Pyrenees. In fact, when seen in the context of comparative European social and economic indices, Portugal vied for the bottom of the ladder with other nations with the same collective 'vocation' for emigration. Thus, the table for 1970/71 concerning the average Gross National Product per head of population placed Portugal, with $527 per annum, ahead of only Turkey ($350) but below Greece ($860), Spain ($733) and Ireland ($1,020).[1]

Moreover, owing to the gross inequalities in income between the landowning, business and managerial classes and the mass of the working population in Portugal, even such international statistical comparisons can be deceptive. In the industrially ad-

1. *Financial Times Yearbook* – 1970/71.

vanced countries of the OEDC, for instance, through institutionalized trade unionism, collective bargaining and pressures
inherent in the consumer society, labour had achieved a share of
some 70 per cent of the national income, while capital earnings
took 30 per cent; in Portugal, the proportion was almost reversed with capital earnings taking 55 per cent and labour, including the managerial classes, less than 45 per cent. Outside
Lisbon and other urban or tourist centres, living conditions for
the mass of the rural and fishing population compared most
closely with those obtaining in non-European, 'developing'
countries. For instance, Portugal during the 1960s was building
less than half the annual number of houses built in the Nether-
lands (10 per 1,000 inhabitants). In study based upon an
official definition of 'inadequate housing' including city slums as
well as rudimentary and decrepit rural stone houses, it was
found that in Portugal 500,000 families, representing one quar-
ter of the population, still lived without piped water, sewers or
electricity.[1] In the early seventies, the then Secretary for Industry stated that one in five Portuguese had no access to electricity,[2] and in fact, as any keen observer travelling through
rural Portugal could see, overhead power cables bypassed
hamlets and villages in many areas, there being no individual
connections to the houses. A large number of rural households
could not cope with the expense involved in either the initial
outlay required for electrical wiring nor with the high unit
charges for power.

Portuguese emigration in the sixties was essentially determined by the same convergence of 'pull' and 'push' factors
which obtained in Spain, Greece, Turkey and Yugoslavia – on
one hand the attraction of higher salaries in the EEC countries,
on the other the desire to get out of the rut of rural stagnation,
poverty, unemployment and oppressive government. However,
in the Portuguese case one finds also the influence of new
factors.

Around half a million Portuguese male emigrants of the

1. Eduardo Ribeiro, *Estudo sobre o problema da habitacão. As Eleições
de 1969* (Europea–America Publications, Lisbon, 1970).
2. *Vida mundial*, 2 June 1972.

sixties were between twenty and thirty; a considerable proportion of these were evading military conscription or were ex-servicemen who did not want to return to their previous rural existence after having been through the disruption caused by years of military service. Reluctance to enter the army had obvious economic motives. During their training period, conscripts received less than 100 escudos a month, subject to deductions in compensation for loss or damage of uniforms and equipment. Since the average price of a cinema ticket was 15 escudos and a packet of 20 cigarettes over 6 for a medium-quality brand, the army of conscripts – over 100,000 a year – regarded military service as a form of imprisonment; accommodation, food, routine and discipline in an army barracks were in fact often little different from the regimen of a penal colony. Money for entertainments had to come from relatives, who typically were poverty-stricken themselves. While on their two-year tour of duty overseas, conscripts' pay rose to the region of 1,500 escudos per month, but as prices tended to be higher than in Portugal this incentive hardly outweighed the risks involved.

Indeed, the prospect of involvement in action on the African fronts was the main factor leading to evading conscription. Although there was a concerted effort on the part of the authorities to understate the number of Portuguese casualties, army communiqués from High Command Headquarters in Guinea-Bissau, Angola and Mozambique regularly published the names of at least some of those killed in combat, as well as indications as to the number of those wounded or victims of 'accidents'. This fragmentary information was systematically collected and put together by opposition groups. During the 1969 elections, an opposition manifesto showed that even if one excluded those wounded, or listed as dead due to accidents or illness, 'the number of men killed up to 1969, in Guinea-Bissau, Angola and Mozambique can be estimated at 3,000. This is equivalent to the number of Americans killed in Vietnam (60,000), given that the population of the United States is more than twenty times larger than that of Portugal'. Other sources put the total for 1970 at over 6,000 dead and 12,000 wounded.[1] Such figures, often exaggerated by rumour, had an understandable deterrent effect on Portuguese youth and their families.

The enormous impetus given to emigration by the colonial wars in Guinea-Bissau, Angola and Mozambique is likely to have long-term demographic consequences, quite apart from the numbers killed in combat. With such a vast outflow of young men, the population of Portugal 'aged' alarmingly. As Professor Almerindo Lessa, Chairman of Social Medicine and Public Health at Lisbon University, explained it in 1972, the active population was emigrating to build a better life elsewhere, leaving behind in Portugal large areas inhabited by people who, owing to their age, cannot make up for the loss in terms of either production or reproduction'.[2] From an economic point of view, the prospect of continuing mass emigration presented the 'Estado Novo' with a serious problem, in part probably irreversible.

1. See *Mundo A ricano Library Notes*, No. 19, 'Portugal's War in Guinea-Bissau', by A. L. J. Venter (California Institute of Technology, Pasadena).
2. *Vida mundial*, 28 July 1972.

Chapter 9
The metaphysics of colonialism

> '*The people who more properly and deservedly merit the title "thieves" are those whom kings put in command of their armies and legions, the government of provinces or the administration of towns, for such people, by cunning or by force, rob and despoil men. The other thieves might rob a man, but these rob entire towns and kingdoms. The other thieves rob at their own risk, but these have no fear of danger. The other thieves, if they rob, are hanged, but these do the robbing* and *the hanging*' –
> ANTONIO VIEIRA (1608–97)[1]

The 'peninsularity' of Spain and Portugal, plus a long tradition of obscurantist and inquisitorial rule, perhaps explain the Iberian propensity for self-deception over sensitive national issues. Under the permanent threat of persecution, even otherwise fairly unconventional observers living inside Spain and Portugal would avoid discussing the roles of the Church or the army; others would only indirectly allude to class conflicts or subordination to foreign capital or strategic interests. But an issue which was seldom mentioned in a critical context was that of the suppressed nations, either inside 'Iberia' or in Portugal's 'overseas provinces'.

Yet, in the same way that the issue of separatism in Catalonia and the Basque country during the last Spanish republic was one of the main emotive factors that came to a head during the Civil War, representative government in Portugal under the constitutional monarchy or the democratic republic was always at the root of disagreement and indecision over colonial matters. Separatism in Angola can be traced as far back as the time of the independence of Brazil in 1820, and in both Angola

1. From *Sermões* (Classicos Sa da Costa, Lisbon, 1954).

and Mozambique there have always existed undercurrents of what the Portuguese call 'nativism', that is to say, aspirations towards independence among educated half-castes, blacks and locally born Portuguese. This feeling often ran parallel with a mood of would-be settler separatism which arose from the divergences between local business interests and those of metropolitan Portugal.

Class antagonisms inherent in the situation in the Iberian peninsula, and the problems that arose from oppressive rule or international politics, might have been the most immediate and primary factors in the tensions and conflicts in internal politics. But censorship and police rule tended to be most rigorous over the question of separatism (in Spanish provinces or Portuguese colonies). Many opponents of both régimes failed to see the common basis of the issue of 'national integration'. The moral justification for the rigours of dictatorship, even among the most liberal and humane of both régimes' supporters, was found in the tacit notion that representative governments had never been, and could not be, compatible with the ideals of 'national unity'. It is significant that in both countries separatists – whether Catalans, Basques, black or white – were treated with a severity which frequently exceeded that meted out to communists. The existence of a colonial or quasi-colonial situation in the political make-up of both countries might be another reason why Spain and Portugal were to remain for so long anachronisms in modern Europe where democratic and parliamentarian governments predominate.

In Portugal and its colonies, repression of 'nativism' had a long and macabre history. The colonialist entrepreneurs, whose interests were identified with classes who owned and controlled the information media in Portugal, always kept a strict censorship over colonial issues, from generation to generation. The very geographical distance between the various component parts of the empire made them inaccessible to anyone but a small class of traders and administrative officials. As in the British and the French empires, it was not until the development of fast, regular air services towards the middle of the twentieth century that it became possible to find the occasional colonial administrator who had visited all the territories of the far-flung Portuguese empire. With white settlement confined to a few coastal towns, only a few administrative officials really knew what went on in the interior. A few decades ago it could be said that 'the darkest thing about Africa was people's ignorance of it'. In fact, although a governor of Portuguese Guinea, Judice Biker, had written a report in 1903 in a limited-circulation Lisbon colonial magazine, more was known abroad than in Portugal itself about conditions in Portuguese-ruled African territories. There are no Portuguese-language translations of or reports equivalent to, those published by the British Henry Nevinson (1906), Charles Swan (1909), William A. Cadbury (1910), John Harris (1913) or the American Prof. Edward Ross (1925).[1] Moreover, whatever rumours of these reports reached the Portuguese by the late 1940s were likely to be dismissed as part of the old and outdated history of international campaigns against Portugal instigated by other imperialist powers. And unfortunately the very fact that such reports had been written by people who had visited the colonies with the permission of the authorities in the republican democratic period, only served to justify greater vigilance on the part of the 'Estado Novo's' framework of consular, 'International Police' and administrative authorities when dealing with outside visitors.

It is significant that the manifesto of the 'National Liberation Board' of 1946–7, which had a circulation restricted to those involved in the movement, contained an extensive programme relating to Portugal itself, but only a single reference to the colonies. The most sensitive issue of the empire was dismissed with a single broad – but deliberately laconic and undefined – call for the 'repeal of the Colonial Act'. There were, no doubt, former colonial administrators among the ranks of the conspirators but these must have been people of moderate views, for the existence of 'democratic experts on colonialism' was, in the circumstances, a contradiction in terms; and certainly those who were better informed on colonial matters also knew that Portugal's politically uneducated population would be likely to

1. See James Duffy, *Portuguese Africa* (Harvard University Press, Cambridge, Mass., 1959), p. 163 ff.

react against anti-colonialist criticism as being 'anti-patriotic'.

After nearly twenty years of the 'Estado Novo', the routine of censorship and police rule had resulted in total public alienation from colonial affairs. Therefore, to be able to understand the system that operated inside the African colonies, and particularly Angola and Mozambique – immense territories almost the size of Western Europe traversed by few roads and railways – one would need to be a man with a rare combination of personal qualities and experience. Such a man would have to be a Portuguese, and a high administrative official or army officer, to be able to travel and stay for long periods at a time in various regions and territories. He would need to have resisted the middle-class values which are inevitably acquired through family influences and secondary and higher education; such a man would need to be humane and with a social conscience and some sociological insight. He should also be proficient in more than one language if he wanted to see his reports in print – but for this he would also need to have the right connections abroad. Moreover he would need to be prepared to transgress sworn undertakings of secrecy on administrative matters and have enough courage to risk his career and police persecution.

Some of these attributes and circumstances are clearly incompatible. As those who have been persistently involved in clandestine politics know, people seldom undergo sudden conversions in later life towards democratic and socialist views. Courage, altruism, rebellious or liberal leanings are as a rule shown fairly early in life, or not at all. No one of strong democratic views would be able to hide certain reactions long enough to succeed in a career leading to high rank in the administration or the army. It would be an extremely rare man who could carry his humanity to the point of consistent dissimulation and eventually write a report for reasons of conscience alone. He would also come up against other moral dilemmas. Since he could only have learned certain facts through the confidences of either fellow officials or missionaries, he would almost inevitably incriminate them by the references, however disguised, necessary in his report to give it documentary validity.

A rare man who did indeed possess some of the qualities needed to break through these almost impregnable barriers was Henrique Galvão – the officer who had fought side by side with Lieutenant Humberto Delgado in the pro-régime barricades of the late twenties. Galvão had in the meantime risen from the position of Director of National Broadcasting and Director of Fairs and Exhibitions, and District Governor of Huila (Angola) to the post of High Inspector of Colonial Administration dealing with 'native policy'. Moreover, he had written extensive semi-official books and monographs on all the colonies, and was one of the three deputies representing Angola in the National Assembly in Lisbon.

In 1947, as his close friend and co-author of books on the colonies, Colonel Carlos Selvagem, was being persecuted for involvement in the movement of the 'National Liberation Board', Galvão decided to draw attention to the situation in the colonies in a debate in the National Assembly. He alleged that he had tried to bring certain facts to the attention of successive colonial ministers but had obtained no response.

In his book *The Santa Maria – My Crusade for Portugal*[1] Galvão describes how he delivered a report to a 'secret' session of the National Assembly which he followed up in 1948 with a more direct, formal approach to the government in the Assembly. The report, although smuggled abroad by members of the Portuguese clandestine opposition at the time, was not noticed in the Western press until Calvão hijacked the ocean liner *Santa Maria* in 1961, but since then it has become a classic indictment of Portuguese colonialism.

In the book Galvão states that 'only the dead are exempt from forced labour'. He describes how the rigours of Portuguese oppression and exploitation had led to the rapid and complete depopulation of a zone of more than 100 kilometres in width along almost the full extent of the inland boundaries of Mozambique and north of the Save river and large sections of Portuguese Guinea. Those Africans who remained behind faced a fate just as bad as slavery. In the days of slavery

1. Weidenfeld & Nicolson, 1961, pp. 45–8.

the Negro, bought as a work animal, was regarded as a piece of personal property which his owner had an interest in keeping healthy and strong, just as in the case of his ox or his horse. Now the Negro is not bought but simply rented from the administration, without losing the label of a freeman. The employer cares little whether the man lives or dies, provided he keeps working while he can; for the employer can demand that another labourer be supplied if the first one becomes incapacitated or dies. There are employers who let as many as 35 per cent of the workers, supplied by government agents, die during what is called the period of 'contract work'.

His report, it must be noted, was written in such general terms as to leave no trace of his sources.

A series of events followed – some predictable, others less so. In the following year, 1948, when Galvão raised the issue openly at the National Assembly the press was allowed to print the substance of his accusations. His situation changed overnight. 'The country looked upon him with sympathy; those in "opposition" thought they had found a potential supporter; but the National Union, and the legion of opportunists it embodied, hated him as the dissident who had dared to expose thefts and thieves, sounding the first alarm against the pillaging of a nation.'[1] Salazar never forgave him for his 'ungratefulness' and was determined to show how the régime treated those who betrayed his trust. In 1948 Galvão's term as deputy came to an end and, therefore, he lost the Portuguese equivalent of 'parliamentary immunity'. Moreover, by his own admission, the exercise of his work as High Colonial Inspector became 'unbearable' and he was forced to resign for 'health reasons'. Galvão, however, did not immediately join the ranks of the opponents of the régime but allowed himself to fall into obscurity.

In fact, much to the disappointment of romantics abroad, the real reasons that led Galvão to write his reports have always been questioned. It is true that Galvão was a man of liberal tendencies, artistic tastes and humane feelings; but he was also an opportunist, and had enjoyed the trust of Salazar for a con-

1. Maria Archer, *Os Ultimos Dias do fascismo portuges* (Editora Liberdade e Cultura, São Paulo, 1959).

siderable length of time. 'I do not know', wrote Maria Archer in a book read in typescript by Galvão before publication,

what truly impelled him to an attitude of rebellion, the risks of which he could not have ignored. Some say he reacted against a decision by the then Governor General of Angola to refuse favours to one of his brothers, Carlos Galvão, who had settled there. But could it be a feeling of solidarity towards the Angolan people, drained of their resources? Was it patriotic concern? Was it a reaction of offended pride for the disdain with which the government learned of his persistent accusations? Reaction of pride prompted by the scorn of those whom he threatened but who remained, with impunity, in power? . . . I know nothing of the months that followed his withdrawal from the public scene, during which he wandered in isolation, without deciding whether to engage in a new adventure, or return to the old comforts.[1]

Indeed, in the following year, the first contested elections for the presidency of the republic since the régime had come to power were to take place, but Galvão did not emerge from obscurity either on the side of the régime's National Union or on the side of the democratic opposition. There can be no doubt that Galvão had had no sudden conversion to democratic ideals and that at best he was to remain only a liberal individualist even after he became a leading adversary of Salazar.

Presidential elections

After the failure of the 1946–7 'National Liberation Board' there seemed to be no hope, either for the opposition or for President Carmona, of relieving themselves of Salazar's guardianship. If anything, the ageing General Carmona had become an even more isolated and distant figure, only occasionally taking part in public functions.

The opposition now pinned its hopes on the fight for power by legal means. The chance would come in 1949, when the opposition intended to avail themselves of the constitutional right of proposing a candidate for the seven-year term of office

1. ibid., p. 29.

as President. All that was required was that a number of citizens support a candidate and that he should be regarded as 'eligible' by the Supreme Court and the Council of State. The opposition, having nothing to lose, would put the régime to a public test at every stage of the constitutional process. In fact, although the electoral rolls were too limited to be regarded as representative (less than 10 per cent of the population could vote), there was at least a theoretical possibility of having a democratic president elected. With the powers conferred upon him by the constitution, the president would dismiss Salazar and appoint a new prime minister and a new government, thus opening the way for what was defined as 'a constitutional *coup d'état*' – a somewhat contradictory concept which nevertheless indicated the sophistry inherent in the constitution.

Moreover, the opposition, organized into support committees throughout the country and in the overseas territories, could always take advantage of the thirty-day electoral period, when censorship was relaxed, to agitate for political ideas – and hope for the best, which could even be either a *pronunciamento* within the army or, preferably, a general uprising of the civilian population.

By 1949, however, despite the apparent political stagnation inside the country the situation had changed. The Movimento de Unidade Democratica, which had operated clandestinely since 1945 and which was still under the influence of the Communist Party, provided a useful degree of organization. But on the other hand Portugal's admission into NATO had influenced the more moderate, or most cautious, sections of the middle class who recognized that the régime was entering a phase in which it would become an accepted member of the Western bloc and a protégé of the United States.

The choice of candidate for the opposition fell on the much-respected General Norton de Matos, a former High Commissioner in Angola, a former Ambassador in Britain and the author of many books on administrative and colonial matters, in which, incidentally, the ideal of a Portuguese 'commonwealth' had first been formulated. He was, however, very much a figurehead. His electoral board of supporters included

Professor Azevedo Gomes, a well-known economist and politician, the historian Antonio Sergio, the writers Alves Redol, Manuel Mendes and Ramada Curto, well-known professors such as Bento Caraça, Paulo Quintela and Rui Luiz Gomes, and many others – in all, a most impressive list of prominent citizens. Among the younger and most active members were Mario Soares, later to become a leading social democrat, and Piteira Santos, later a member of the board of the Front for National Liberation, based in Algiers.

Norton de Matos's electoral programme was tantamount to an end of the 'Estado Novo' and the restoration of democracy. However, the opposition itself was very divided and reflected the ideological divergences which were being debated throughout Europe among middle-class intellectuals and party leaders. A series of books well publicized in the West[1] – by David Rousset, Albert Camus, Arthur Koestler, Jean-Paul Sartre, George Orwell, Victor Kravtchenko – which, in one way or another, attacked the Soviet Union and established Communist parties were having a disturbing and divisive influence in literate circles of the middle-class opposition in Portugal who were permanently engaged in making ideological choices, even before they fought to have the right to choose.

Divided or united, however, the opposition had no means of imposing free elections or overthrowing the régime. Reading the democratic literature of the time, and even allowing for the care with which such issues as the 'overseas empire', the Church, the army and 'national security' had to be dealt with for fear of persecution, one sees that few people in the opposition movement had grasped the implications of the newly acquired NATO membership for the survival of the régime in Portugal.

Some of these implications, however, are reflected in the events surrounding the election and the final statements made by General Norton de Matos himself. On the eve of polling day, in a gesture designed to discredit the elections both at home and abroad, General Norton de Matos, having received no

1. See Mario Soares, *Portugal's Struggle for Liberty* (Allen & Unwin, 1975).

guarantees of genuinely free elections, handed in to the Supreme Court his formal withdrawal from the candidacy. In a public statement explaining his decision he complained of the lack of civility he had found everywhere, and the speculation that had been made about his atheistic views. He specifically accused the Minister of War, Colonel Santos Costa, of having interfered with normal electoral campaigning 'by ordering nationwide air force and army exercises all the week preceding the elections and on polling day itself'.

Yet one of the passages of his closing statement indicates his own moderate political views and nationalistic feelings:

> Today more than ever Portugal wants to maintain the place to which it has a right in the world, to gain in grandeur and prestige, to retain zealously its independence and sovereignty and cooperate internationally for the consolidation of universal peace, using for those ends its enterprising spirit, its colonizing genius, and its natural goodness that only justice and violence could alter.[1]

Apart from a significant allusion to Portugal's 'colonizing genius', which was one of General Norton de Matos's cherished beliefs, the 'colonial question' was once again expediently avoided. Despite the fact that independent India was now claiming that both France and Portugal should follow the example of Britain and leave their remaining small coastal possessions in the sub-continent, the opposition had not formulated any alternative to the colonialist policies of the 'Estado Novo'. The 'colonial question' was still regarded at this late date as a marginal issue. The situation had crystallized into an antagonism between those who supported the régime and who contented themselves to be defined just as *'situacionistas'* (those for the *status quo*), and a broad front of *'oposicionistas'* (those who opposed the régime), and these latter were too divided even to agree on a radical programme. Except for the Communist Party, who had a clandestine, cohesive organization, the 'opposition' was really an association of individuals, mostly lawyers, who read French books and who knew all about dialectical

1. Serafim Ferreira and Arsenio Mota, *Para Um Dossier da oposição portuguesa* (Nova Realidade, Tomar, 1969).

materialism. The overwhelming majority of peasants and urban workers, however, could hardly understand the 'opposition' political manifestos and even after the literate read to them an electoral article or interview some peasants and workers were not exactly sure on which side a certain '*senhor doutor*' might be. Unlike the régime, which had powerful backing from neighbouring Spain and many friends in NATO, the opposition had little more than a nuisance value.

On 13 February 1949, those whom the government authorities had appointed to count the votes agreed on a figure of 80·3 per cent in favour of the unopposed National Union candidate President Carmona who, in the meantime, had been raised to the status of Marshal for 'services rendered to the nation'.

Divine Providence, however, did not always work in favour of the régime. Marshal Carmona, then in his eighties, had reached an advanced age for the role that was demanded from him, and on 18 April 1951 he died. A new election had to be called.

Essentially, though, the new elections only served to emphasize Salazar's absolute power. The régime's National Union chose as its new candidate General Craveiro Lopes, whose life and career, even when embroidered by official propaganda, were not particularly impressive. But the opposition was more divided than ever. After the last elections a new grouping had emerged, the Movimento Nacional Democratico, but many of its sponsors, including the Communist Party's General Secretary, Alvaro Cunhal, were arrested, and it presented no electoral challenge. Of the two candidates who did stand, one was Prof. Rui Luiz Gomes, a much-respected mathematician who rose through the ranks of the youth wing of the Movimento de Unidade Democratica and who had now matured enough to command the movement nationally. The other candidate was Admiral Quintão Meireles, who derived his support from a group of surviving democratic republican leaders whose ideas had by this time been completely overtaken by events.

The novelty in the campaign was that Admiral Meireles also had the support of a group of former followers of the régime, including Captain Henrique Galvão who had finally decided to reappear on the scene. However, as politicians, Captain Galvão and his group of dissidents proved to be a disappointment.

Admiral Meireles's electoral propaganda was directed by Captain Galvão himself. But all the manifestos and statements revealed a form of opportunism and political parochialism which is peculiar to many undeveloped countries. One of the main features of Admiral Meireles's campaign was an emphasis on 'protecting religious freedom', as if a hint had been taken from the previous bitter experience of atheist General Norton de Matos that to win in politics in Portugal you must claim to be on the side of God – whether he wants you there or not. The other feature was an obsessive concern with the threat to national security allegedly seen in communism. One can understand upper-middle-class people being afraid of communism as a social doctrine, for its rise to power would eventually mean that they might end up having to work. But anti-communism in undeveloped countries appears, more often than not, masked as anti-Sovietism and a concern with 'national independence'. In the case of Portugal such postures could only be an act of contrivance. Portugal is so small a country, and so secluded behind Spain and Western Europe, that only a megalomaniac or a fool could feel unduly insecure or threatened by the Soviet Union. Unlike the United States, Portugal had no nuclear weapons or other targets of primary strategic, economic or political value in a modern global war. It had such a low standard of living that any foreign army would have to think twice before invading it for fear of having to share its rations with the population. Moreover, since by 1951 the country had already been deprived of fundamental freedoms for over twenty-five years the average Portuguese might not even have been able to tell the difference had there been a change in the type of dictatorship.

Nevertheless, in the midst of underdevelopment, or perhaps because of it, Portugal always had its fairly well-advanced share of professional anti-communists, even outside the régime. Many an author, anxious to establish a good relationship with the censors, would temper his mild criticisms of the régime with the most intemperate attacks on the Soviet Union or China, countries which the Portuguese really knew very little about and which most of them could hardly afford to visit as tourists. In the case of political groups, this contrived anti-communism was often intended to impress both the naïve inside the country, and United States Embassy staff who, because of the more direct American involvement in worldwide strategy and ideological conflict, were often receptive to such tactics.

The first pointer to the character of Admiral Meireles's electoral campaign was a statement to the effect that 'no understandings are contemplated or desired, or relationships wanted, with the group which proposes the candidacy of Prof. Rui Gomes, or with any groups or parties who are, directly or indirectly, dependent on a foreign power'. The second was the manifesto's concluding statement that Admiral Meireles did not intend or wish to 'overthrow a régime, to promote a convulsion, to agitate a new ideology or suggest a solution dangerous to the continuity of Portuguese public life'. One can clearly detect, here, the naïvety of Captain Galvão in wishfully thinking that he could divide the régime and eventually replace Salazar as Prime Minister.

The ultimate consequence of the stand taken by Admiral Meireles's supporters was that Prof. Rui Gomes was further isolated. With the régime's designs converging with those of Meireles's group, Prof. Gomes was declared 'ineligible' by the Supreme Court, that is to say, lacking in *idoneidade* (fitness or suitability) to be President. Consequently he was subjected to such personal abuse and danger that at an electoral session near Lisbon, when one of his supporters questioned the validity of the Cult of Fatima, a number of pious PIDE agents actually assaulted him and his followers in public. On the following day the pro-régime press attacked him as if they were exorcizing the devil. Ironically, however, in their turn Admiral Meireles and his supporters did not escape the scorn of both the democratic opposition and the régime, and Admiral Meireles, much for the same reasons as General Norton de Matos before him, was forced to withdraw his candidacy on the eve of election day. On 22 July 1951 the National Union candidate was elected unopposed, the official count in his favour being, once again, over 80 per cent of the total votes cast. For the sake of formality, as soon as the new president was inaugurated in August, Salazar and the cabinet tendered their resignation and the new president immediately reiterated his trust in them and had them re-appointed. It was the wisest thing he could do.

Although, as President of the Republic, General Craveiro Lopes retained the power to dismiss and appoint the Prime Minister, only in appearances could Salazar be regarded as a 'dictator by proxy'. Salazar was by now a gigantic national figure compared with the rather modest general he had picked for President. Moreover, Salazar had already introduced a de-fensive catch into the constitution that showed how he could dismiss his own and only 'boss'. A former judge and lifelong opponent of the régime, Sebastião Ribeiro, described the con-stitutional catch in this way:

In accordance with Article 80, Paragraph 1, the Council of State – made up of ten members appointed by the Government (Salazar) for life – was empowered to judge the 'permanent incapacity' of the President of the Republic. The Prime Minister (Salazar) in his turn has the power to convoke the Council of State to meet for that purpose; and has also the power to declare in the official *Diario do Governo* [*Daily Law Record*] the vacancy of the Presidency, should the Council agree upon the incapacity of the President. And the Council would certainly agree, if it was so ordered, made up as it was of trusted pillars of the régime.[1]

With the election over and another seven-year term of undis-puted rule in view, Salazar had his day of reckoning with the rebellious Galvão. When the curtain of censorship again de-scended over Portugal, the PIDE infiltrated the semi-clan-destine Organização Civica Nacional (National Civic Organization) where Galvão was plotting against the régime with former republican ministers, such as Cunha Leal, and dis-gruntled army officers alike. On 6 January 1952 he was arrested, 'to begin a long, hard martyrdom, the vengeance of the régime and the dictator'. In fact, having first been sentenced to only

1. Sebastião Ribeiro, *Anotações ao presente* (Lisbon, 1972), Vol. 2.

three years in jail, Galvão was subjected to a series of trials which extended his imprisonment indefinitely.

By 1958, when President Craveiro Lopes's term of office was coming to an end and new elections fell due, it almost looked as though Salazar had succeeded in turning the Portuguese into 'one of those happy peoples who do not have to think'. Past failures together with renewed Western support for the régime combined to demoralize the traditional opposition. This mood was reinforced by a widespread feeling that Salazar would soon disappear from the political scene, either through old age or death, and that the collapse of the régime would inevitably follow. But if the opposition had its troubles, the elections of 1958 uncovered serious splits within the ranks of the régime itself.

On 3 May the central board of the National Union Party announced that, for personal reasons, President Lopes had declined to stand for re-election. He was to be replaced by Admiral Americo Thomaz, a man whose main claim to distinction was his lifelong loyalty to Salazar. He had entered the cabinet in 1944 as Minister for the Navy, and was credited with having modernized the merchant fleet and helped to expand trade and communications with the empire.

Initially the democratic opposition, including the Communists, gave their backing to the Lisbon barrister and painter Arlindo Vicente. But Vicente withdrew in favour of an independent candidate, General Humberto Delgado, a man whom the pro-régime press had for years been hailing as a dynamic organizer and Portugal's worthy representative at NATO. He had apparently become disenchanted with the régime after visits to the overseas territories and long tours of duty in countries 'where life moves faster and people are not treated like a flock of sheep'. He had also evidently become '*estrangeirado*', for he dared to introduce into Portugal the direct, person-to-person campaigning methods he had seen in foreign countries.

As Delgado's electoral campaign proceeded, his message got through to the discontented middle class and the oppressed workers, young and old, and echoed throughout the empire.

200

Much to the alarm and rage of Salazar, Delgado proclaimed that if elected he would dismiss the dictator, and this act of defiance was hailed with mass demonstrations of support in Oporto and Lisbon, involving hundreds of thousands of people.

Delgado was obviously winning the election by popular acclamation, but winning officially was quite another matter. On the day following the poll, Admiral Thomaz was attributed 758,998 votes, and Delgado 236,528. The true figures may never be known. As the iron curtain of censorship descended once again, Delgado appealed to the Supreme Court and addressed letters of protest to the new president inviting him to have the dignity to resign. He also wrote an appeal to his former friends and colleagues, Generals Botelho Moniz, Lopes da Silva, Costa Macedo and Beleza Ferraz, who all still held key positions of command, calling on them to rebel. When this came to nothing, Delgado became involved in a conspiracy to start a military uprising under an 'Independent Military Movement' which included Captain Vasco Gonçalves,[1] Captain Varela Gomes and the Catholic socialist leader Manuel Serra. The plot was uncovered on 12 March 1959, and most of the conspirators were arrested. After attempts on the part of the régime to silence Delgado with the offer of a well-paid scholarship in Canada, he was forced to take refuge in the Brazilian embassy in Lisbon. In the meantime, perhaps because Delgado's activities had absorbed all the attention of the PIDE, Henrique Galvão managed to escape from Lisbon's Hospital of Santa Maria, where he had temporarily been sent for treatment, and took asylum at the Argentine embassy.

Delgado's electoral campaign had nevertheless shaken the régime, and moved Salazar to plug the last hole in his constitutional dam by abolishing direct suffrage for the Presidency of the Republic. In future, 'The President will be elected by the Nation through an electoral college composed of the members of the National Assembly and representatives of various local

1. Later Prime Minister in the second Provisional Government after the *coup* of 25 April 1974.

authorities from each district or overseas province.'[1] This amendment, the most important since the constitution had been enacted in 1933, meant that never again would it be possible to achieve a 'constitutional *coup d'état*' by getting a president elected who could dismiss the prime minister and the government and open the way for the dissolution of the régime. It therefore marked the final consecration of single-party rule.

Deprived of all legal means of opposition, Delgado made his way to South America, where he was reunited with Galvão, and reorganized his forces into the Independent National Movement. He also formed an alliance with the most combative Spanish exile groups, and created a joint Iberian Revolutionary Directorate of Liberation, known by its Spanish and Portuguese initials as DRIL. DRIL was intended to act as a 'technical agency of liberation', above the organizational problems which kept the various political groups disunited. This short-lived alliance will be best remembered for the capture of the 25,000 ton Portuguese liner, the *Santa Maria*, off the Venezuelan coast on 23 January 1961. This act of 'piracy' captured the world's headlines and was to have a significant impact on political developments in Angola.

Subsequently Delgado re-entered Portugal secretly, to lead the abortive assault on the army barracks at Beja in January 1962. He also paid a secret visit to Mozambique to study conditions for a local rebellion. He continued to use Brazil as a base, but as soon as newly independent Algiers offered hospitality and support, he decided to set a base nearer Portugal.

Upon arrival in Europe at the end of 1963 he was painfully disappointed to realize that he was now barred from visiting most Western European countries, including Britain, whose institutions and parliamentary system he cherished as a model for Portugal. He discreetly visited the Soviet Union, and went to Prague to attend several meetings with other exiled leaders who were then reorganizing the Patriotic Front for the Liberation of Portugal (FNLA), to be based in Algiers. He was elected President of the FNLA's newly created Revolutionary Board in

1. Decree No. 43528, first announced in 1959 and finally enacted on 21 March 1961.

January 1964, but, still insisting on immediate armed rebellion and urban guerrilla activities against the régime, he soon clashed with the more disciplined and cautious members of the Board, and began to conspire without their knowledge.

PIDE agents, taking advantage of General Delgado's isolation as well as the dangerous conditions of exile and conspiratorial life, had infiltrated his circle of supporters and Delgado ended up by unknowingly conspiring with them. At a meeting held in Paris in December 1964, he was lured to a supposed secret conference with fellow conspirators from Portugal to take place near the Spanish border town of Badajoz on 13 February 1965. Later investigations proved beyond doubt that the PIDE directorate had planned to kidnap him and his secretary in Spain and bring him to Portugal where he had already been sentenced *in absentia.* Instead Delgado and his secretary were shot by one of the agents, Casimiro Monteiro, a Goanese whose background suggests he might have been a hired professional assassin. Their bodies were found two and a half months later, on 27 April, in a shallow grave at Villa Nueva del Fresno, near the Spanish-Portuguese border. It remains unclear whether Delgado was murdered because the PIDE agents could not subdue him, or because there had been a double plot whereby, without the acknowledgement of other officials, only Monteiro had been secretly instructed to liquidate Delgado on the spot.

The 'overseas provinces'

While these comparatively irrelevant domestic events were taking place, Salazar was more absorbed with new, complex questions of foreign policy and the survival of the empire.

On one hand he had already succeeded in turning the colonies into rewarding propositions. He had nationalized the port and railways of Beira, which served the vast hinterland comprising Southern Rhodesia, Northern Rhodesia, Nyasaland and Katanga, and gave Portugal a useful share in the profits from handling the exports of rich commodities such as copper, lead and tobacco – in fact, nearly 80 per cent of the sea-borne traffic of this rich, land-locked zone. He had interested Portuguese capitalists in new ventures which combined nicely with Portugal's economic interests. The production of raw materials (such as cotton, essential for the development of Portugal's only viable major industry – textiles – and sisal, which had been in great demand during the Korean war) were earning good rewards. Portugal was now getting all its supplies of foodstuffs – sugar, coffee, tea – from Angola and Mozambique, while being able to step up colonial exports to a host of hard-currency countries. The escudo was becoming one of the world's strongest currencies, thanks to the systematic exploitation of the colonies.

TAP, the national airline, had been expanded and sea routes improved with the extensive programme for the renewal of Portugal's merchant fleet which, because of its virtual monopoly of shipping between the empire and Portugal, was an extremely profitable proposition.

Moreover Salazar's long rule had coincided with a period of vast scientific and technological development throughout the world, and tropical Africa, with the advent of effective means of combating malaria, was now more propitious for white settlement. The white populations of Angola and Mozambique had doubled since systematic colonization had begun towards the end of the nineteenth century, and by 1950 had reached levels comparable with territories such as Kenya, Northern Rhodesia, Southern Rhodesia, the Ivory Coast and the Belgian Congo, of a similar scale and administrative character.

Not content with these beginnings, which escaped the attention of most people in Portugal but were very noticeable in the overseas territories and certain foreign circles abroad, Salazar was personally studying a series of six-year development plans for the combined development of Portugal and the overseas territories. These included settlement schemes in both Angola and Mozambique which would stave off the need for agrarian reform in Portugal, and new railways, dams and airports, which would create new jobs for a considerable number of technicians and public servants, as well as widening the opportunities available for many families of middle-class settlers.

The trouble with such long-term schemes, however, was that

they ran against the new trend in world politics which was beyond Portuguese control. Although internally Portugal and the empire were firmly under the control of the police and the military–civilian administration, Portugal was confronted with increasing problems in foreign policy. India was stepping up its demands for negotiations over Goa; the British, the French, the Belgians and the Dutch were all under pressure in their colonies and faced with an irresistible movement towards decolonization. Red China was emerging as a potential revolutionary threat of decisive importance for the future of the world. In Korea the combined might of UNO-sponsored Western forces could go no further than accept a truce; in Indochina France was fighting a losing war. The only comfort Salazar could take was from the contact he had with frequent visitors from foreign governments, and information gleaned by Portuguese diplomats in Britain, the United States and elsewhere.

Despite the fact that he never visited those countries, he had long grasped that despite widespread delusions of democracy and progressive trappings, the biggest Western nations were firmly in the hands of conservative establishments. Embarrassing questions might be raised in the American Senate or the British Parliament, but those who had the finger on the trigger and the control of strategic policy were the extreme right-wing and nationalist sectors of the establishment. This was particularly true of external affairs, for no matter which of the two main parties was in power the difference in foreign policy was hardly noticeable. Even after the war, when the British Labour Party formed a government which pursued radical policies at home, Foreign Minister Ernest Bevin, a close friend of the then Portuguese Ambassador, the Duke of Palmela, was a source of much comfort to Salazar. The British Ambassador in Lisbon, Sir Nigel Ronald, captured the tone of Anglo-Portuguese postwar relations in a comment that is as revealing of Salazar's considerate manners as of Ronald's own character as a British diplomat:

In this shy, lonely bachelor there was a marked streak of kindliness ... One day I had to see him on business at the little seaside fort, converted into a convent school, which he liked to occupy

205

during the school holidays. In the passage there was the finest Scarborough lily I had ever seen. I asked him where he got it. When I got back to the embassy the lily was there waiting for me. Its descendants are with me [in England – 1971] and about to flower.[1]

The United States had by then inherited the cloak of British international influence and was a new, important factor in Portuguese foreign policy. But with the Americans, if anything, Salazar felt even more at ease. As far back as 1946, George Kennan, a former United States representative in Portugal and widely reputed as an influential theorist of the Cold War, had stated that 'the United States of America undertakes to respect Portuguese sovereignty in all Portuguese colonies'.[2]

By all accounts Salazar had a great knowledge of men. Now he needed as many diplomatic fools as he could find to overcome the next hurdle in Portuguese foreign policy: admission to the United Nations, from which Portugal was still banned by the opposition of the Soviet Union and the Communist bloc, as well as those Western European nations more directly victimized by Hitler during the war. Nehru's India, however, was anxious for Portugal's admission in the hope that Salazar would be cornered by the international legal implications of holding on to 'non-self-governing territories'. The least that could happen was that Portugal might be forced to send regular reports to the United Nations and be internationally answerable for conditions in the territories and measures taken for their eventual independence.

There followed another constitutional expedient, the success of which only the obscurity of Portugal and the 'cover' provided by Western diplomacy can explain. By an amendment introduced in 1951, the 'colonial empire' underwent a thorough verbal 'revolution' whereby all colonies were regarded as overseas 'provinces' of a single country. The words 'empire' and 'colonies' suddenly disappeared, which was no small task since they were printed on millions of items of stationery, coins and

1. *Listener*, 27 August 1971.
2. Department of State Bulletin 1082 (1946); see also William Minter, *Portuguese Africa and the West* (Penguin, 1972).

notes, government institutions, trade marks and names of private concerns. Moreover, the background of the constitutional manipulation unmasked one of the biggest blunders made by the wise men of the régime with their famous 'Colonial Act' of 1930. Briefly the constitutional position was this:

In common with a long Latin tradition, initiated by the Romans and followed by both the Spaniards in their Latin American empire and later the French in some of their colonies, including Algeria, the Portuguese constitution of 1820 and Constitutional Charter of 1826 had effectively used the term 'provinces' to describe the overseas possessions.

In 1910, however, with the republican revolution and the promulgation of a new constitution, the territories were named 'colonies' to emphasize the transient nature of Portuguese rule. In other words, Portugal had adhered to the then internationally held view that colonization would eventually lead to self-government after the colonial powers had discharged themselves of the 'white man's burden' and the colonies of their riches. But in 1930 the Salazar régime saw no need to revert to the old style of 'provinces', and used the term 'colonies', 'colonial' and 'empire' in all appropriate places. However, in 1951, when Portugal was applying for admission to the UN, this caused some embarrassment and the régime had no one but itself to blame. Probably, in a democratic and parliamentarian country this blunder would have brought about a reckoning and a change of government – but not in Portugal. The Corporative Chamber and the National Assembly duly approved the new constitutional amendment without anyone in Portugal being able to expose its implications. The few foreign diplomatic and press observers accredited to Portugal – all of them of course from the West – either did not see or did not want to probe too closely.

Obviously the 1951 constitutional reform was a regression from the point of view of the status of the territories. It was tantamount to a permanent territorial annexation by unilateral decree without any consultation with the populations involved.

Portugal: fifty years of dictatorship

The United States, determined to provide cover for Portugal, sanctioned the principle. In 1955, one year before Portugal was to be admitted to the United Nations, Secretary of State Foster Dulles pointedly referred to Goa as an 'overseas province of Portugal'. After protests from India, he was to repeat the substance of the statement upon being questioned at a press conference in December 1955. His answers proved him either ignorant or plain dishonest:

Q. Does this government regard Goa as a Portuguese province?
A. As far as I know, all the world regards it as a Portuguese province. It has been Portuguese, I think, for about 400 years.
Q. Mr Secretary, did you say 'province' or 'colony'?
A. Province.[1]

In the following year, 1956, after much bargaining between the Soviet and the Western blocs over the admission of some questionable prospective members, Portugal was admitted to the United Nations. The UNO's Secretary General promptly reminded Portugal of the need to report on 'non-self-governing territories'. But Portugal was by now sufficiently covered by legalistic forms and by its powerful Western friends to be able to resist any pressures by India, the Soviet bloc and other members hostile to Portuguese colonialism. Inside Portugal and the 'overseas provinces', perhaps to hide its feelings of guilt and embarrassment, the government was to strengthen its repressive legislation to such a point that criticism of the overseas administration, or any mild questioning over the continuity of Portuguese rule, were regarded as an attempt to undermine national integrity and security and, as such, tantamount to treason. In fact, when Prof. Rui Luiz Gomes, the former 'ineligible' democratic presidential candidate, dared to question the anachronistic oddity of clinging to 1,542 square miles of separated enclaves in Goa (south of Bombay), and Damão and Diu (north of Bombay), together inhabited by 700,000 people, at a time when the more powerful British had just ended their rule over the remaining 1,143,267 square miles and its 400,000,000 people, he was quietly forced out of the country into exile in

1. Minter, op. cit., p. 49.

208

Brazil. His lonely word of advice was to be dramatically confirmed when only a few years later, in December 1961, India expelled the Portuguese army and civilian administration in a military operation that lasted less than twenty-four hours.

Meanwhile, there were outbreaks of rebellion in Portugal's African 'provinces' which already contained the seeds of later liberation movements. There had been an attempted uprising in São Tome in 1953. More recently there were insurrections at Pidgiguiti in Guinea-Bissau in 1959, and Mueda in Northern Mozambique in 1960. The episode of the capture of the *Santa Maria*, temporarily renamed the *Santa Liberdade,* by the Portuguese group centred around Delgado and Galvão also had important repercussions in Angola. Galvão was well known for his former association with the colonial administration, and when a number of foreign journalists converged on Luanda in Angola in the expectation that the captured liner would arrive there, MPLA supporters from the city's *musseques* (hill slums) attacked the main prison of São Paulo de Luanda at dawn on 4 February 1961. This first major explosion of African nationalism in Angola after nearly four decades of repression by the 'Estado Novo' came as a shock to the local settler population, who were already looking apprehensively at events in neighbouring Congo-Léopoldville which had become independent the year before.

The uprising was curbed within a matter of weeks by the local authorities, who ruthlessly eliminated all visible traces of resistance to Portuguese rule. However, on 15 March 1961 Angola was shaken by the news that groups of armed Africans, apparently coming from Congo-Léopoldville, had attacked several farms, plantations and administrative posts, leaving hundreds of settlers – men, women and children – slaughtered in their wake.

The Portuguese reaction was instinctively brutal. Despite the fact that at the time military forces in the whole of Angola totalled only 3,000 men, or one soldier for every 500 square miles, the Portuguese civilian population was sufficiently superior in technological resources and mobility to improvise their own defence. Once the spark of racial hatred had caught light, the

209

settlers waged a genocidal war. The history of this tragic episode will never be accurately written; estimates of the dead vary from 20,000 to 60,000. Incalculable misery was inflicted upon over 200,000 Africans who fled to the Congo, many dying on the way from exhaustion, disease and starvation. Eye-witness accounts allow one to conclude that this was one of the greatest tragedies in Portuguese colonial history.

The uprising, however, left many questions about security unanswered. Thousands of Africans belonging to a group called the UPA (União das Populaçoes de Angola), led by Holden Roberto, had been able to organize a fairly large-scale attack from just across the border in the Congo, apparently with help and training from the Congolese army, yet the authorities had been taken completely by surprise. The extensive northern frontiers had only an average of one soldier for every $2\frac{1}{2}$ miles.

As if to confirm that the régime was aware of the danger, the government suddenly announced in Lisbon that it had dismissed the Minister of Defence, General Botelho Moniz, with Salazar himself taking over the Ministry for the period of emergency. It turned out that Botelho Moniz had been among a group of senior officers, which included the then Colonel Costa Gomes,[1] who held the view that there would be 'no military solution' in the colonies in the event of widespread guerrilla wars in areas many times the size of Portugal itself.

The existence of this group was discovered, and Salazar once again managed to outsmart the main conspirators who wanted to force him into retirement. While Botelho Moniz was detained and others removed from their positions, Salazar himself, perhaps to suggest that he had no direct responsibility for the lack of military provision in Angola, made a speech on TV, announcing the 'nation's determination' to remain in Africa to 'defend Western and Christian civilization'. With an accumulated gold reserve of over £300m., a new fleet of modern ocean liners and growing numbers of military and air transports, Portugal was able to rely on its own resources to transfer over 50,000 troops to Angola in a few weeks.

1. Later President of the Republic.

This ability to cope with the situation was seen by many of the régime's supporters as further confirmation that Salazar's long-term policies of national survival, based on economic recovery and empire-building, were now bearing fruit. Salazar himself took to emphasizing that Portugal could stand 'proudly alone' in its fight against the trends of history.

This xenophobic attitude was reinforced by the deterioration of relations with the US. With the election of President Kennedy, Salazar became more distrustful than ever of American policies. He had been brought up within living memory of US expansion in Spanish America in the second half of the nineteenth century, and he believed that American liberalism in Africa was merely a tactic for furthering American interests at the expense of those of Europe. He began to increase pressure on the US base in the Azores, refusing to grant more than short-term extensions of the original agreement. With the encouragement of the PIDE, the Portuguese press carried a lot of anti-American copy; there were even demonstrations of protest against the US in Lisbon, Luanda and Lourenço Marques.

But the overall impact of the uprising in Angola and the loss of Goa to India in 1961 was to force a dramatic change in both colonial and foreign policies. Showing the first signs of old age, fatigue and disappointment, Salazar began to surround himself with younger collaborators. He delegated unprecedented powers upon men such as Dr Franco Nogueira and Dr Adriano Moreira, respectively Foreign and Overseas Ministers. They were to deal with the national emergency and prepare for a new strategic and political situation in the colonies.

Both new ministers were men in their forties, brought up under the régime and by a notable coincidence, both had been fairly liberal in their young adulthood. Franco Nogueira was literary critic on the magazine *Vertice*; Adriano Moreira was a lawyer who had once been detained by the PIDE after acting as counsel in a criminal case against former Defence Minister Santos Costa.

Although, because of his secluded life, Salazar might not have fully grasped the implications of the internationalization of Portuguese colonial issues at the UNO and elsewhere, he had, nevertheless, had long experience of fluctuations in the political climate. He had lived through the First World War, the period of the League of Nations, the Spanish Civil War, the Second World War and the Cold War, and had survived many international and internal threats and pressures. At any rate, he was capable of making quick political adjustments. Although for decades he had presented himself as a 'man of peace', he was now warning that the wars in Africa might become a permanent feature of Portuguese life. And although he had pursued a xenophobic policy of national-capitalism, he suddenly became receptive to the need for foreign capital and involvement in the empire. The role of Portugal as a bastion of 'Western civilization' and loyal member of NATO was emphasized in all official statements. Portugal was to embark upon a new phase of 'imperialism on credit'.

Franco Nogueira saw that whether the Western powers acted in concert, or whether their actions were prompted by their individual interests, they would eventually rally behind Portugal. Britain had explicit economic and strategic reasons for preferring Portugal's presence in Angola and Mozambique to seeing her replaced by less predictable and really independent-minded African governments. France and West Germany harboured the suspicion that the success of African nationalism might only result in consolidating Anglo-American hegemony in the area, without significant advantage to French and West German interests.

Therefore, while through its NATO and EFTA links Portugal was able to obtain extensive British economic support, the régime also began to look for closer ties with West Germany and France. The resumption of good German–Portuguese relations was made easier by the fact that Salazar, in a gesture of loyal respect to his former friends, had not confiscated German assets in Portugal in 1945. Moreover, with Germany outside the UN, there was little risk of inconvenient criticism from her. In 1963 an agreement was concluded with the West German government for a German Air Force training base to be established in Beja, Portugal. In exchange, West Germany supplied loans and credits, facilities for specialized medical assistance in

Germany for Portuguese soldiers seriously mutilated in the African wars, and provided arms, aircraft and technical training.

France acquired its own air base at Flores, in the Azores, to operate as a tracking station for French missiles. De Gaulle was pursuing the idea of a 'Euro-Africa' as a means of opposing American expansionism at the expense of European interests, and so France was to become one of the main sources of support and practical assistance to Portugal. Moreover, at a time when an oil boycott of South Africa was being suggested in many quarters, France was expanding its trading interests, including the marketing of oil, in the area, and French industrialists began to pay increasing attention to the surveying of possible oil and mineral resources in Angola and Mozambique. French ship-yards built eight frigates and submarines for Portugal, while aircraft factories supplied planes and most of the helicopters for the Portuguese Air Force.

At the same time, Adriano Moreira, who had been for many years a leading professor on colonial administration, introduced extensive reforms in the colonies which were consistent with the need to meet international pressures, including those of Port-ugal's NATO allies. In September 1961 the régime repealed its Native Statute of 1954 and granted equal rights of citizenship to Africans, including the right to vote subject to educational or property qualifications essentially similar to those obtaining in Portugal. A new Code of Rural Labour, likewise hurriedly in-troduced in 1961, was also, by its wording, clearly designed to confuse the international critics of Portuguese rule. It author-ized equality of pay for equal work, irrespective of race or sex, freedom of choice of work and the prohibition to labour re-cruitment through the intervention of administrative officials. Another decree, revoking all previous legislation governing the compulsory cultivation of cotton, set heavy penalties for co-ercion and other abuses by local administrative authorities and trading concessionaries.

Since at the time the implications of the internationalization of colonial issues were a far more immediate threat than internal opposition, these reforms were clearly introduced to harmonize with Franco Nogueira's new drive in foreign policy.

213

Adriano Moreira himself echoed Nogueira's views with the following comment:

We are living in an age when self-sufficiency is no longer possible, since no country is capable of maintaining itself in splendid isolation and no people can manage to survive without the aid of reliable allies. To establish a set of national values depending exclusively on one's own human and material resources is a challenge to history, often attempted in the past, but which will never be practicable again ... There is no chance of finding any but a collective solution for the major problems facing the countries within the area covered by NATO. Not merely in the field of military security but also in that of the economy, it has become manifest that solutions not based in international cooperation are bound to end in failure.[1]

This new approach did have an immediately beneficial effect on the Portuguese economy. Foreign currency was made available in the form of loans and other aid from NATO countries, and this, together with the temporary decline in the activities of the UPA in Angola, ensured the restoration of the value of the escudo on the world money market after its decline in the wake of the disturbances of 1961.

But in the meanwhile, the African nationalist movements were regrouping in preparation for more systematic and concerted attacks on colonial rule. Dr Agostinho Neto had escaped from detention in Portugal with the help of the Portuguese democratic opposition, and was now in the Congo-Léopoldville reorganizing the MPLA; Amilcar Cabral was preparing the PAIGC for the launching of a guerrilla war in Guinea-Bissau in 1963; and Eduardo Mondlane had assumed command of Frelimo, which was to begin guerrilla attacks in Mozambique in 1964. In order to meet these threats, Portuguese military expenditure rose astronomically – to nearly 40 per cent of the entire budget by 1963; the national debt had jumped between 1960 and 1963 from 1.9 billion escudos to 6.3 billion.

In order to overcome scepticism and despondency, the régime announced a series of projects designed to instil a sense of purpose and achievement for Portugal's role in Africa. Some of

1. Adriano Moreira, *The Extent of Europe* (Agencia Geral do Ultramar, Lisbon, 1962).

these new schemes had in fact more of a psychological than tangible effect. Plans to set up a Portuguese Escudo Free Trade Area were expedited, and on 1 January 1964 all customs duties on imports from the 'overseas provinces' were abolished – while, on the other hand, a 'consumer tax' on overseas imports was introduced. But other schemes, although at first announced in propagandistic terms, had wider economic and political implications. Among these were two large-scale dams and land-settlement schemes, to be built at Cabora Bassa, near Tete, Mozambique, and the basin of the river Cunene in Southern Angola, which together would allow for the settlement of $1\frac{1}{2}$ million Portuguese in Mozambique and Angola.

In order to meet both the commitments and loans already contracted and the increased expenditure that was needed for defence, Salazar had to swallow his pride and abandon his policy of excluding foreign investments. This dramatic reversal came in the form of Decree No. 46412, which by coincidence was published on his seventy-sixth birthday, on 28 April 1965. It guaranteed foreign investors the free transfer of interest, dividends and capital gains obtained with 'lawfully imported capital', as well as the right of complete repatriation of such capital. Portuguese banks, departing from their rather conservative traditions, began to campaign for foreign capital, and adopted a style resembling that of enterprising travel agencies. One of their brochures on investment opportunities in Portugal provides a list of 'features of attraction':

1. Fairly low wages and cost of living, and abundant disciplined and adaptable labour capable of attaining the same standards of productivity as in the industrial countries of Europe. This fact has permitted industries such as clothing, electronics and textiles to compete favourably with countries and territories such as Singapore, Formosa and South Korea.
2. Professionally trained personnel – engineers, chemists, agronomists, architects, economists, etc. – and managers of European standard who are not normally to be found with the same facility and level of training in countries in the process of development.
3. Special treatment within EFTA which accords to Portuguese industrial goods duty-free access to a market of over 100 million

215

consumers with a high purchasing power whilst, at the same time, the home market benefits from protection until 1980.

4. A fairly satisfactory infrastructure and network of inter-industrial relations able to offer important external economies to firms.

5. The most favourable tax system in Europe for private enterprise, whereby taxation of profits, including all local taxes, does not exceed 38 per cent of actual profits.

The invasion of the 'overseas provinces' by foreign capital involved the South African government and South African-based concerns, such as the Anglo-American Corporation, in projects ranging from both the Cabora Bassa and the Cunene dams to oil and mineral prospecting, together with inerests in various other ventures; the Americans in Cabinda Gulf oil; the Germans and Japanese in Angolan iron ore. A host of other non-Portuguese concerns, including British banks, carried the internationalization of Portuguese colonialism to the point of actually entering into partnership with Portuguese companies. In many cases, as in the exploitation of oil, it was a 50–50 association with the government, but in others Portugal contented itself with a smaller share in the form of profit taxes, concession rights and royalties, export taxes, payment for local labour and materials and all the fringe benefits that go with business activity where previously there existed stagnation.

In fact, when measured in terms of expansion in exports and budgetary revenue, and particularly when taken in the context of the economies of African countries (which often declined after independence), the development of Angola and Mozambique in the first decade of guerrilla warfare is little short of spectacular. The investing countries were attracted by the fact that the Portuguese, hard pressed for money and support, could offer better terms than any other rulers who might more legitimately come to govern these territories; and the political support given by the NATO powers to Portuguese rule greatly encouraged this drive for profits. For their part, the Portuguese official and business *élite*, negotiating over what was after all other people's property, could only find the régime's new policy of 'imperialism on credit' a rewarding proposition.

Chapter 10
The collapse

> *'The system that oppresses and exploits*
> *the peasant in Portugal is also the system*
> *that oppresses and exploits the Angolan,*
> *with different motives, different methods,*
> *but always with the same purpose –*
> *exploitation. And between the Portuguese,*
> *the Angolans, the Mozambicans and the*
> *Guineans it is possible to establish just*
> *relationships, relationships which will*
> *prevent the exploitation of man by man.*
> *The racial factor will play only a minor*
> *role and will last only a little longer, once*
> *the relationship between master and slave*
> *is brought to an end'* – AGOSTINHO NETO[1]

SALAZAR ruled Portugal for nearly forty years, yet the circumstances of his disappearance from the political scene were anticlimactic to the point of absurdity. On 6 September 1968, as he was enjoying a normal day at his seaside residence in Estoril, he fell from a deck-chair and developed a cerebral stroke. After a series of operations, on the advice of American neurosurgeons flown in by courtesy of the State Department he was declared incapacitated.

Opponents and apologists alike generally expected that there would be a major upheaval leading to the downfall of the régime, since it appeared so dependent on Salazar's personal ability to preserve a balance between the various groups within the power *élite*. Moreover, Salazar had made no provision for a successor, leaving the future of Portugal dangerously uncertain. One possibility was a return to overt military dictatorship, as during the first phase of the régime in 1926. Brazil had taken this road in 1964 and Greece in 1967, and they seemed to presage a renewed international trend towards this kind of Fascism.

1. 'Quem e o inimigo ?', text of a lecture given at Dar es Salaam University on 2 February 1974, edited by 'Maria da Fonte' (Lisbon, 1974).

Another option was the restoration of the monarchy, a system admittedly not very popular since its overthrow in 1910 but one which nevertheless had a residual core of supporters within the régime. As in Spain, there was a pretender already living in the country, so that a move towards monarchism could not be ruled out.

But as it happened, the succession crisis was resolved with a minimum of dislocation. Salazar was left for the last twenty months of his life to fade away undisturbed in his official residence, nursed by socialites and devout ladies under the supervision of Portuguese doctors who were not even supporters of the régime. He was granted the honours of his position 'for life' on 26 September, when it was clear that he was beyond recovery. At the same time the President called upon Professor Marcello Caetano to become Acting Prime Minister.

Salazar rapidly began to fade from the nation's memory. There is an element of tragic justice in the fact that in this last period of physical incapacity and mental alienation, Salazar was made to live in an officially contrived make-believe world. The titular President of the Republic, Admiral Thomaz, who had always looked up to Salazar as if he were his protecting master, engaged in a pious conspiracy with some of the dictator's closest collaborators and Ministers to shield him from the news that he been replaced by none other than his one-time protégé Marcello Caetano. In a press interview given to a French journalist, the first and last since his incapacity, Salazar referred to Caetano as being out of politics, so totally unaware was he of what was going on.

By all accounts, until the end, Salazar was spared from the shock of reality. Even at that late stage, his life-long 'housekeeper' Dona Maria de Jesus, was trying to persuade him to 'retire' on account of his advanced age and poor health. But each time Salazar would reply that 'he could not go, as there was no one else'.

Salazar died in July 1970. There is a story that some weeks previously he had married Dona Maria; but if he had, it was of little use to her. For a while she was allowed to mourn her late master, but then she was abruptly given a few hours to pack her modest effects and leave the palace. Apparently the man she had so reverently addressed as '*Senhor Doutor*' and faithfully served since his student days had been so lacking in normal feelings of affection and gratitude, or so detached from practical reality, that he had failed to make any provision for the only dependant who was to survive him. It seems also that, through superstition or lack of concern, Salazar had left no will.[1]

The circumstances which brought Caetano to power were strikingly similar to those surrounding Salazar's own early career in the late twenties. Like Salazar, Caetano was a professor invited to step into the government as a saviour who could resolve the tensions within the ruling clique. Like Salazar, too, Caetano was a man with an impeccable sense of timing. He had in fact resigned from the government seven years previously after disagreements with Salazar, and had been waiting patiently for the call ever since. As far back as 1959, he was predicting the shape of things to come:

> Unpleasant as the prospect may be, it is inevitable: Salazar is not immortal ... The continuation of the Estado Novo will not be a problem precisely because we have his doctrine and his work, which have laid the basis for our system and have educated an entire generation. And in the day – which, may God permit, is far off – on which His designs demand that another man take Salazar's place, I hold the firm hope that the Estado Novo will remain easily on its planned course, provided that Portuguese nationalists, faithful to the invaluable guidance provided by so many years of intelligent government, prove themselves capable, in those inevitably critical hours, of practising three personal and political virtues: unity, serenity and common sense![1]

In style and temperament, though, Salazar and Caetano were very different men; and this is largely attributable to the contrasts in their upbringing. Unlike Salazar, Caetano was a product of the urban middle class, the son of a senior customs official. Born in Lisbon in 1906, he was, therefore, some

1. *The Times*, 22 August 1970.
2. Marcello Caetano, *Paginas inoportunas* (Lisbon, 1959), pp. 169, 184.

seventeen years younger than Salazar – a fact that had a crucial importance in his political calculations in later years.

He had been a militant Fascist since his student days and editor of the extreme-right-wing magazine *Ordem Nova*. In 1931, when Salazar was Finance Minister and beginning to assert his position as the custodian of Fascism in Portugal, Caetano graduated as a lawyer. His first relevant service to the régime was assistance in the drafting of many of the constitutional laws which laid the foundations of the 'Estado Nova'. In 1933, the year that Salazar finally consolidated his position as Prime Minister, Caetano, then twenty-seven, was appointed Professor of Law at Lisbon University.

Caetano held a succession of posts and positions, ranging from commissioner for the 'Portuguese Youth Movement' to Minister for the Colonies. During his first official visit to South Africa in 1945 he was received by President Smuts, and welcomed by aspiring young Afrikaner politicians such as Malan, Strydom, Verwoerd and Vorster. In 1954, he wrote in one of his many books dealing with constitutional and colonial issues: 'The natives of Africa must be directed and organized by Europeans but are indispensable as auxiliaries ... The Africans did not yield any useful inventions or any technological advancements and did not make any meaningful contributions to the evolution of mankind ... Therefore, the Blacks in Africa must be seen as productive elements organized, or to be organized, in an economy directed by Whites.'[1] His signature as a member of the Cabinet was attached to most of the régime's repressive legislation.

Caetano was a family man who had often travelled abroad, and he had earned himself a reputation for pragmatism and a flexibility of approach. Though he began his political career somewhat to the right of Salazar, he evolved into what was variously described as 'liberal Fascism' and 'forward-looking traditionalism', and resembled the type of conservative one finds in positions of power in the United States, West Germany, Britain, France and other countries of the West. He had undoubtedly long cherished ambitions to command and 'serve the

1. Marcello Caetano, in *Os Nativos na economia africana* (Lisbon, 1954).

nation' at the highest level. In a book devoted to discussing the qualities required of leaders, *A Missao dos dirigentes*, he emphasized that 'there is a scarcity . . . of people with the ability to lead and command . . . To command is not a freedom – it is a form of slavery.'[1]

Since 1947, according to his own testimony in *Paginas inoportunas*, Caetano had hoped that Salazar could be persuaded to step up to the Presidency of the Republic, leaving the Prime Minister's office vacant for that rare man, presumably himself, whose executive abilities could measure up to the task. But in this hope he was finally frustrated in 1958, when the departing President was replaced as National Union candidate, not by Salazar, but by a minor figure, Admiral Americo Thomaz. This meant that for the next seven years at least there would be little chance for Caetano to succeed Salazar as Prime Minister. Disagreements between the two men came to a head soon after the elections, and Caetano resigned as Minister for the Presidency. In January 1959 he chose to return to academic life, and took up the Rectorship of Lisbon University while he awaited a more favourable turn of events.

The cherished opportunity nearly came in 1961, when a group of dissident generals including the Minister of Defence, General Botelho Moniz, attempted a *coup* with the limited aim of forcing the resignation of Salazar; but this came to nothing. In 1962, a year of intense political unrest, with strikes, demonstrations and student actions, Caetano decided to take an open stand against the government. He wrote an article in the monarchist-Catholic newspaper *A Voz* – where, ironically, Salazar had made his name in the 1920s – criticizing the restrictions imposed on the autonomy of universities by new laws introduced by the régime. Then, while retaining the position of life member of the Council of State, Caetano pointedly resigned from the executive board of the National Union. And soon afterwards, as the police invaded Lisbon university to curb a student demonstration, he resigned from his position as Rector.

1. Marcello Caetano, *A Missao dos dirigentes*, quoted in *O Tempo e modo* (Lisbon, 1968), Nos. 62–3.

Some observers commented at the time that, far from being prompted by liberal feelings of outrage, Caetano was merely resentful of the fact that he had not been consulted by the authorities beforehand. Others suspected that, always a practical man with a wife and children used to a high standard of living, he had merely been looking around for a suitable opportunity to resume his lucrative career as a legal consultant. Either way, he was young enough to bide his time.

As it turned out, Caetano had only seven years to wait to prove his assertion that Salazar, at least politically, was not immortal. When the succession crisis came up in 1968, Caetano had the backing of most of the key figures in the régime, with the exception of a few disgruntled Ministers and former Ministers who harboured their own ambitions, and a few generals who regarded him as too liberal and unpredictable. By and large, his temporary disengagement from the régime stood him in good stead, since the bulk of the middle class, whether in favour of the *status quo* (the *situacionistas*) or opponents of Salazar (the *oposicionistas*), found it possible to look towards Caetano for leadership.

His first speeches as Prime Minister were well calculated to soothe the nerves of the oligarchy and the middle class. Of Salazar's disappearance, he said: 'Life must go on. Men of genius turn up sporadically, sometimes with an interval of centuries ... The country has been accustomed for a long time to being governed by a man of genius; from today it will have to adapt itself to being governed by common men.' He certainly did not look like a 'rich man's steward' illuminated by some high and long-term vision, but had the demeanour of a relaxed company director. Adopting old international slogans which were nevertheless somewhat new for Portugal, Caetano, paraphrasing de Gaulle, stated that he was 'neither left nor right – but for the country'. And, following the old pattern set by Roosevelt and democratically elected leaders in other countries, he started a series of regular and seemingly informal *Conversas de Família* (Family Chats) on the Government-controlled TV channel.

He was really trying, successfully to some degree, to please everyone, centre, right and left – in that order. He did not upset the 'ultra-Salazarists' with dramatic changes and, at first, only replaced a few Ministers; but even those that remained, like the young Minister of the Interior Gonçalves Rapazote, whose functions were to supervise the PIDE and the apparatus of repression, adopted a more liberal posture, promising a 'political spring'. Caetano had a consoling word even for those whom he was dismissing after many years of dedicated service to his predecessor. Upon accepting the formal resignation of Franco Nogueira, the star Foreign Minister under Salazar, he commented that this well-known 'ultra' was only 'transferring to a new trench' in the national battle, an unwittingly ironic remark in view of the fact that Nogueira had just joined the board of directors of several private companies, including the British-owned Benguela Railways Co., of Angola. It also transpired at the time that Caetano had given 'guarantees to the army' in exchange for their support against eventual pressures from the extreme right.

He took immediate steps to ensure that some of the most striking injustices inherited from his unforgiving predecessor were corrected. Some prominent exiles, notably the Bishop of Oporto, Antonio Ferreira Gomes – who had been prevented from re-entering Portugal after a visit to Rome in the aftermath of the 1958 elections contested by Delgado – were discreetly allowed to return; others returned on their own initiative, but were not unduly disturbed by the state police. And although, according to reports appearing in the press, the redoubtable Salazar had begun to regain consciousness, Caetano (probably after seeking further medical advice) went ahead with even more spectacular decisions. He ordered that a deportation order which had kept Mario Soares, a Lisbon lawyer and a leading opponent of the régime, in the tropical islands of São Tome for nearly a year, be rescinded. Soares, the son of a former Republican Minister, had been active in politics since his student days. In 1949 he had been a secretary of the Board supporting General Norton de Matos's Presidential campaign; subsequently, when democratic groups had again been driven underground, he became the leader of the youth wing of DUM

(Democratic Unity Movement) which influenced a generation of leading opponents of the régime. His activities had earned him the honourable record of twelve arrests before he was forty. He had incurred Salazar's displeasure once too often by the time he became lawyer to General Delgado's family: when Delgado was assassinated, he tried to press for the arrest of the PIDE officials named in the Spanish judicial inquiry. In the 1965 National Assembly elections he had once again been among the most active opposition leaders. In December 1967, accused of responsibility for leaking to the foreign press a scandal involving the sexual corruption of minors by members of the government, bankers and other pillars of the establishment, Soares was summarily deported to São Tome by order of Salazar. He had been living there for some ten months, and was facing an uncertain future, when Salazar was taken ill. Observers believed that Caetano, embarrassed by the glaring injustice done to Soares, wanted to have the problem out of the way. In a major speech scheduled for the re-opening of the National Assembly in November 1969, Caetano was to reaffirm his desire for national reconciliation. Soares, however, was something short of tactful. On arrival back from exile he remarked to a reporter from a Lisbon newspaper:

More important than words would be institutional changes that could give substance to the good intentions that are being professed. As for changes to ensure a return to normal participation by all citizens in the political life of the country, without depending on favours from the régime, we must admit that nothing relevant is happening at the moment. We have passed the stage of accepting promises and concessions.

The first real test of Caetano's government came in the National Assembly elections in the autumn of 1969. No changes were made in the rather selective voters' roll, which included less than 1·5 million people out of a total population in Portugal and the 'overseas provinces' of more than 22 million; and the pattern of the election was in other respects the same as under Salazar. There were token gestures: on the government slate there appeared a handful of 'liberal' candidates, such as Sa Carneiro, Miller Guerra and F. Balsemão, though even these men subsequently resigned from the National Assembly in protest at the new Government's obduracy. The 'opposition' was harassed in much the same way as in the past, and in various districts of Portugal, Mozambique and Angola it was not represented at all. One way and another, Caetano managed to get the results he wanted.

Change was slow in coming, but in some significant ways changes there were. For example, the Church was already planning the retirement of Cardinal Gonçalves Cerejeira, the life-long friend of Salazar, with the intention of replacing him with Dom Antonio Ribeiro, a man who could be expected to pursue a low-key policy. In this way the Church hoped that people might forget the role it had played in bolstering Salazar's régime at home and in the colonies.

Caetano himself took seriously the famous dictum of ruling classes in despair to the effect that if 'we want things to remain as they are, things will have to change'. In one of those periodical verbal revolutions in which Portuguese rulers have indulged through the ages, Caetano changed the names of institutions and introduced superficial reforms and social improvements, making many people inside and outside the country believe that if the Portuguese had not achieved a parliamentarian democracy, they had at least moved on to the stage of 'Fascism with a human face'. The régime's single party, the National Union, became Popular National Action; the PIDE became the DGS (Directorate General of Security) – a title which, unimaginatively enough, brought it into line with that of Franco's police in Spain; the Propaganda Secretariat was renamed the Information and Tourist Office; the Censorship Board became the Previous Examination Board. In time the verbal revolution extended to the overseas territories, which were promoted from 'overseas provinces' to 'states', while local Legislative Councils became Legislative Assemblies. In an apt turn of phrase, Dr Almeida Santos, then a lawyer in Lourenço Marques and a life-long opponent of the régime, called these moves a 'signboard policy'.

But despite varying degrees of relaxation and repression in police methods and censorship criteria which reflected transient factors and pressures, no substantial reform was ever made. The whole situation can be summed up in the following announcement which appeared in a Lisbon newspaper:

> Previous examination: The new Press Statute, published on 4 May 1972, becomes law from today, 1 June. Establishing the rules of the new Press Law (5/71) of 5 November 1971, the Statute lays down the following: 'It is lawful for all citizens to use the Press in accordance with its social role and with respect to other people's rights, society's demands and moral principles.'
>
> There is an exception: the rule of previous examination. 'The publication of texts and images in the periodical press can be liable to previous examination in cases when a state of emergency or martial law have been decreed.'
>
> Given that we are presently in a 'state of emergency' (decreed by a resolution of 20 December last in view of the wars in Africa) the periodical press is therefore subject to previous examination. Thus, censorship, which until yesterday was the rule (requiring previous administrative permission for the publication of texts and images) is, as from today, the exception.[1]

Had Portugal been an island in the middle of nowhere, the régime might have succeeded in suspending the process of advance. But despite censorship, repression and passive acquiescence, the transition between the last years of Salazar's rule and the Caetano régime coincided with a period in which Portuguese life was undergoing a process of accelerated change. This reflected the impact of industrialization and involvement in modern international politics in Africa and elsewhere.

The wars in Africa, increasing the demand for better-educated soldiers and the introduction of such novelties as women nurses and auxiliaries in the armed forces, had become another factor compelling modernization. This process of change was visible mainly in Lisbon, Oporto and other large towns where Portuguese youth, despite censorship, was following the same patterns of thinking in matters of ideology and sex, in dress and hairstyle, as prevailed among their counterparts in the Western world. TV shows, pop groups and beauty contests, as much as

1. First page of the then 'previously examined' *Diario de Lisboa*, 1 June 1972.

226

rebel priests wanting to do away with celibacy vows and the dogmas about birth control, were part of the new scene.

In more significant ways, too, there was a genuine attempt to break with convention. The styles of personal treatment became less formal, with *'voce'* (you) replacing the old pompous *'v.exa.'* (your excellency), and professional men refusing to be addressed indiscriminately as *'doutor'* at social functions and middle-class parties. Domestic workers, traditionally known as *'criadas'* ('servants'), were re-named 'domestic employees', and benefited from a noticeable improvement in pay and working conditions. The popular *fado* song, too fatalistic and melancholy, and tending to embody the romantic, masochistic values of a society given to male domination and self-pity, was replaced by the more vigorous protest song. And while the famous Amalia Rodrigues, formerly the entertainer of the power *élite*, and other fashionable *fado* traditionalists catered for tourists, the home market formed by middle-class professionals and the more aware youth turned towards Zeca Afonso and other singers who protested against the inequities of war and class exploitation. Even in smaller towns there were ever more motor-cars, supermarkets, frozen food, TV sets, record players, as well as pollution, traffic jams, bank robberies, and all that goes with the modernization of life.

Moreover, whereas in the past it had been possible to keep identifiable enemies of the régime under control, the coming of age of generations brought up under dictatorship and born wise to police informers and functionaries of repression had made the task of the DGS increasingly difficult. Since the early sixties an underground political culture, predominantly revolutionary, had developed particularly amongst students and certain professions such as journalism, but also in public departments, company offices and factories. With well over three quarters of the population educated under the régime, most people had learned ways of exchanging views, information and illegal literature, or prompting debates at professional meetings and social gatherings without running too much risk.

The illegal Communist literature of the time was full of denunciations of social injustice, together with competent Marxist

227

analyses of Portugal's problems. A number of publishing 'cooperatives', formed by Communist, Socialist and progressive Catholic groups – such as Editora Norte, Pragma, Devir, Livrelco, Vis, Proelium, Eudoxio and Ateneu Cooperativo – produced valuable work before they were finally suppressed in 1972. Moreover, in order to keep within an 'optimum' balance of repression, the government allowed the holding of Republican and opposition congresses, such as those at the town of Aveiro in preparation for elections for the National Assembly in 1969 and 1973, and the many theses presented to these meetings provided a guideline for democratic thinking.

Reading this body of literature a picture emerges of a country which, despite the surface illusion of urban prosperity, was really heading towards bankruptcy. The policy of imperialism on credit had led to the mortgaging of the country's future to international banks in New York, London and elsewhere. The end of protectionist policies and restrictions on foreign capital had meant that, in Mozambique and Angola, the exploitation of large-scale resources in hydroelectric power, oil and iron ore had come into the control of United States, West German companies or international groups. Since this increased even further the disproportionate share of foreign capital in both territories, Portugal was rapidly assuming the role of a 'flag of convenience' for international interests.

At home, where the economy was dominated by a few large monopolist industrial and banking groups, such as CUF (Companhia União Fabril), Espirito Santo, Champalimaud, Portugues do Atlantico and Borges & Irmão, new Western European and American consortia, such as ITT, Timex, Ford Renault, Grundig, British Leyland, Plessey and Heinz had arrived to take advantage of low wages and repressive labour conditions. As a result of the open-door policy, most recent industrial developments had been undertaken by foreign companies, whose stake in Portuguese industry increased from only 1·5 per cent in 1960 to 27 per cent in 1970.[1]

While profits accrued to big international and Portuguese

1. Luiz Salgado Matos, *Investimentos estrangeiros em Portugal* (Seara Nova, Lisbon, 1973).

businesses and to the political and military ruling clique, the consequences of Portugal's colonial wars, in terms of social disruption and human suffering, were increasingly alarming. This is how an opponent of the régime, J. P. Silva, attending the Aveiro Congress in April 1973, summed up what he described as 'the tragic situation caused by the wars':

(1) Mobilization of Portuguese youth into one of the longest and most arduous military conscriptions in the world; (2) 10,000 dead; (3) 20,000 wounded and mutilated; (4) immeasurable psychological consequences; (5) heavy increase in taxation; (6) substantial rise in the cost of living; (7) loss of markets in countries opposed to colonialism; (8) piecemeal sale of the country to foreign enterprises; (9) reinforcement of the political power of certain economic groups which benefit from the continuation of the wars. The government's policy is thus anti-patriotic.[1]

In fact, in order to keep the edifice of the régime and the empire intact, half of the entire budget was absorbed by the armed forces and the security network, more than the combined total allocated for education, social assistance and the administration of justice. A similar picture emerged in the budgets of both Angola and Mozambique, territories which, owing to the centralized control of currency in Lisbon, were now accumulating debts to Portugal and rapidly heading towards financial insolvency.

In desperation, a number of urban guerrilla groups such as the LUAR, led by Palma Inacio, the Revolutionary Brigades sponsored from Algiers, and the ARA, said to be the 'direct-action' wing of the Communist Party, carried out a number of raids and acts of sabotage. But although their stand was of considerable psychological significance, they had a long way to go before they could become an effective 'fourth front' united in common struggle with the guerrilla armies of Africa.

The established opposition could do little of significance other than to protest against the policies of the government. However, they were working towards a realistic assessment of the political situation. At the 1973 Aveiro Congress at least two

1. Borga and Cardoso Rodrigues, *O Movimento dos capitães e o 25 de abril* (Moraes Editora, Lisbon, 1974), p. 215.

of the most prominent speakers recalled the role of the armed forces in bringing about and sustaining the Fascist régime. They pointed out that successive presidents had been generals, and denounced the role of senior officers heading the Censorship Boards, commanding the police, the Republican Guard and the Portuguese Legion as well as acting as directors and highly paid 'government delegates' in public and private companies. One of the speakers, Professor Armando Bacelar, concluded his address by pointing out that although the army was the mainstay of the régime, it would not be fair to accuse all officers of being Fascists and colonialists. He added that the armed forces were becoming increasingly aware of the deception into which they had fallen and that an appeal should be made to them to seek ways of intervening to restore democracy. It is known that some young captains revealed unprecedented curiosity about the stand taken at the Congress, particularly concerning the role of the army and colonial issues.[1]

Despite the fact that the manipulation of censorship and official propaganda minimized the effect of adverse news originating abroad, the mass of Portuguese was by now aware that Portugal was grouped with racialist South Africa and Rhodesia as one of the outcast countries at the UNO and elsewhere. The worldwide sensation provided by reports of massacres in Mozambique, which reached the headlines in mid-1973, also had moral repercussions in Portugal.

Moreover, the social and economic situation was now rapidly deteriorating. After Britain's desertion from EFTA into the EEC, Portugal was further isolated. The rate of inflation, at over 20 per cent, was one of the highest in Europe and even Mozambique and Angola, beset by overwhelming pressures in foreign currency earnings, could not be of much help. With a disproportionate amount of resources being spent in Guinea-Bissau, there were indications that certain capitalist circles in Portugal and in Western European countries were receptive to the idea of a neo-colonialist stripping of assets through selective decolonization. Coincidentally, the Arab oil boycott and an escalation in the cost of fuel, raw materials and foodstuffs, were

1. Borga and Cardoso Rodrigues, op. cit., p. 213.

further evidence of an irreversible trend towards a major crisis.

In the last months of 1973 rumours began to circulate that there was a 'Movement of Captains' afoot agitating against the régime, but only a small number of inveterate optimists within the ranks of the opposition placed much faith in their success. There were other contradictory rumours of plots and counter-plots, sometimes involving reputedly liberal generals such as Spinola and Costa Gomes, sometimes involving die-hard pillars of the régime such as Generals Kaulza de Arriaga, Alexandre Trony, Luz Cunha and others. Given the long habit of social self-segregation in the military class, they were all unknown quantities to most civilian professionals or to the mass of the population.

One event, however, brought home to everybody the debate going on within the armed forces. This was the publication of a book by General Antonio Spinola, *Portugal and the Future*, which demolished many of the régime's cherished myths about Portugal's colonialist role. Spinola had, however belatedly, come to recognize that a liberal solution for the African colonies was both morally valid and inevitable and expedient. He argued that Portugal was on a dangerous course of self-deception in claiming it possessed a divine mission to convert and 'integrate other peoples into Western civilization', or that it 'remained in Africa to defend the West'. He proposed a plan (similar to that of General Delgado ten years before) for a federation of self-governing states instead of a 'single nation' made up of far-flung overseas provinces subject to centralized government in Lisbon. In the prevailing climate, the book had explosive consequences, not so much because of what it said, but because it had come from one of the leading figures in the established ruling class.

The impact of General Spinola's book can be grasped from the following statement by Marcello Caetano:

On 18 February 1974 I received a copy of *Portugal and the Future* with a kind dedication from the author. I could not read it on the same day, nor on the following day because of a Cabinet meeting. Only on the 20th, after 11 p.m., I managed to start reading it.

231

I did not stop until the last page, which I read in the small hours of the morning. And when I closed the book I had understood that the military *coup*, which I could sense had been coming, was now inevitable.[1]

The immediate outcome, however, was that General Spinola, who had only recently been appointed by Caetano to the newly created position of Deputy Chief of Staff of the Armed Forces, was abruptly dismissed together with his superior, General Costa Gomes, who had authorized publication of the book. The military establishment, apparently with the support of President Thomaz, was closing ranks against a serious threat to the régime. They had, indeed, manifest reasons for feeling perturbed. On 16 March 1974 there was an officers' uprising originating in the town of Caldas, which was frustrated only as the insurgents approached Lisbon.

These checks initially only reinforced the pervasive feeling of scepticism. In a dictatorship that had lasted so long that it had shaped a national culture and a tacit code of civil behaviour, most people had learned to live within their natural social 'cells' made up of relatives, school friends or work colleagues. They had learned to view with suspicion all strangers – particularly those that went around spreading bits of provocative but fragmentary news on political and military conspiracies. Such plots as those alleged to involve a new 'Armed Forces Movement', or the 'Captains' Movement', as it was variously called, were by their very nature secretive and their outcome conjectural. Thus the Portuguese public had no reason to believe that these persistent rumours amounted to much more than the many recurring fantasies that had come and gone before in a lifetime of dictatorship.

The 25 April *coup*

Then, suddenly, in the morning of 25 April 1974 the news spread that units of the army had taken over broadcasting stations and key government buildings, and that both President

1. Marcello Caetano, *Depoimento* (Record, Rio de Janeiro, 1975).

Thomaz and Prime Minister Caetano, together with most of the government's Ministers, were under detention. In less than twenty hours a régime that had lasted nearly half a century had collapsed.

Events moved so fast that suddenly there were no longer any experts on Portuguese politics, but only historians. The 'April Revolution' found its symbol in the seasonal red carnation and was singularly deprived of feelings of revenge. Even the two people who died outside the besieged DGS headquarters in central Lisbon were shot at by a handful of police agents in panic. The takeover had combined the most modern operational efficiency with a timeless sense of adventure. A young peasant soldier standing guard on a Lisbon street corner was asked by a middle-class passer-by what he was doing there; he replied that he had been ordered to keep an eye on insurgent troops. Upon being told, 'but *you* are the revolutionaries!' he shouted to a colleague: 'Manuel, we are the rebels – *Viva!*' The mass demonstrations on 1 May 1974 were one of the happiest explosions of liberal acclaim any country could ever see. It recalled the mood of victorious nations at the end of the war and for many people the belated defeat of Portuguese Fascism came as a confirmation of the ultimate unpredictability of life. Freedom had been late in arriving but when it came it had generosity and style.

It was only in retrospect that political writers and sociologists began to understand how events had evolved. Since the Salazar–Caetano régime had always been able to watch, and eventually suppress, even the most incipient conspiracy, clearly the *coup* was something more than a mere plot. And in fact, prosaic as some of its original factors may have been, the 25 April *pronunciamento* was undeniably part of a wider revolutionary process that had been fermenting in Portugal for many years.

The sequence of events is fairly simple to explain. The extensive involvement in three colonial wars had led to a widening of the structure of the armed forces and a consequent increase in permanent cadres. In mid-July 1973, with the publication of a decree which gave conscripted officers exceptionally favourable

233

conditions for permanent integration in the forces, there had been a clash of interests between career officers, from the military and naval schools and academies, and the commissioned and conscripted officers who outnumbered them. The issues revolved around promotion, pay and status, and led to a series of gatherings, which went under the name of 'picnics' and were therefore outside the provisions banning the right of association.

Coincidental with these narrow professional issues, the armed forces were deeply divided over the colonial policies of the régime and the ideological, political and strategic implications of the wars in Guinea-Bissau, Angola and Mozambique. In June 1973 a Fascist group calling themselves the 'Congress of Veterans' had tried to meet at Oporto to express their support for the régime's hardliners, but their meetings had not been authorized for fear of creating a precedent. But now a more progressive and liberal-leaning group, which included a hard core of ideologically committed officers, had found an opportunity to hold meetings and debate the great national issues of the day.

Originally numbering 136 middle-rank officers, the 'Captains' Movement' expanded and gained strength. By October 1973 the Caetano government was confronted with a threat of mass resignation by hundreds of officers who demanded the repeal of the new laws on NCOs. Significantly their statements began to mention other issues, including changes in the army leadership, the policies towards the African territories, and the social-economic situation in Portugal. It was at a meeting on 24 November that a lieutenant-colonel, about to leave for the war in Guinea-Bissau, firmly rejected the 'paper war' in which the captains and lieutenants were engaged and openly suggested a *coup*.[1]

From then on the Armed Forces Movement was set on its revolutionary course. Although the ubiquitous DGS had some difficulty in gaining access to the officers' meetings there is evidence that they had indirect, if imprecise, knowledge, that a plot was afoot. This could have been obtained through informers

1. Borga and Cardoso Rodrigues, op. cit. p. 333.

within the army, or by keeping an eye on the movements of some of the main suspects. But the process was by now too far advanced and, finding themselves outmanoeuvred, the DGS were unable to prevent the *pronunciamento*.

The eventual operational details of the 25 April *coup*, which were coordinated by, amongst others, Otelo Saraiva de Carvalho, are now part of the new folklore. As the government surrendered unconditionally, the Junta was in such complete control of the situation that they accorded full military honours to President Thomaz, Prime Minister Caetano and other Ministers, who they then promptly sent to Madeira on their way to exile in Brazil. Curiously enough, the only complaint raised by Prime Minister Caetano was that the guards who escorted him were armed and commanded only by a sergeant-major.[1]

For those who lived through those days, liberation and fraternity ceased to be abstract concepts and hopes, and became a real experience. There was an explosion of genuine collective joy at the news of the release of political prisoners at Caxias and Peniche and the labour camps in Guinea-Bissau, Angola and Mozambique, where thousands of Africans were kept in captivity. Some of the long-term Portuguese prisoners had twenty, fifteen and ten years' experience of imprisonment. Many had given up hope of ever resuming normal life with their families. A few gave accounts of new DGS methods of psychological torture, involving the use of drugs and sensory deprivation techniques. Well-known exiles returned from distant countries to embrace comrades who had lived 'clandestinely' inside the country, operating in the underground anti-Fascist resistance.

There can be no doubt, after placing the statements, manifestos and Programme of the AFM in the psychological and political context of the time they appeared, before and after the 25 April *coup*, that the original aims of the movement were essentially twofold. The paramount one was the attainment of a 'political', and by implication, peaceful, solution to the African wars through a process of decolonization. The other was the restoration of democracy through free elections and the conse-

1. Marcello Caetano, *Depoimento*, op. cit.

235

quent withdrawal of the army from direct involvement in domestic politics.

In a document circulated illegally in January 1974, and entitled 'The Movement, the Armed Forces and the Nation', the AFM described the colonial wars as 'the gravest question which underlies the overall crisis within the régime', and called for a 'political solution which safeguards national honour and dignity'. Allowance must be made for the fact that conspiratorial literature has to foresee the possibility of it being used as evidence in legal proceedings should repression gain the upper hand. But at the time, when the date of the *coup* was not yet fixed, the terms of reference had to be adequately mild and broad to get the support of the politically heterogeneous mass of conspiring officers.

In the same document the officers, after denouncing the role of the military in upholding the repressive régime at home and sustaining the ruinous wars in Africa, attacked the 'myth that our armed forces are politically neutral'. This understatement touches on a fundamental issue in Portuguese politics.

Traditionally, power in Portugal, as in Spain and other Southern European countries, has been alternately disputed and shared between two main classes, the military and the lawyers, sometimes with the blessing, and other times with the curse, of the Church. The army, one must not forget, was the mainstay of the Salazar régime. Salazar himself, incidentally, on more than one occasion referred to the 'glorious armed forces' that kept him in power.

In a natural reaction against this historical fact, the AFM was now aiming at evolving a democratic system in which the armed forces would ultimately cease to have any direct involvement in domestic politics. The AFM Programme published in April 1974 established the institutional process leading to democracy. A seven-man National Salvation Board, under the President and heads of the three branches of the armed forces, was empowered to disband the previous régime and restore civil rights; the President would appoint a provisional civilian government made up of representatives of main opposition groups to carry on the task of governing within certain democratic and socialist guidelines laid down in the Programme. A National Constituent Assembly would be elected by direct suffrage within one year from 25 April to draft and approve a new constitution. Regarding the future role of the armed forces the 'final points' of the Programme could not be more clear: 'Once the National Constituent Assembly and a new President of the Republic are elected by the nation, the National Salvation Board will be dissolved and the activity of the Armed Forces restricted to their specific mission of external defence of national sovereignty.'

General Antonio Spinola, whose book expressed liberal ideas that the bourgeoisie identified with the broad aims of the *coup*, was chosen as President and head of the National Salvation Board – equivalent to a Presidential Council – which included General Costa Gomes, who had been reinstated as Chief of Staff. The other five members had all been former army, air force or naval commanders in the African territories, a choice designed to ensure cooperation of the armed forces overseas.

For a country beset with so many problems and undergoing such a major dislocation, the degree of discipline and cohesion displayed by the military and civil administration, both in Portugal and in the far-flung empire, was quite remarkable.

At this stage the armed forces were anxious to maintain a low profile. During the 1 May celebrations President Spinola stayed at home to allow the returning exiled leaders, like Alvaro Cunhal and Mario Soares, to receive the popular acclaim. The AFM leaders were still engaged in the operational work of consolidating the *coup* in Portugal and in the overseas territories, and discussing the purge of officers compromised with the previous régime. The few officers who surfaced as spokesmen emphasized the collective character of the AFM leadership and their intention to refrain from interfering directly in the information of the civilian provisional government.

The delicate task of achieving the cooperation or peaceful surrender of all army commanders was only paralleled by the difficulties faced by President Spinola in appointing a civilian government. According to the AFM Programme the cabinet

237

had to be made up of representatives of the main political groupings in order to establish a tacitly satisfactory balance of representation. Ironically, since under the Salazar–Caetano régime, all opposition activity had been illegal, to begin with the only three qualifying political parties of major significance were Communist or Socialist. One was the Portuguese Communist Party, whose monthly newspaper *Avante* had been published for nearly forty-three years. The party had been founded as far back as 1921, and had had its first congress in 1923. It had been banned in 1927, soon after the overthrow of the Republican régime and even before Salazar had started his career as Finance Minister. At its third congress in 1933 it had established two main points for action: (1) the setting up of a united front of opposition groups; and (2) taking advantage of the possibilities of legal activity, mainly during electoral campaigns. Over the years, at the cost of immense sacrifice and dedication from its nucleus of militants,[1] the party developed into a fairly well-organized structure. Its members were advised to participate in legal social life, entering the trade unions, corporations, social clubs, students' bodies and so forth. At underground level it followed the usual cellular pattern, and had over all other opposition groups the advantage of organized support abroad, mainly in the Soviet Union, Czechoslovakia and other Eastern European countries as well as from the Communist parties of the West. Portuguese-language broadcasts from Moscow, and from 'Radio Free Portugal', based in Prague, were of considerable help. All these factors ensured that, although the PIDE/DGS was occasionally successful in infiltrating some of its cells, the party never ceased to publish and circulate *Avante* even when regional printing presses fell into the hands of the police.

The party's exiled leader, Alvaro Cunhal, who had his own share of experiences of imprisonment and torture, had consistently anticipated the inevitability of overthrowing the régime by force. In his report to the party's fourth congress in

1. One of the Communist Party's claims in the run-up to the April 1975 elections was that their 247 candidates for the Constituent Assembly had served between them 440 years behind bars.

1946 he stated that 'one must secure the participation and neutralization of a large section of the armed forces' to attain that end. In fact the PC outlived all other opposition groups through the years and was for long periods the main driving force keeping anti-Fascist resistance alive.

The second legal party was the Socialist Party, led by Mario Soares, which had been formed at a meeting held in West Germany in 1972 by members of a grouping known as Socialist Action. This group had evolved from socialist opposition factions in previous electoral campaigns in Portugal but had gained a new impetus in exile and migrant circles abroad since the Caetano régime had forced its leader Mario Soares into exile in Paris soon after the 1969 elections. Outside Portugal, in addition to Mario Soares, there were two other well-known leaders, Tito de Morais and Ramos da Costa, later joined by another young exile, Jorge Campinos, a law lecturer in France. The group had developed useful connections with the Socialist International and its affiliated social-democratic parties in Western European countries, including the British Labour Party. Inside Portugal the Socialists counted on the leadership of, among others, Salgado Zenha, Sottomayor Cardia, a noted socialist theoretician, and Antonio Macedo, a lawyer from Oporto. While claiming to be, like the Communist Party, essentially a working-men's party, the Socialists aimed at a 'classless society' and a 'multi-party democratic system'.

Finally, there was the CDE, the Democratic Electoral Commission, which claimed to represent the traditional united front formed by Communists, Socialists and other left-wing groups operating within the régime's legal framework, particularly during electoral periods. Their continued existence as a front met with considerable resistance, especially from the Socialist Party, but eventually it re-emerged as the CDE/Portuguese Democratic Movement and gained status as a party. Although this party adhered to the principle of anonymous collective leadership, some of its leaders, namely Pereira de Moura, an economics professor, Jose Tengarrinha and Lindim Ramos gained individual distinction.

In order to counterbalance the left wing in the new government, a third, anti-Communist, social-democratic grouping was improvised into a new party – the Popular Democratic Party. Evolving from the token liberal wing of ex-National Assembly members and from fairly forward-looking technocratic factions within the previous régime, the PPD was founded in early May 1974 by F. Sa Carneiro, Magalhães Mota and Pinto Balsemão, the editor of the influential Lisbon weekly *Expresso*.

Eventually a government emerged which included, not only two representatives from each of the main parties, but a number of independent personalities as well. The Prime Minister was a well-known Professor of Law, Palma Carlos; Mario Soares emerged as Minister of Foreign Affairs; Alvaro Cunhal and Sa Carneiro as Ministers without Portfolio. Another independent, Almeida Santos, was appointed as Minister for Overseas (renamed Interterritorial) Affairs, on the strength of his past democratic militancy and his experience as a resident of Mozambique for twenty-five years. Significantly, the ratio of lawyers to other professionals, including the military, in the first Provisional government, was 95 per cent of the total. Such men, all faced with the immense task of resolving the manifold problems resulting from the collapse of the previous régime, were for the most part unacquainted with each other and, unlike in normal democratic situations, they had no clear picture of each other's way of thinking.

The 'overseas question' was the most immediate issue confronting the new government. Their terms of reference were contained in the rather terse Point 8 of the AFM Programme:

The overseas policy of the Provisional Government, having regard to the fact that it will be defined by the nation, will be guided by the following principles: (a) recognition of the fact that the solution for the overseas wars is a political and not a military one; (b) creation of conditions for a frank and open debate, on a national level, of the overseas problem; (c) launching of the bases of an overseas policy that will lead to peace.

Once the Provisional Government was headed by a Professor of Law, Palma Carlos, who fully adhered to the conventional concepts of constitutional right denied by the previous régime, it was not difficult for President Spinola and his supporters to gain an ally for the scheme of achieving decolonization through a process of democratic consultation. In the African context, since there were rival movements and factions amongst African nationalists, it appeared that to seek a solution through negotiations with the strongest of them would still be an act of colonial rule, tantamount to making a last convenient deal over the heads of the African peoples concerned. It seemed obvious at the time that Portuguese and international support for a summary transfer of powers to the PAIGC in Guinea-Bissau and Frelimo in Mozambique was based upon ideological sympathy rather than an understanding of the overall Portuguese situation. Had the same movements been supported by the wrong neighbour, as was the case with the FNLA in Angola, the left would have seen the need for referenda.

Despite all appearances and protestations to the contrary, the AFM leaders were keeping a close control of civilian government behind the scenes. All ministers, for instance, had officers attached to them as aides, shadowing their movements inside and outside the country, who became known as 'army fiscals' among the civilians who resented their presence. Another delayed side-effect of the Salazar–Caetano period was that individuals and classes viewed each other with suspicion, many civilian democrats being justifiably bewildered at finding suddenly so many revolutionary socialists in high-ranking uniforms. It was clear that, for all the validity of their belated stand, the armed forces, as a group, were also covering up for their responsibilities for the situation that Portugal had been led into. The most cynical observers knew that as a nation confronted with defeat, Portugal was following the historical pattern of other nations in making of forced surrender an ideological virtue.

The 'open and frank debate' called for in the AFM Programme had somewhat contradictorily been made impossible after the publication of a decree on 22 June setting up *ad hoc* commissions with extensive powers of intervention in the activities of the media. Under this decree it became a crime of 'ideological aggression' to criticize the principles of the AFM, or incite or provoke military disobedience or lack of respect for military laws and regulations. Fines of up to 500,000 escudos and suspension of up to sixty days could be imposed on any newspaper or broadcasting station that 'published or divulged false reports' contrary to the implementation of the Programme. These measures prevented anyone from probing too deeply into the past careers of individual officers or questioning certain forgotten issues such as inquiries on atrocities.

Not everyone in the new government was happy to have an improvised civilian cabinet go down in history for carrying out a far-reaching process of decolonization without any clear constitutional mandate. The Programme of the AFM specifically stated that the 'overseas policy of the Provisional Government would be defined by the nation'. A departure from this principle could bring about a decisive split between the various factions within the armed forces which had concerted or otherwise adhered to the Programme before or after the 25 April *coup*. In order to break the stalemate which was hindering the Provisional Government in many other issues as well, Prime Minister Palma Carlos proposed another solution. This would entail giving wider powers to the President, while at the same time anticipating the whole process of elections, leading to a new constitution and representative institutions. Instead of waiting for one year, as provided for in the Programme, the process should be initiated forthwith.

This marked the first major clash between two concepts of the 25 April movement – one abiding by the conventions of Western traditions of the rule of law and bourgeois liberalism, the other turned towards a new revolutionary ethical code which regarded certain rights and needs of the masses as being self-evident. Since both these concepts were sincerely held and both derived coherent arguments either from conditioning, or from a discovery that there was something fundamenally wrong in the inherited class system, the clash became imbued with emotionalism. By then objective reasoning in Portugal had not gained much from a situation in which censorship and police rule had given way to partisan media, determined to programme national thinking. In order to placate both sides, it might have been possible, as Minister Almeida Santos tried to do, to convince both sides that there was no point in quibbling over constitutional niceties in a situation when the 25 April *coup* had been by definition a 'revolution'. An open and frank re-assessment of the Portuguese situation in Africa might also have gone a long way to explaining why referenda were unpractical, time-consuming and unlikely to produce the peaceful solution envisaged in the Programme.

Instead, without any immediate public clarification of the issues involved being provided, Prime Minister Palma Carlos was forced to resign in disgrace. Minister without Portfolio Sa Carneiro, who had assisted in the drafting of the project, resigned with him, but President Spinola survived this first major crisis in the new régime. A new government emerged with less lawyers and more military officers. The new Prime Minister was Brigadier Vasco Gonçalves, described as one of the masterminds behind the *coup*; Majors Melo Antunes and Victor Alves became Ministers without Portfolio. At the same time most of the leading figures in the AFM emerged from anonymity and assumed open control of key positions within the régime.

In mid-July the new Provisional Government found a curious device to open up the way for African independence by promulgating the repeal of the 1933 constitution, which defined Portugal as a single country made up of home and overseas provinces. On 28 July, certainly under considerable pressure, President Spinola made a formal declaration accepting the principle of independence for all African territories. This was received with mixed feelings by many people who still wanted to cling to some of the last and richer remnants of the 500-year-old empire, and resulted in a further blow to Spinola's prestige among the more conservative sections of the population.

From then on negotiations with the African liberation movements proceeded at full steam. Army officers, such as Major Melo Antunes and Brigadier Otelo Saraiva de Carvalho, who had hitherto hidden behind the apparent negotiators, Foreign Minister Mario Soares and Overseas Minister Almeida Santos, now sat openly side by side with them, or without them altogether, at conference tables in Algiers, Lusaka and Dar es Salaam. In less than six months, both Guinea-Bissau and Mozambique, where the Portuguese military position was most desperate, had firm dates for independence.

A mutual desire for peace, African partisan and Portuguese national interests were among the main factors which promoted speedy agreement with the PAIGC and Frelimo. More than a decade of guerrilla warfare had resolved the colonial dilemma for Portugal. Guinea-Bissau had long been a liability, absorbing human and financial resources out of all proportion to its economic interest to Portugal; Mozambique was on the verge of bankruptcy. By coming to terms with the African liberation movements, the Portuguese could still play a relevant role in the new independent countries. Moreover, decolonization would lead to a positive reversal in foreign policy, with the opening up of trade and diplomatic connections with the Soviet Union, Eastern European countries, and the Arab, African and Asian markets closed to the previous régime. In diplomatic terms the policy paid immediate dividends, culminating in the overwhelming acclaim accorded to Portugal at the 1974 UN General Assembly.

However, in the meantime, Portugal was beginning to feel the full impact of the economic and social deterioration which had begun under the Caetano régime. Increases in the price of oil, sugar and other foodstuffs, and raw materials had pushed the domestic inflation rate to 30 per cent, one of the highest in Western Europe. International inflation had also precipitated a sharp decrease in revenue from migrants' remittances and tourism, which traditionally provided some 30 per cent of total foreign currency earnings. With the dislocation caused by a badly needed increase in wages and improvement in working conditions, many small and medium concerns had closed down. The return of soldiers from Guinea-Bissau and disgruntled settlers from Mozambique had helped to bring the number of unemployed to over 200,000. By mid-1974 it was estimated that the year would end with a balance of payments deficit of some US $600m. or nearly 20 per cent of the gold and foreign currency reserves inherited from the previous régime.

Moreover, the search for democracy was having some disturbing side-effects in the social field. The crisis in education, which had led to a complete standstill in many schools and faculties since the events of 25 April, was the culmination of a growing rebellion by Portuguese youth, which some compared to similar phenomena in other European countries in the sixties. The suspension of classes and the disruption of the educational system could be attributed to a minority of students who sometimes claimed to be, and were sometimes accused of being, ultra-left Communists or Maoists. They apparently wanted to impose a revolutionary curriculum as well as introduce student rule and teacher subordination. They appeared to have mistaken the aims of 25 April with those of their ideology. And since there were many features in their stand which seemed to conform to the prevailing trend, the authorities were somewhat undecided and inhibited about how to tackle the situation. On top of this, the sudden explosion of applications for secondary and higher education had led to a situation whereby, for lack of adequate facilities and staff, the enrolment of some 30,000 new students had to be deferred. The suggestion that they might do a term of voluntary work was resisted by many as aggravating the unemployment problem. This massive disruption was causing a loss of time and money to thousands of students' families, and the whole situation was blamed on the new régime.

It would be irrational to expect that in the short space of a few months a régime that was still trying to assert itself could succeed in reversing an adverse trend in the economic and social situation, which reflected also the influence of many international factors beyond Portuguese control. Moreover since private banking and industry retained control of foreign exchange and employment, the economy was obviously highly vulnerable to sabotage.

Large sectors of the middle class in the towns and the mass of peasants in certain regions were either retreating into alienation or beginning to voice opposition to the new régime. The ideological campaigns of re-education were also proving counterproductive and turning people away from the media.

On 10 September President Spinola vented his emotions and

sense of frustration in a dramatic address marking the formal recognition of Guinea-Bissau's independence, just a few days after the signing of the Lusaka agreement setting out the terms for Mozambique's independence in June 1975. He stated that the 'process of decolonization should not consist in a mere transfer of power to the party organization that sustained the armed struggle against the former régime', and warned against the dangers of 'one-party' states. Turning to the situation at home he remarked that Portugal might also be faced with the risk of evolving a situation where 'the future would not be shaped in consultation of the Portuguese people ... It has been recognized that the trend in modern societies is towards socialism; but socialism should not be understood to be built at the cost of human liberty and dignity.' He urged the Portuguese to 'wake up to defend themselves against extremist totalitarians that fight in the shadows'.

This address was taken as a battle-cry for the 'silent majority' to whom President Spinola, paraphrasing the then discredited President Nixon, specifically referred. Within little more than two weeks, on 28 September, a *coup* within the *coup* took place. Most of what is known about the mysterious events surrounding the claims of *coups* and counter-*coups* at that time is contradictory and partisan. A raid by the COPCON, the new Home Operational Command or security force led by Brigadier General Saraiva de Carvalho, on the headquarters of the so-called Nationalist Party at Oporto revealed an incipient pocket of armed resistance to the new régime. It was run by members of the former régime's single party, the APN, and the disbanded Portuguese Legion. A plot to assassinate Prime Minister Vasco Gonçalves was alleged in most of the media. On the other hand, Brigadier Saraiva de Carvalho later disclosed in a press interview that the detention of nearly 100 leading figures in the former régime as suspects had been merely a coincidence, for the arrests had already been ordered beforehand as a routine security measure.[1] In a situation where one was forced to accept the tacit and the conjectural as if it were evidence, the only visible fact was that thousands of left-wing militants took

1. Interview in *Sempre Fixe*, 25 January 1975.

to the barricades and enforced on-the-spot road checks for arms in cars allegedly taking part in a middle-class 'March on Lisbon' to provoke a Presidential *putsch*. The almost universal revolutionary cry, 'reaction will not pass', last heard in the Iberian peninsula during the Civil War, echoed again in Portugal.

In the event President Spinola, confronted with the imposition of the summary dismissal of some of his closest supporters in the junta and the government, decided to resign. In his farewell address he again reverted to the theme of decolonization, stating that it had been 'distorted with the deliberate intention of introducing anti-democratic measures harmful to the true interests of Africans'. The AFM had also wanted to promote 'harmony amongst all political creeds', but this had become impossible because of the use of violence by political groups and psychological coercion through the media. He said that old laws were being scrapped without new ones being enacted to regulate the political, social and economic life of the country. He protested that 'the peace, progress and well-being of the country were compromised by the economic crisis to which we are hastening due to unemployment, uncontrolled inflation, decrease in trade, cutting back on investments and inefficiency of the central power'. He again warned against the danger of a new slavery.

After President Spinola's replacement by General Costa Gomes, the AFM asserted its role as a 'shadow' military government. Its institutionalization was achieved through a powerful structure of interlocking councils and committees, connected with COPCON. The organic structure, in the form of a pyramid, was headed by the Superior Council of the AFM (also known initially as the Council of Twenty, because of the number of its members). The chairman was the President of the Republic, who also presided over COPCON. The other six members of the National Salvation Board, plus all the military ministers and seven members of the Programme Coordinating Committee all had seats in the Council. The Superior Council was supported by the AFM General Assembly, interconnected with nine councils and assemblies. The Assembly was thus the decisive policy-making organ with some 200 members representing the three branches of the armed forces as well as regional commands.

The clash of two concepts

Revolutions, like nations and empires, can hardly be made according to plan, since they are shaped by social and economic circumstances. Like most of their fellow countrymen, the officers of the Armed Forces Movement must have been surprised with the very process they had helped to set in motion after the 25 April *coup*. Indeed, Prime Minister Vasco Gonçalves for one was quoted a few days after the *coup* as saying that he was only too anxious to be able to return to his army barracks. In fact, after forty-eight years of dictatorship the Portuguese people, including those in uniform, were like blind men who, upon recovering their sight, were dazzled and stumbled. Allegations of a long-term political conspiracy between the army officers and leaders of both the Communist and Socialist parties have been convincingly denied by army leaders who, even weeks after the *coup*, had not met those with whom they were supposed to have plotted.

There is evidence that even those officers who plotted the *coup* were soon overtaken by events – and the best symbol of the situation was the scene when ordinary people pushed the army tanks with their bare hands up a hill to the Carmo Barracks in Lisbon, where Prime Minister Caetano and other Ministers had taken refuge. Within the short space of two months there were no less than fifty different political parties, some with independent factions or affiliated youth groups. Inevitably there was an upsurge of opportunism and reciprocal accusations between the parties that many people were taking advantage of the massive purge of former government officials to promote their own followers into key and rewarding positions. In fact, all the main parties, including the Communist Party and the Socialist Party, as well as the AFM, ran the risk of having their hard core of veteran supporters vastly outnumbered by newly converted members.

As the April 1975 elections for the National Constituent Assembly approached, and the main parties submitted their applications for legal recognition on the bases of a minimum 5,000 membership, it became possible to determine that there would be at least five main parties dominating the political scene in the foreseeable future. In addition to the three parties represented in the government – the Socialists, the Communists and the Popular Democrats – two other parties, the left-wing MDP/CDE (Democratic Party) and the right-wing CDS (Centre Social Democrats) had come to the fore. Although the right wing had its fair share of factions, only two parties, the Christian Democrats and the Monarchists, were worth mentioning. On the far left there were the PCP (M–L) (Communist Party (Marxist–Leninist)), the MES (Left Socialist Movement), the LUAR (League of Unity and Revolutionary Action: populist), the PRP (Revolutionary Party of the Proletariat), the MRPP (Movement for the Reconstruction of the Proletarian Party: Maoists), and the LCI (International Communist League: Trotskyists).

This diversity of parties, and the somewhat confusing literature they circulated, led many people to despair of the possibility of a coherent political analysis. But in fact, if one adopts fairly simple points of reference instead of the conventional theoretical ones, it is possible to sketch an outline on the developing situation.

First, one must grasp that the agitation was still a delayed side-effect of the former régime. Owing to the lack of mobility between the classes and the lack of communication between individuals and groups it was not possible in the short space of one year to achieve a more cohesive national debate. The situation could be compared by analogy with a radio operating on various parallel wavelengths which never meet each other. Secondly, in addition to the usual social contradictions and class antagonisms among the urban population of industrial workers and middle-class, white-collar professionals, more than half the Portuguese population are peasants living in conditions of medieval simplicity. Such people still lived divorced by low income and poor communications from the world beyond the horizon; they were God-fearing souls kept in the condition of wards of the local priest. Progress had by-passed their villages and hamlets, and like the traffic on the highroad it had no connection with local rural life. Over the years there had been some attempt to expound to their children the benefits of a somewhat sterilized primary education, but by and large they were an amorphous mass reacting by instinct to innovation. Since their holdings were the equivalent of the tools of workers or the diplomas of the professionals they had an emotional attachment to the idea of property. Under the previous régime they were left out of the restricted suffrage on account of their lack of educational and other qualifications, or because they did not even care to go through the complicated formalities of applying for voters' registration. This is reflected in the following table showing the percentage of voters in relation to the total population:

Year of elections	Population	Voters	Percentage
1938	6,985,000	743,930	10·6
1945	7,563,000	909,456	12·0
1949	7,956,147	1,140,000	14·6
1953	8,024,853	1,161,932	14·4
1958	8,360,760	1,213,381	14·5
1961	8,562,271	1,236,000	14·5
1965	8,610,200	1,278,387	14·8
1969	8,700,000	1,700,548	19·54

After the 25 April *coup*, the right to vote was extended to all adults over the age of eighteen. Thus while, owing to massive emigration, the total population remained in 1975 about the same as for 1969, the number of voters jumped to over 6,000,000, or nearly 70 per cent of the total population. The peasant class all of a sudden acquired a decisive political significance by sheer weight of numbers. But they remained an unknown electoral quantity, like a pool of non-committed voters that could easily sway the balance of power.

Party political activity was mostly confined to the larger towns and villages and, while the struggles between the various groupings embodied the conflict of interests between the classes, they eventually polarized in two different concepts of democracy – the bourgeois and the revolutionary. The first was rooted in the values transmitted from generation to generation through the conditioning of a hierarchical society. The other was the product of a discovery that the traditional system of free enterprise and property perpetuates privilege, and that the attainment of democracy must be made through a socialist system in which the rights of workers and peasants are paramount.

In Portuguese politics the bourgeois camp would include all parties to the right of the Socialist Party and the Popular Democratic Party which, in varying degrees, believed in a classless society where the workers and peasants would in time be integrated into the standards and values of the middle class. The other camp, to the left of the Communist Party, believed that the difference beween the former bourgeois dictatorship and the bourgeois democracy was one of methods and degree, not of aims. From the point of view of the working and peasant class it might in the end amount to no more than the difference between armed robbery and a confidence trick.

The bourgeois camp believed in the traditional notion of 'one man one vote' and electoral and institutional democracy, and wanted to safeguard Portuguese society from coercion, harassment and intimidation. They derived from recent experience an emotional resistance to dictatorial rule, afraid that religious and nationalistic obscurantism would give place to programmed conformity to ideology and single-party rule. The revolutionary camp suspected that the vote is not the weapon of the people, but the weapon of the bourgeoisie. For the paternalistic Communist Party above all, the classical liberal notion of parliamentary democracy might be of little value in a society where intense poverty and economic inequality combined with a new set of problems which the uneducated masses were unable to understand.

One must also take into account Portuguese experiences over ten years of wars which, owing to the rotation of conscription, perhaps involved nearly 1 million people, or over 10 per cent of the population. No one goes to war without asking why. Thus large numbers of servicemen and students liable for 'military duty' became exposed to the influences of the African liberation movements. Portugal was in the singular situation of

251

simultaneously possessing the last old-style empire and being it-self colonized by foreign capital. With fairly substantial gold reserves accumulated through the exploitation of masses of white and black workers the Portuguese were like the richest poor men in Europe.

The AFM absorbed ideas of liberation through years of dis-cussions at student gatherings, at sergeants' and officers' train-ing schools, in officers' messes or even while travelling on patrol. Moreover, the fact that the wars had compelled an in-crease in conscripted officer cadres at a time when attendance at regular military institutes had considerably declined and the number of career officers decreased, had created a situation where the armed forces were truly a people's army.

After the 25 April *coup* the officers of the AFM were further exposed to new influences. At leadership level this was par-ticularly noticeable in the negotiations with the three main An-golan liberation movements in early 1975. While negotiations with the PAIGC and Frelimo had taken place outside Portugal, the summit conference with the MPLA, FNLA and UNITA leaders was held at the Algarve with the direct par-ticipation of AFM leaders. When the firm date for inde-pendence on 11 November 1975 – the anniversary of the founding of Luanda by the Portuguese four centuries before – was agreed upon, the Angolan and Portuguese representatives looked more like comrades-in-arms than diplomatic nego-tiators. At all levels in the army after the ceasefire, much was learned from African guerrillas in the fraternizing that went on during joint operational security actions.

The impact of all these influences permeated through the political campaigns of education of the AFM via their own newspapers, radio and TV programmes and direct practical teaching to peasants. In their meetings with peasants, they would explain rudimentary notions of equality between the classes and the sexes, or denounce the abuses of priests and the puerility of superstition.

The AFM programme had always embodied a dual purpose: on the one hand a return to democracy through free elections, and on the other the pursuit of a socialist restructuring of the country. The latter was to be guided by an Economic and Social Plan, devised with the help of civilian experts but ultimately sponsored and presented by the military Minister without Portfolio, Melo Antunes, on behalf of the AFM. The central, non-partisan role of the AFM was emphasized when some of its representatives stated that the movement would continue to play a part in political development by guaranteeing security and political freedoms and ensuring that the Economic and Social Plan would be carried out.

But by the early part of 1975 the objectives of democracy and of socialist reconstruction began to pull the AFM in different directions. On 1 February the operational head of COPCON was quoted in *Expresso* as saying that 'the party that gets the biggest number of votes will not necessarily reflect the real will and true interests of the Portuguese people'. It became increasingly hard for the armed forces to maintain their impartial role and plan for a speedy withdrawal from politics. Curiously, the major civilian parties, Communists, Socialists and Social Democrats, themselves welcomed the continued presence of the AFM. Portugal was caught at a particularly difficult time economically and socially, and while the future promised an improvement in conditions, in the meanwhile the country was still reeling under the impact of one of the greatest political and economic dislocations in its history. The AFM offered itself as a stabilizer. More deviously, perhaps, it appeared to the civilian parties to be wise to encourage the army to participate in government over this difficult period: in this way it would be co-responsible for developments, and it would be more difficult to justify a military take-over in the event of a deterioration in the situation.

Eventually the AFM emerged as a 'fourth liberation front', so called in an allusion to the PAIGC, Frelimo and the MPLA, the three African liberation movements with which it was more closely identified. It had become a movement in its own right, sharing power and influence side by side with the civilian parties and retaining a decisive political role. Though elections were called for April 1975, as undertaken in the Programme, the AFM resolved to maintain an institutional presence lest the forces of convention succeeded in reversing the revolutionary process through electoral and legalistic means.

The experiment might well be the one best suited to steer Portugal through the transition from half a century of dictatorship towards democracy; but only the next few years will tell whether the armed forces, for forty-eight years turned against the people, have really succeeded in becoming an army of the people. All the indications are that Portugal will have to strike an optimum balance between extremes both in home and foreign policies. A turn to the extreme right might mean the final severing of connections with the new African countries, where socialist-orientated régimes have emerged. A turn to the extreme left might imply the artificial grafting of an alien ideology on to a country which ultimately will have to find its place in the Western European economic context. There might even be a role for Portugal, as a small country, to play in a future united Europe. All the major European nations – Britain, Spain, France, West Germany – are really mosaics of smaller nationalities, in some cases integrated into a bigger national *bloc* through the vagaries of history, at other times ruthlessly suppressed in their aspirations to nationhood and autonomy. As one sees the aspirations of smaller nations still fermenting, often with violence, one realizes that a belief in cultural plurality does not invalidate a belief in economic integration. Portugal must now return to its Iberian and European origins, and the way to avoid the continued hegemony of Britain, France and Germany might well be to think in terms of a more representative political division of Europe.

A few months after the *coup* the new régime had already an impressive roll of achievements. First and foremost were the liberation of captive African nations and the assistance given to the building of the new states of Guinea-Bissau, Mozambique, Angola and São Tome Island. This must have far-reaching repercussions on the balance of power in Africa and the development of democracy in the West generally, and Southern Africa in particular. At home it had released the working class from its condition of chattels of an oligarchy, establishing strong trade unions and a minimum and maximum wage to emphasize the egalitarian character of the new Portuguese society. It had given the right to vote to millions of people who had never known their natural rights, while cushioning the shock and despair of a middle class so conditioned to believe in its own righteousness that it often failed to understand the positive meaning of the revolution taking place.

On 11 March 1975 another attempted counter-*coup* took place involving former President Spinola and other officers who had played a prominent part in the AFM and the overthrow of the Caetano government. Finding no adequate support General Spinola fled with some of his aides to Spain, and subsequently sought asylum in Brazil. Copies of his book *Portugal and the Future*, which only one year before had provided the guidelines for a new republic, were burnt by young revolutionaries who had assaulted Spinola's home in Lisbon.

From then on the pace of the revolution accelerated decisively. The Military Revolutionary Council, assuming open control of government, ordered the nationalization of all Portuguese banks and insurance companies and many industrial and transport concerns. The pledge to hold elections within one year was qualified by restrictions on party political power and preconditions for the constitution to be evolved by the Constituent Assembly. On the first anniversary of the régime, and within the deadline set out in the original AFM Programme, the first free elections in half a century were held. The result was an impressive victory for the Socialist Party, who gained 38 per cent of the vote, followed by the Popular Democratic Party (28 per cent), the Communist Party (13 per cent), the Social Democrat Centre (8 per cent) and the MDP/CDE – Portuguese Democratic Party (5 per cent).

From an international point of view the trend towards a socialist revolution seemed irresistible. The world had changed so dramatically in the half century since the high tide of Fascism and Nazism gave rise to the Salazar régime that few nations still held capitalism as a political dogma. Asia and Africa had emerged from colonialism. Half of mankind lived under socialist régimes. The masses in the newly independent nations of the Third World could no longer fail to see the contrasts produced in a few decades between the social and technological development of the Soviet Union, Eastern Europe and China compared with India, Latin America or other areas of comparable size and importance, which were still riddled with poverty, disease, malnutrition and illiteracy. The Arab *bloc* was reasserting itself politically and economically; the anti-Communist régimes in Vietnam and Cambodia, for so long propped up by the United States, had collapsed. Nearer home there was renewed unrest in Spain. The terminal physical state of the old dictator Franco seemed to herald the disintegration of the nationalist régime and brought hope of a return to democracy.

Ultimately, given the balance of internal political forces and external pressures, a new Portugal may be able to achieve, if not a revolution, at least a process of accelerated evolution capable of achieving socialism in the context of a freer society. In this way the struggle of the colonized peoples of Africa against Portuguese domination has helped to free the people of Portugal itself from the oppressive rule of their middle class.

Epilogue

One year after the *coup* of 25 April a visitor to the small cemetery which stands on a hill at Vimieiro, near the village of Santa Comba Dão, will find a modest grave simply inscribed 'A O S – 1970'. Antonio de Oliveira Salazar lies here, by the side of his parents as he had always wished.

Although half a century of oppression seems a long time to some of us who lived through it, and despite the pervasive after-effects of his régime, Salazar has been almost completely forgotten. Those who do still remember him remember only an old man living in a make-believe world of empires and colonies. This book attempts to record for posterity the man and his régime as they really were.

Like the legendary ruler who, born blind, forbade the manufacture of lamps on the ground that they were an unnecessary luxury, Salazar never understood the meaning of the democratic and socialist ideals he so resolutely suppressed. Consequently the so-called 'National Revolution' which his régime imposed, on his terms and at his pace, was never a response to the needs of ordinary Portuguese men and women. It stemmed from an obsession with Portugal's 'standing' in the world.

Apologists for the régime point to advances which Portugal made during Salazar's rule. Illnesses like malaria and tuberculosis were eradicated; air, sea and land communications were developed. And one must remember, so the argument runs, that when Salazar came to power Portugal was one of the poorest and most backward nations in Europe.

In actual fact, none of the advances made by Portugal before the *coup* of 1974 can be credited to the Fascist régime. The twentieth century has seen the greatest explosion of new ideas, inventions and technical achievements man has ever known; it is hardly surprising that Portugal should have benefited to some degree from the import of advanced methods developed elsewhere. Even the substantial gold and currency reserves accumulated by Portugal up to 1970, the pride of the régime, were created by remittances from emigrant labourers, income from tourism and investments from abroad – all reflections of economic prosperity which Portugal played no active part in creating. The cruel fact is that, if Salazar inherited a poor nation, when he handed it to Caetano forty years later it was still the most backward and the poorest nation in Western Europe.

If nations can be known by the heroes they celebrate, then if Salazar is ever transferred from that simple grave to a national mausoleum – beware.

Bibliography

This book is based on some twenty-five years of reading, writing and lecturing on the subject of Portugal and the dictatorship. Over this time I have accumulated a library containing more than 2,000 books, pamphlets and other documents on Portugal, Angola, Mozambique, Guinea-Bissau, Brazil, and Southern African countries, most of which are presently available only in Portuguese. The following is a selection of works in English to which the reader could usefully refer:

ABSHIRE, D. M., and SAMUELS, M. A., *Portuguese Africa: A Handbook*. Pall Mall Press, 1969; Praeger, 1969.

ANDERSON, PERRY, 'Portugal and the End of Ultra-Colonialism'. *New Left Review*, 1962.

ATKINSON, WILLIAM C., *A History of Spain and Portugal*. Penguin, 1960.

AXELSON, ERIC, *Portugal and the Scramble for Africa*. Wittwatersrand University Press, Johannesburg, 1967.

BARRENO, MARIA ISABEL, HORTA, MARIA TERESA, and DA COSTA, MARIA VELHO, *New Portuguese Letters*. Gollancz, 1975.

BIRMINGHAM, DAVID, *The Portuguese Conquest of Angola*. Oxford University Press, 1965.

BOXER, C. R., *The Portuguese Seaborne Empire*. Hutchinson, 1969, and Penguin, 1973; Knopf, 1970. See also Boxer's many other works.

CABRAL, AMILCAR, *Revolution in Guinea*. Stage 1, 1969; Monthly Review Press, 1972. See also Cabral's many other essays.

CASTLES, STEPHEN, and KOSACK, GODULA, *Immigrant Workers and Class Structures in Western Europe*. Oxford University Press, 1973.

CHILCOTE, RONALD H., *Portuguese Africa*. Prentice-Hall, 1967.

CHILCOTE, RONALD H., (Ed.), *Protest and Resistance in Angola and Brazil: Comparative Studies*. University of California Press, 1973.

CUTILEIRO, JOSE, *A Portuguese Rural Society*. Oxford University Press, 1971.

DAVIDSON, BASIL, *The Liberation of Guiné*. Penguin, 1969. *In the Eye of the Storm*. Longman, 1972, and Penguin, 1975; Doubleday, 1973. See also Davidson's many other works.

DELGADO, HUMBERTO, *Memoirs*. Cassell, London, 1964.

DUFFY, JAMES, *Portuguese Africa*. Oxford University Press, 1959; Harvard University Press, 1959. *Portugal in Africa*. Penguin, 1962.

259

DUNCAN, T. BENTLEY, *Atlantic Islands*. University of Chicago Press, 1972.

EGERTON, F. C. C., *Salazar, Rebuilder of Portugal*. Hodder & Stoughton, 1943.

FERREIRA, EDUARDO SOUSA, *Portuguese Colonialism from South Africa to Europe*. Aktion Dritte Welt, Freiburg, 1972.

FERRO, ANTONIO, *Salazar: Portugal and Her Leader*. Faber, 1939.

FIGUEIREDO, ANTONIO DE, *Portugal and Its Empire: The Truth*. Gollancz, 1961. *Angola: Views of a Revolt*. Oxford University Press, 1962.

FREYRE, GILBERTO, *The Portuguese in the Tropics*. Lisbon, 1961.

FRYER, PETER, and PINHEIRO, PATRICIA, *Our Oldest Ally*. Dobson, London, 1961.

GALVÃO, HENRIQUE, *The Santa Maria – My Crusade for Portugal*. Weidenfeld & Nicolson, 1961; World Publishing Co., 1961.

HAMMOND, RICHARD J., *Portugal and Africa, 1815–1910*. Oxford University Press, 1967; Stanford University Press, 1966.

HARRIS, MARVIN, *Portugal's African 'Wards'*. American Committee on Africa, 1958.

HASTINGS, ADRIAN, *Wiriyamu*. Search Press, London, 1974.

HUMBARACI, ARSLAN, and MUCHNIK, NICOLE, *Portugal's African Wars*. Macmillan, London, 1974.

KAY, HUGH, *Salazar and Modern Portugal*. Eyre & Spottiswoode, 1970.

LIVERMORE, H. V., (Ed.), *Portugal and Brazil: An Introduction*. Oxford University Press, 1953.

MARCUM, JOHN, *The Angolan Revolution. Vol. 1: The Anatomy of an Explosion*. MIT Press, 1969.

MARQUES, A. H. OLIVEIRA, *History of Portugal*. Columbia University Press, 1972.

MARTINS, HERMINIO, *Portugal, Offprint from European Fascism*. Weidenfeld & Nicolson, 1968.

MINTER, WILLIAM, *Portuguese Africa and the West*. Penguin, 1972.

MONDLANE, EDUARDO, *The Struggle for Mozambique*. Penguin, 1969.

NOWELL, CHARLES, *History of Portugal*. Macmillan, London, 1953; Van Nostrand, 1952.

PINTADO, XAVIER, *Structure and Growth of the Portuguese Economy*. EFTA Publications, 1964.

RIBEIRO, AQUILINO, *When the Wolves Howl*. Jonathan Cape, 1963; Macmillan, New York, 1963.

RODRIGUES, JOSE HONORIO, *Brazil and Africa*. Cambridge University Press, 1965; University of California Press, 1965.

SALAZAR, ANTONIO DE OLIVEIRA, *Doctrine and Action: Internal and Foreign Policy of the New Portugal, 1928–1939*. Faber & Faber, 1939.
SIDERI, S., *Trade and Power: Informal Colonialism in Anglo-Portuguese Relations*. Rotterdam University Press, 1970.
SOARES, MARIO, *Portugal's Struggle for Liberty*. Allen & Unwin, 1975.
SPINOLA, ANTONIO, *Portugal and the Future*. Perksor, Johannesburg, 1974.
TREND, J. B., *Portugal*. Benn, London, 1957; Praeger, 1967.
VINTRAS, R. E., *The Portuguese Connection*. Bachman & Turner, London, 1974.
WHEELER, D. L., and PELISSER, R., *Angola*. Pall Mall Press, 1971; Praeger, 1971.

Many of the works of the great novelist Eca de Queiroz are available in English, and provide a good insight into Portuguese culture and life. They include:

Cousin Basilio. Reinhart, 1953; Farrar, Strauss, 1953.
The Relic. Reinhart, 1954.
The City and the Mountains. Reinhart, 1955; Dufour, 1963.
The Sin of Father Amaro. Reinhart, 1962; Dell, 1964.
The Maias. Bodley Head, 1965; St Martins, 1965.
The Mandarin and Other Stories. Bodley Head, 1966; Ohio University Press, 1965.
The Illustrious House of Ramires. Bodley Head, 1968; Ohio University Press, 1968.

Finally, mention must also be made of the useful *Portuguese and Colonial Bulletin*, which for over twelve years published news on Portugal and the wars, and articles by Portuguese democrats in London; and the press-cutting service provided by *Facts and Reports* published in Amsterdam by the Angola Committee, in English and French.